Eating Disorders in a Capitalist World

Women, Economy and Labour Relations

Series Editor: Martina Topic, Leeds Beckett University, UK

This series aims to publish monographs and edited collections that tackle the position of women in the economy as well as explore labour relations. By labour relations, it means studying human relations in work in its broadest sense and analysing how labour relations affect social inequality with particular reference to women. In terms of social inequality, this series particularly welcomes analyses of women and class and broader analyses of labour relations. The series will publish perspectives from around the world and thus the series fits into the understanding of labour relations through both work relations in a Western sense and non-Western forms of labour. The series is also interested in studies of the position of women in worker's unions, the stance on women's affairs within workers' unions and the position of women and women's affairs in labour movements. Both historical and contemporary perspectives are welcome. Studies in industrial and economic sociology are particularly welcome.

The book series aims to publish books from a variety of perspectives, e.g. the series will equally accept both theoretical and empirical perspectives. Also, the book series will accept case study perspectives on women working in various industries. We would particularly like to hear from authors who research the position of women in working-class jobs, e.g. factory workers, supermarket workers, etc. Studies on women in feminised industries (e.g. nursing, teaching, PR) and masculine industries (construction, business, finance) are equally welcome. This book series's main aim is to deconstruct women's position in the economy and explore labour relations from a feminist perspective. All feminist perspectives are welcome, which includes liberal feminist perspectives, as well as analyses of the position of women from radical and socialist feminist positions. In the case of the latter, we particularly welcome proposals that tackle the economic system and inequalities with special reference to the position of women. The proposed books should particularly focus on analysing structural problems that bring about inequality, the distinctiveness of women's contributions to the economy, work conditions and masculinities in organisations and wider societies and differences between men and women. Besides, books that tackle economic systems and link this to the position of women are also welcome.

Eating Disorders in a Capitalist World: Super Woman or a Super Failure?

BY

JELENA BALABANIĆ MAVROVIĆ

Centre for Eating Disorders BEA, Croatia

United Kingdom – North America – Japan – India – Malaysia – China

Emerald Publishing Limited
Emerald Publishing, Floor 5, Northspring, 21-23 Wellington Street, Leeds LS1 4DL

First edition 2024

British Library Cataloguing in Publication Data
A catalogue record for this book is available from the British Library

ISBN: 978-1-80455-787-7 (Print)
ISBN: 978-1-80455-786-0 (Online)
ISBN: 978-1-80455-788-4 (Epub)

Printed and bound by CPI Group (UK) Ltd, Croydon, CR0 4YY

INVESTOR IN PEOPLE

Table of Contents

About the Author

Jelena Balabanić Mavrović was born in Split on 16 June 1972. She graduated in 1998 after completing a single major study of Sociology at the Faculty of Humanities and Social Sciences, University of Zagreb. That same year, she enrolled in a 5-year study of psychotherapy at the European Institute for Reality Therapy in Kranj, Slovenia, where she studied intermittently and graduated in 2015. From 2001 to 2005, she studied at the Department of Sociology and earned her Master's degree, her thesis being 'The concept of reflexive modernisation in contemporary sociological theory' completed under the mentorship of Prof. Rade Kalanj, PhD.

She finished her doctoral studies in 2022 at the Department of Sociology at the Faculty of Humanities and Social Sciences in Zagreb.

She is professionally active in the non-profit sector, where she has headed several associations focused on the promotion of health. In 2012, she started specialising in mental health problems, i.e. prevention and provision of psycho-social support to patients with eating disorders. She is one of the founders of the NGO BEA Centre for Eating Disorders, where she still works. She works closely with the Day Hospital for Eating Disorders at the Sveti Ivan Psychiatric Hospital and with other institutions treating patients with anorexia, bulimia and other specified feeding or eating disorder.

She authored the eating disorder prevention programme '*Tko je to u ogledalu?*' ('Who is that in the mirror?'), which has been implemented in secondary schools in the Republic of Croatia since 2009 and is the co-author of the prevention programme '*Baš je dobro biti JA*' ('It's good to be ME') for elementary schools. She works as a counselling therapist at the BEA Centre, helping people suffering from anorexia, bulimia and other specified feeding or eating disorder and their family members on a daily basis. She regularly designs and implements training programs for experts, parents and the wider community aimed at prevention and identifying and treating patients with eating disorders. She organised expert visits by top therapists and authors in the field of eating disorder treatment from the United Kingdom, the United States and Italy for the purpose of building a system of prevention and treatment of eating disorders in the Republic of Croatia. She is a member of HURT (Croatian Association for Reality Therapy) and EAP (European Association for Psychotherapy).

Acknowledgements

I would like to thank my interviewees, 30 brave young women who placed their trust in me and made it possible for me to write this book. They share their valuable life experience through this volume with everyone who would like to understand what it means to have an eating disorder. My interviewees speak for hundreds of thousands of women and men whose voices are not heard and who struggle daily with the demons of a disturbed relationship to food and the body.

I owe many thanks to the management of the Sveti Ivan Psychiatric Hospital and the fantastic team at the Day Hospital for Eating Disorders, led by Dr Handl, who supported this research. These kind and dedicated people treat young men and women with eating disorders every day, restoring hope to those who had lost it.

I would like to thank my translator Marko Majerović for his refined translation of this book.

I also thank my mentors Branka Galić and Ksenija Klasnić for their support and guidance. Branka Galić kept reminding me of the importance of maintaining a feminist perspective, and Ksenija Klasnić kept a watchful eye on methodology, never losing sight of the bigger picture, helping me to put the various parts together into a meaningful whole.

Heartfelt thanks to Jelena Ogresta, who gave a significant contribution to this book by selflessly sharing her knowledge of qualitative methodology.

This research would never have happened without the amazing women on the BEA Centre for Eating Disorders team, my regular port of call and professional home. Tončica, Maja, Martina, Ivana K.V., Ivana J., Nikolina E., Irena and my other colleagues made discrete contributions to every page of this book. Our many discussions and case analyses from our practice pervade the whole of this text. Miriam, Tina and Antonela, whether far away or close by, you are always here.

I would like to thank my supervisor, Dr Karin Sernec, who, like an angel sitting on my shoulder, keeps guiding me on my professional (and private) journey.

Thanks to Danijela and Maša for their friendly advice and support.

Thanks to the teachers of Reality Psychotherapy who passed on their knowledge to me, with which I grew into a therapist. Their influence is indelible.

I would like to thank my colleagues from Zagreb hospitals, University Hospital Centre Sisters of Mercy Zagreb and University Hospital Centre Zagreb, who keep helping patients with anorexia and bulimia. Orjena, Ivan, Darko, Maja B.,

Lena, Ivana, Barbara, Marija... Thank you for being with us all these years. Thank you, Božidar, Ana P. and other experts in the health system, for not giving up on the prevention and treatment of these severe and often misunderstood mental disorders.

And finally, I give thanks to my wonderful family – my husband Željko and my children, who patiently waited for Mum to finish her book. With their support, everything was possible. I thank my parents Nađa and Šime for teaching me to finish what I start, and that it is never too late to do the right thing.

Chapter 1

Introduction

This book explores sociological aspects of the body, eating and gender role expectations in women with eating disorders. This is a very current topic as eating disorders are on the rise, and scientists are still struggling to find the right way of interpreting them (Bulik et al., 2019; Munro et al., 2017). We can say that the conceptualisation of eating disorders is incomplete, and no theoretical model has yet offered an exhaustive explanation for the development, maintenance and treatment of eating disorders (Pennesi & Wade, 2016). This is evident in the fact that outcomes of eating disorder treatment are relatively poor (Bulik, 2014; Smink et al., 2012) since it is a very lengthy and expensive process (Toulany et al., 2015), with anorexia having the highest mortality rate of all psychiatric conditions (Smink et al., 2012).

In this book, we shall focus on the socio-cultural context of how eating disorders develop and are maintained, but this does not mean that we mean to diminish the importance of genetics, the biological basis of eating disorders (Bulik et al., 2019), personality traits (Culbert et al., 2015) and family dynamics (Gander et al., 2015), which have been proven to be associated with the development of eating disorders. The biopsychosocial model of understanding eating disorders has been called into question in recent years with the discovery of a biological basis of anorexia ('anorexia as a disease of the brain' Bulik, 2014; Treasure et al., 2014). Some authors have announced a paradigm shift in terms of treating anorexia as a metabolic as well as a psychiatric condition (Bulik et al., 2019) and accepting a biopsychiatric model (Treasure et al., 2014) as opposed to the current paradigm of recovery (Treasure et al., 2014) or the socio-cultural model of understanding eating disorders (Stice et al., 2017).

No matter how we conceptualise eating disorders, the fact remains that millions of children, women and men all over the world suffer profoundly or even die because of their disturbed relationship to their body and food. The fear of gaining weight, the obsession with being thin, starving oneself or excessive consumption of food followed by vomiting, fasting or obsessive exercising all lead to fatal consequences: poor health, stunted growth and development of children and young people, heart disease, digestive disorders, bone loss, tooth decay, kidney failure, brain starvation and also death as a result of medical complications or suicide (Crow et al., 2009). People with anorexia can be equally detached from the normal psychosocial functioning as people suffering from schizophrenia (Martin

Eating Disorders in a Capitalist World, 1–12
Copyright © 2024 Jelena Balabanić Mavrović
Published under exclusive licence by Emerald Publishing Limited
doi:10.1108/978-1-80455-786-020231001

et al., 2015; Treasure et al., 2001) to the extent that people with chronic anorexia do not finish school, are not employed and cannot live independently.

Such a serious decrease in life expectancy, quality of life and psychosocial functioning of the affected individuals encourages clinicians, theorists and researchers to continue the search for answers as to why eating disorders occur in the first place and what sustains this self-destructive behaviour.

I carried out the research presented in this book in 2019. I conducted semi-structured interviews with 30 women, who were or had been patients of the Day Hospital for Eating Disorders at the Sveti Ivan Psychiatric Hospital in Zagreb, Croatia at the time, and I performed a thematic analysis of these interviews. I included the interviewees in the research as an expert by experience (Tehseen, 2013), and it was important for me to understand the actual experience of the interviewees, their views and perspectives on the research topic. In order to reduce the traumatic potential of conducting the interviews, I chose interviewees for whom this was not the first time that they talked about their disorder to someone they did not know and who were taking part in a professional help programme. During the in-depth interviews, I also asked for procedural consents (Allmark et al., 2009): as soon as I noticed discomfort or hesitation in an interviewee, I would remind her that we could end the conversation then and there, and that she could decide which questions she would answer and which she would not. It was important to me that the interviewees felt safe during the interview and that I protected their dignity and well-being as much as possible at all times.

Some authors recommend that, before conducting semi-structured in-depth interviews with vulnerable groups, interviewers first spend some time working in that particular environment (Ensign, 2003) or even attend counselling training sessions to make sure that, when they communicate with members of vulnerable groups, their words or behaviour would not lead to misunderstandings or psychological harm for the interviewees (Parkes, 1995). In this research, this condition was met by the fact that I had completed a 5-year education programme for a psychotherapist in reality psychotherapy (EAP certificate). My many years of experience as a counselling therapist for people with eating disorders also proved invaluable.

As a researcher and the author of this study, I acknowledge three professional roles that have influenced my work: the role of a sociologist and social scientist, a therapist working in a counselling centre specialising in people with eating disorders and finally an activist promoting the need for prevention and treatment of eating disorders. The fact that these roles overlap has its advantages and disadvantages. Advantages include in-depth knowledge of the research area, and many years of practice in counselling, preventive and educational work with patients with eating disorders and their families, which has earned me my insider status. Most of the interviewees had heard about my work in advocating the rights of patients with eating disorders and were eager to participate in the research. It was easier for them to trust me since I had demonstrated sensitivity to the specific issues of this population in the past. At the beginning of each interview, I introduced myself and my research, but in most cases, the interviewees had already come with a positive attitude and were very much open to dialogue, which

I attribute to my earlier professional work in the field of eating disorders. This is supported by how they used the words 'us' and 'them' during the interviews: placing people with eating disorders and those who understand them in one group, while the other referred to the 'rest of the world' supported by the media which associate eating disorders with vanity, self-indulgence and 'weak will' while simultaneously insisting on the 'perfect appearance' of women and 'health food'. As a researcher, I was perceived either as part of the 'us' group or as an intermediary, a person who could help to dispel myths about eating disorders through her research. Generally, I see myself as a bridge between people with eating disorders and the scientific community, and I feel a double loyalty: on the one hand, to the academia, which is interested in research results and on the other hand, to people with eating disorders, whose attitudes, experiences and feelings I want to 'translate into scientific discourse' as faithfully as possible while still maintaining their authenticity.

1.1 Sociology and Eating Disorders

Insufficient research of eating disorders in a social context represents a challenge for every researcher who decides to delve into this topic. I believe it is crucial to shed light on the relationship between eating disorders and the social meanings attached to the body, food, eating and abstaining from food and especially gender roles as an important factor of one's personal identity related to the experience of physicality.

In this book, I adopt the definition of gender as a 'social construct of femininity/masculinity, i.e. the meaning these categories take on through the processes of socialization and construction of gender roles in society' (Galić, 2002, p. 227). Gender, gender roles and gender identity are cultural terms that suppose socially constructed and expected differences between men and women (Galić, 2008). Different norms, values and conventions, as well as representations, images and expectations, are thus attributed to the biological sexes (Galić, 2008). The female gender is biologically (through its reproductive role) and culturally connected with the meanings of the body (Grosz, 1994), and it is, therefore, important to look at the incidence of eating disorders through the sociological prism of gender construction.

To social scientists studying eating disorders, the relationship between eating disorders and cultural influence is particularly interesting and has been interpreted in various ways, from completely negating the existence of any connection to emphasising cultural influence as a key factor in the development of the disorder (eating disorders as a culture-bound syndrome, Swartz, 1985). The phenomenon of eating disorders has, therefore, been interpreted in various ways, and the quest for a clear interpretation is nowhere near over yet.

In medical circles in the early twentieth century, anorexia was defined as a disease of the pituitary gland (Dell'Osso et al., 2016), or in terms of psychoanalysis, as a subconscious fear of oral impregnation (Brumberg, 1989), and the starvation of young women (and occasional young men) was not brought into connection with any wider social influence. After the Second World War, the German psychiatrist Hilde Bruch, who worked in the United States, laid the foundations for the modern study of anorexia as a developmental personality disorder. She treated anorexia as a serious psychiatric illness and not as a difficulty in eating (Treasure & Cardi, 2017) and pointed out that the starvation of young girls represented a struggle for autonomy and confidence (Almeida et al., 2019). Many of Hilda Bruch's ideas are still fresh today and are consistent with contemporary understanding of eating disorders (Treasure & Cardi, 2017).

In the second half of the twentieth century, attempts were made to attribute the cause of eating disorders to family relationships, so concepts such as the 'anorexogenic family environment' (Dell'Osso et al., 2016) emerged, focusing on insecure attachment between mothers and children with eating disorders.

In the 1970s, the 'desire for thinness' was introduced into the diagnostic criteria (Dell'Osso et al., 2016), and 10 years later, with the recognition of bulimia as a separate form of eating disorder, there was a strong shift towards socio-cultural theories of the causes and rising prevalence of eating disorders. Such an understanding of eating disorders was facilitated by the rising rates of anorexia and bulimia among young people (Hall & Hay, 1991; Hoek et al., 2005; Jones et al., 1980; all according to Keel & Klump, 2003), which was interpreted as a consequence of the objectification of the female body in the media, the western cultural pressure for women to be thin and the new diet culture and the fitness industry (Hesse-Biber, 1991). Such social trends encouraged late twentieth century feminist theoreticians to link media pressure towards a thinner appearance in women with the greater prevalence of eating disorders. Through a series of influential books and the popularisation of original but also controversial concepts such as 'anorexia as a hunger strike' (Orbach, 1986) or 'anorexia as a crystallization of culture' (Bordo, 1993), these authors deepened their criticism of patriarchal society and the media's objectification of women. Feminist theorists based their criticism on the 'continuity theory' (Tylka & Subich, 1999), believing that there was nothing pathological in anorexia and bulimia, but that these forms of behaviour were only a radicalisation of the experience of 'being a woman' in modern Western society, in which all women were more or less constantly compared to ideal images of the female body found in the media and were thus hindered in the realisation of their own authentic personality. These authors offered gender theory as the key to the interpretation of eating disorders by analysing the specificity of the bodily aspect of the woman's experience in contemporary society.

Parallel to the feminist approach, an increasing number of researchers, mainly psychologists, wanted to operationalise the influence of the environment on the development of eating disorders, and influential models were created that are still used in research today: the tripartite influence model (Thompson et al., 1999) and the dual pathway model (Stice, 2001). These emphasised the influence of parents, peers and the media on the development of body dissatisfaction in young people, and emphasised the internalisation of the thin ideal and social comparison as mediators of these influences. In addition to these two models, especially influential is the transdiagnostic model (Fairburn et al., 2003), as the basis of the cognitive behavioural therapeutic approach to eating disorders. According to the transdiagnostic model, there is a fundamental psychopathology common to all types of eating disorders (i.e. anorexia, bulimia and other specified feeding or eating disorder), and that is a dysfunctional cognitive scheme which includes low self-esteem, high perfectionism, intolerance of 'bad' moods and difficulties in maintaining relationships with other people (Brytek-Matera, 2021).

Even though there are many inspiring theories and approaches, we are still faced with limited knowledge and insufficient effectiveness of current treatment methods for eating disorders. This creates a kind of uncertainty in research and clinical work. Relatively poor success rate and long-term psychotherapy (Pennesi & Wade, 2016) make the field of eating disorder studies open, self-reflexive and, ultimately, self-critical (Aradas et al., 2019; Bardone-Cone et al., 2018; Escobar-Koch et al., 2010; Hay, 2012; Holmes, 2019; Lilienfeld et al., 2013; Lock & Le Grange, 2018; Strober & Johnson, 2012).

The self-reflexivity of scientific efforts in the understanding and treatment of eating disorders strengthens the awareness of the historical basis of knowledge, so that the system is very flexible and is continuously searching for new solutions. As there is currently no 'silver bullet' for eating disorders, either in the form of pharmacotherapy or efficient psychotherapy with predictable outcomes (Keski-Rahkonen, 2007), we can conclude that the system does generate uncertainty, but at the same time encourages researchers and clinicians to keep a historical perspective and to be innovative and self-critical.

In this book, I shall deal with the issue of gender and gender stereotypes in women with eating disorders. Ever since the first cases of anorexia were recorded, this mental disorder has been associated with young women (Witztum et al., 2008), and gender issues were an integral element in the interpretation of anorexia, which was even called hysterical anorexia in the late nineteenth century (Lat. anorexia hysterica, Dell'Osso et al., 2016).

During puberty, a woman's body changes from that of a child to that of an adult, and symbolically it exhibits the need to assume the female role. For people with eating disorders, the body becomes the arena of internal struggle. Along with a number of other factors (genetic predisposition, neurological vulnerability, family situation, etc.), psychological conflicts intensify due to external pressure towards an unrealistically perfect appearance presented through the media, but also through social coding of femininity as the weaker sex (Bordo, 1993). The thin ideal as an ideal of female beauty, prevalent in Western society since the 1960s, has become the dominant way of expressing idealised femininity which symbolises self-discipline and the ability to succeed in competitive societies (Malson, 2009).

In addition to defining eating disorders in terms of gender, the twenty-first century has brought an objective increase in obesity in developed post-industrial countries and, consequently, a 'global war on obesity' (WHO, 2000). Scientists and doctors have now added to aesthetic demands on the female body by advocating weight loss, thus providing legitimacy to body monitoring and assessing health through the body mass index. The body as the basis of identity stems from a broader cultural understanding of health, desirable body weight and even morality. Numerous studies indicate that in Western society, in addition to aesthetic qualities, thin and obese bodies are also associated with moral qualities. Therefore, in addition to thin bodies being beautiful and desirable, they are also seen as healthy and they testify to responsible behaviour, self-control and moral virtues of the individual (Riley et al., 2008). In contrast, fat bodies are labelled as ugly and sick, and they are signs of overindulgence, greed and laziness (Malson, 2009).

In such a public health atmosphere, the prevention and treatment of eating disorders is even more challenging (Levine & McVey, 2015) since the values that inspire patients with eating disorders are in full agreement with the generally accepted values of 'the war on obesity' (Malson, 2009).

Despite all these challenges (or maybe precisely because of them), research in the field of eating disorders in the context of today's society is intriguing and exciting. It offers the possibility of shedding further light on these enigmatic and fascinating mental disorders, the way they are sustained and connected with social meanings that determine our gender identities, our relationship to food and the perception of different forms of the female body.

This book consists of two parts. In the first, theoretical part, we shall present the historical paradigms of interpretation of eating disorders and place them in the context of various social and technological changes that occurred over the past 100 years, namely the development of psychiatry, the feminist movement, the social processes of globalisation, industrialisation and urbanisation but also the technological development of science that enabled new ways of studying the genome and the functions of the brain. As was already mentioned, the twenty-first century has seen another paradigm shift (Bang et al., 2017; Bulik et al., 2019), and eating disorders are increasingly studied and defined as biologically based illnesses (Schmidt, 2003). After presenting an overview of the key achievements in the conceptualisation of eating disorders and of the fundamental research conducted so far, I shall move on to the findings of my own research. The second part of the book brings a description of the research and the results of the thematic analysis.

1.2 Eating Disorders

Eating disorders are mental disorders associated with a range of negative consequences which include medical complications and disruptions in an individual's cognitive, emotional and social functioning (APA, 2013). They constitute the third most common chronic diagnosis in the adolescent population after obesity and asthma (Kakhi & McCann, 2016), and anorexia is the mental disorder with the highest mortality rate (NICE, 2017). The Diagnostic and Statistical Manual of Mental Disorders describes eating disorders as 'characterized by a persistent disturbance in eating or eating-related behaviour that results in the altered consumption or absorption of food and that significantly impairs health or psychosocial functioning' (APA, 2013) (Table 1).[1]

---

[1]Types of eating disorders as classified in the 2013 American Psychiatric Association DSM-V manual include the following diagnoses: anorexia nervosa, bulimia nervosa, binge-eating disorder, pica, rumination disorder, avoidant/restrictive food intake disorder (ARFID), other specified feeding or eating disorder (OSFED), unspecified feeding or eating disorder (UFED).

Table 1. Anorexia Nervosa.

Anorexia Nervosa	
Lifetime prevalence	EU sample of 6 countries: 0.9% women; no recorded male ANs (Preti et al., 2009) Finnish sample: 2.2% women; 0.24% men (Keski-Rahkonen, 2007) USA sample: 0.9% women; 0.3% men (Hudson et al., 2007)
Malnutrition Dieting – starvation	Restriction of energy intake relative to requirements, leading to a significantly low body weight in the context of age, sex, developmental trajectory and physical health. (DSM-V, 2013)
Fear of gaining weight	Intense fear of gaining weight or of becoming fat, or persistent behaviour that interferes with weight gain, even though at a significantly low weight (DSM-V, 2013)
Distorted body image Attributing central importance to body weight Denying the health consequences of one's extreme thinness	Disturbance in the way in which one's body weight or shape is experienced, undue influence of body weight or shape on self-evaluation or persistent lack of recognition of the seriousness of the current low body weight. (DSM-V, 2013)
Other physiological effects of anorexia	Amenorrhoea (the absence of menstruation) or delayed menarche in girls, (no longer a diagnostic criterion in DSM-V) Dry flaking skin, fine downy hairs on neck and face, brittle nails, the yellowing of the skin, bradycardia, obstipation, low body temperature and muscle weakness (Mehler & Brown, 2015)
Health complications include	Osteopenia/osteoporosis, low blood pressure/orthostatic hypotension, heart arrhythmia, impaired kidney function, damage to the digestive system, stunted growth, infertility (Sidiropoulos, 2007)
Mortality	6% – of which 1.2% are suicide deaths (Arcelus et al., 2011)

Anorexia and bulimia are predominantly female mental disorders with a ratio of 9:1 in favour of female patients in anorexia (Micali et al., 2013), and 7:3 in bulimia (Dell'Osso et al., 2016). They typically develop in adolescence – most diagnoses of anorexia and bulimia are made between the ages of 15 and 24 (Smink et al., 2012). Anorexia and bulimia were first recorded in young high-class girls (the so-called golden girls from rich bourgeois families) (Bruch, 1973). Although anorexia and bulimia are different mental disorders, the transition rate between these two disorders is higher than between either of them and any other psychiatric diagnosis (Smolak & Levine, 2015). Therefore, we shall analyse the cultural context related to two of the three typical forms of eating disorders (the third typical form being the binge-eating disorder; Galmiche et al., 2019) since they represent a clearly differentiated sample of similar socio-demographic characteristics (Table 2).[2]

In addition to anorexia and bulimia, there is a category of 'other specified feeding or eating disorders'. This group of disorders, which used to be called eating disorders 'Not Otherwise Specified' in the DSM-IV, is actually the most common form of eating disorders. They include a disturbed relationship with food and the body which does not meet the diagnostic criteria of the so-called 'pure' anorexia, bulimia or binge-eating disorders (Table 3).

1.3 Diagnostic and Epistemological Controversies

The understanding of eating disorders has changed over time – the young science of psychiatry corrected and expanded the definitions of anorexia and bulimia in each new DSM manual since 1952. Until 1987, anorexia and bulimia were classified as one disorder, and in the DSM-III revised edition, they were split up into separate subtypes of eating disorders. The same thing happened in DSM-V (2013) with binge-eating disorder, which broke away from the group of not otherwise specified eating disorders into a separate diagnosis.

The high ambivalence and resistance which patients with eating disorders feel towards treatment should be emphasised, as well as the shame due to the strong

---

[2]Binge-eating disorder or compulsive overeating is a disorder that involves consuming a large amount of food in a short time (so-called binges or episodes of overeating), after which a person feels strong guilt and shame. In this book, we focus on anorexia and bulimia, and compulsive overeating will only be included sporadically since patients with binge-eating disorders are treated differently (da Luz et al., 2018); they often suffer from obesity (Hudson et al., 2007; Villarejo et al., 2012) and have a different socio-demographic profile. In order to compare the socio-demographic profile of people with anorexia and bulimia on the one hand, and people with binge-eating disorder on the other, we shall list the basic differences. In binge-eating disorder, the ratio of female and male patients is 3.5:2 (Hudson et al., 2007). People can develop it at any point in their lives, the peak being in the period of middle age (NIMH, NCS-R: 2001–2003). They suffer from social stigma because of their physical appearance (Palmeira et al., 2016), and there are studies which indicate greater prevalence of binge-eating disorder among the lower classes (Kim et al., 2020; Nicholls et al., 2016).

Table 2. Bulimia nervosa.

Bulimia Nervosa	
Lifetime prevalence	1.5% women; 0.5% men (Hudson et al., 2007)
Episodes of binge-eating Objectively large quantity of food Inability to control one's eating	Recurrent episodes of binge eating. An episode of binge eating is characterised by both of the following: Eating, in a discrete period of time (e.g. within any 2-hour period), an amount of food that is definitely larger than what most individuals would eat in a similar period of time under similar circumstances. A sense of lack of control over eating during the episode (e.g. a feeling that one cannot stop eating or control what or how much one is eating). (DSM-V, 2013)
Self-induced vomiting, misuse of laxatives, diuretics, etc. Fasting or excessive exercise	Recurrent inappropriate compensatory behaviours in order to prevent weight gain, such as self-induced vomiting; misuse of laxatives, diuretics or other medications; fasting; or excessive exercise. (DSM-V, 2013)
Frequency	The binge eating and inappropriate compensatory behaviours both occur, on average, at least once a week for 3 months
Self-evaluation is based on body image	Self-evaluation is unduly influenced by body shape and weight
Other physiological effects of bulimia	Russell's signs, nosebleeds/epistaxis, burst blood vessels in one's eye, tooth decay, swelling of the salivary glands/sialosis, difficulty swallowing/dysphagia, dehydration, constipation (Mehler & Rylander, 2015)
Health complications include	Oesophageal lesions with a higher risk for cancer (Brewster et al., 2015), damage to the digestive system, electrolyte imbalance, swelling of the extremities, heart failure (Mehler & Rylander, 2015)
Mortality	3.9% (Crow et al., 2009)

Table 3. OSFED/EDNOS Other Specified Feeding or Eating Disorders.

Other Specified Feeding or Eating Disorders OSFED/EDNOS	
Significant distress or impairment Symptoms do not meet the full criteria of anorexia or bulimia	This category applies to presentations in which symptoms characteristic of a feeding and eating disorder that cause clinically significant distress or impairment in social, occupational or other important areas of functioning predominate but do not meet the full criteria for any of the disorders in the feeding and eating disorders diagnostic class. (DSM-V, 2013)
Anorexia without malnutrition	Atypical anorexia nervosa: All of the criteria for anorexia nervosa are met, except that despite significant weight loss, the individual's weight is within or above the normal range. (DSM-V, 2013)
Bulimia of low frequency or of limited duration	Bulimia nervosa (of low frequency and/ or limited duration): All of the criteria for bulimia nervosa are met, except that the binge eating and inappropriate compensatory behaviours occur, on average, less than once a week and/or for less than 3 months
Binge-eating disorder of low frequency or limited duration	Binge-eating disorder (of low frequency and/or limited duration): All of the criteria for binge-eating disorder are met, except that the binge eating occurs, on average, less than once a week and/ or for less than 3 months
Purging disorder without binge eating	Purging disorder: Recurrent purging behaviour to influence weight or body shape (e.g. self-induced vomiting; misuse of laxatives, diuretics or other medications) in the absence of binge eating
Night eating	Night eating syndrome: Recurrent episodes of night eating, as manifested

Table 3. *(Continued)*

Other Specified Feeding or Eating Disorders OSFED/EDNOS	
	by eating after awakening from sleep or by excessive food consumption after the evening meal. There is awareness and recall of the eating. The night eating is not better explained by external influences such as changes in the individual's sleep-wake cycle or by local social norms. The night eating causes significant distress and/or impairment in functioning. The disordered pattern of eating is not better explained by binge-eating disorder or another mental disorder, including substance use, and is not attributable to another medical disorder or to an effect of medication
Mortality	5.2% (Crow et al., 2009)

stigma attached to mental disorders, which leads to estimates that presently only about 30% of patients with eating disorders are treated within the health system (Forrest et al., 2017; Hoek & van Hoeken, 2003; Keski-Rahkonen et al., 2008). Therefore, the collected data on the prevalence of anorexia and bulimia in the general population can only be considered relevant in terms of indicating the trends of this phenomenon, but not as realistic numerical indicators.

A certain 'elusiveness' of eating disorders in public health records makes it much more difficult to understand these complex phenomena and their correlation with the cultural and historical context. Studying eating disorders in different societies and time periods becomes more complicated since it is difficult to conduct a transcultural comparison of the presence of the aforementioned behaviours (and their meanings for the people involved) in different ethnic and racial groups at different stages of modernisation (Galmiche et al., 2019; Habermas, 2015).

All of the above strongly influences the understanding of the phenomenon of eating disorders. We can conclude that two processes are taking place at the same time, which makes it difficult to study these mental disorders objectively. Firstly, the diagnostic criteria are changing significantly, redefining our understanding of anorexia and bulimia and their statistical monitoring (Galmiche et al., 2019), and the disorders themselves are also changing due to their strong social components and relationships with environmental influences (Habermas, 2015).

Intense social changes over the last 50 years, which is how long the diagnostic defining and study of eating disorders in modern medicine has been in progress (bulimia was mentioned as a possible diagnosis as late as in 1979, in Russell's text *Bulimia nervosa: an ominous variant of anorexia nervosa*), strongly affect the understanding of the phenomenon of eating disorders, which 'change as we talk about them' (Nasser et al., 2001, p. 14). We can conclude that epistemological questions – what exactly eating disorders are and what the diagnostic criteria for them, their causes and pathogenesis are – still spark controversy (Smolak & Levine, 2015).

Chapter 2

In-depth Interviews With Women With Eating Disorders

In the context of historical and current perspectives in the study of eating disorders, I will present the findings of my research conducted in 2019 with a group of girls and women suffering from anorexia, bulimia and other specified feeding and eating disorders. The aim of the study was to determine, analyse and explain the social aspects of the body, eating and expected gender roles in women with eating disorders.

Given that the data were collected using qualitative methodology, i.e. the method of in-depth semi-structured interviews, and that setting hypotheses is not in accordance with this methodology, I was guided by the following research questions:

1. What gender stereotypes do women with eating disorders associate with male and female gender roles?
2. What social meanings do women with eating disorders associate with particular shapes of the female body (thin/fat) and food, eating and abstaining from food?

I conducted the research on my own. The structure of the protocol was determined in advance in order to gain insights into how the interviewees think and perceive the topics of interest to this research, but during the interview, I allowed them to free associate, digress and speak freely, in order to encourage their contribution to the creation of the study subject itself. Relying on the approach of observing the interviewees as an 'expert by experience' (Tehseen, 2013) and in accordance with the thematic analysis as the chosen method of qualitative data analysis, I wanted to ensure that the interviewees would be able to make contributions during the interviews as much as possible. I took this position while collecting the data guided by the awareness that the interviewees were experts on their own experience and that their insights and answers would not only enable the research questions to be clarified, but that the process might also open up additional topics important for the understanding of this field.

Eating Disorders in a Capitalist World, 13–22
Copyright © 2024 Jelena Balabanić Mavrović
Published under exclusive licence by Emerald Publishing Limited
doi:10.1108/978-1-80455-786-020231002

When determining the size of the sample for conducting a thematic analysis on the data collected through semi-structured in-depth interviews, I relied on the Braun and Clarke's recommendation (2013), and I selected 30 interviewees.[1]

The sample was purposive, and, therefore, it does not allow quantitative generalisations, but it enables the making of an analytical generalisation (Polit & Beck, 2010) through a deeper analysis of the collected data (Slišković, 2020).

The participants were members of the target population of female adults with experience of eating disorders (anorexia and bulimia). The sample is heterogeneous in terms of subtypes of eating disorders, which means that we included people with anorexia, bulimia and their mixed forms (other specified feeding and eating disorders, OSFED, DSM V, 2013). I decided on a heterogeneous sample in terms of psychiatric disorder subtypes in order to cover various forms of eating disorders and to investigate whether there were certain social aspects of attitudes towards gender stereotypes and social meanings which eating disorder patients associated with attitudes towards food and the shape of the female body. In this study, I did not conduct tests to determine the type or severity of the participants' eating disorders separately, since the involvement in psychiatric treatment for eating disorders alone qualified each individual for participation in this research. I did not consider comorbidities as relevant, since they are not the focus of this research.

Female interviewees were chosen for two reasons: they represent the majority of patients with eating disorders who seek psychological or medical help in the aforementioned institutions (90% of patients with anorexia and bulimia are female), and they represent a gender-homogeneous group which allows us to draw relevant conclusions about the research topic.

2.1 Method of Data Collection

I collected the data by conducting semi-structured in-depth interviews and through a questionnaire with the socio-demographic characteristics for each of the participants. I was aware that my own perspective could potentially influence the collecting of the data during the semi-structured in-depth interview, so I relied on double consciousness or an analytic 'eye' or 'ear' (Braun & Clarke, 2013) in the data collection process, which means that I simultaneously listened empathetically to the interviewees and critically analysed what they had said.

I believe that my involvement and empathy were beneficial because this led to a better understanding of the personal experiences of the interviewees (Slišković, 2020). Therefore, in the data collection process, I focused on achieving a balance between maintaining control over the direction of the interview which followed our original research questions and allowing the interviewees to redefine the research subject in order to gain new knowledge (Slišković, 2020).

---

[1]Some authors believe that six participants are sufficient for researching the personal experience of participants (Morse, 2000), while Guest (2006) believes that thematic saturation is achieved with 12 participants.

2.2 Ethical Considerations

In order to conduct research with patients with anorexia and bulimia from the Day Hospital for Eating Disorders at the Sveti Ivan Psychiatric Hospital in Zagreb (Jankomir), Croatia, I obtained the consent of the Research Ethics Committee at the Department of Sociology at the Faculty of Humanities and Social Sciences of the University of Zagreb and the Ethics Committee of the Sveti Ivan Psychiatric Hospital.

To ensure anonymity and confidentiality of the data, the interviewees were informed that any information regarding their names, the names of cities, hospitals, doctors and the like would be removed from the transcripts, which was carried out.

Since the participants in this study were individuals with lived experience of eating disorders, I estimated that the participation in the interview alone could have a disturbing effect for them. Therefore, it was important to me that psychological and psychiatric support was available for the interviewees at the Sveti Ivan Psychiatric Hospital after the interview.

I approached the problem of the power imbalance between the researcher and the interviewees by following the advice of Finch (1993), who recommends that the interviewer openly acknowledges that access to the intimate world of another individual is a great privilege.

When I conducted the interviews, I followed the point of view that I should maintain my position as a researcher and not assume the role of a therapist or activist (Rosenblatt, 1999; Smith, 1992). On several occasions during the interviews, I clearly stated this to the interviewees, gently reminding them that this was a research interview and not a therapy session. I empathically instructed the interviewees that if they felt they needed to work through the issues they had brought up, they should do so with their therapist.

In one of the interviews, the interviewee asked me to turn off the mobile phones which were used to record the sessions so she could share with me some extremely intimate information that she did not want 'entered in the study'. I followed the interviewee's request and the recording of the session was interrupted for five minutes in order for the interviewee to share a very emotional story which included a sexual trauma. I concluded that this was in accordance with the ethical principles of protecting the psychological well-being of the interviewees during the data collection process.

Furthermore, during the data collection process, several interviewees brought up memories of sexual abuse during their childhood or adolescence. I did not encourage the interviewees to expand on these topics, since they were not the focus of this study, but I listened to the interviewees when they chose to share these experiences in connection with the questions asked. The design of the research anticipated the possible disturbing potential of the interviews, and it was important that the participants should have available psychological and psychiatric support while they participated in the research.

This was not the first time that the participants shared their sexual traumas, and as a researcher I had no moral or legal obligation to react to testimonies of sexual abuse of minors in terms of sharing this knowledge with social services or the police.

After the interview was over and the cell phones used for recording were turned off, I spoke with each interviewee about their participation in the interview and asked them how they felt afterwards, how they had felt during the interviews, and I thanked them once again for their contribution. Some of the interviewees preferred that this conclusion of the conversation be short and others longer. I felt it was important to end the interviews in the most natural way possible, so that the interviewees would not feel like the objects of research, but as equal participants in the conversation.

All interviewees were offered the possibility to contact me later if they had additional questions or comments about the research. Two interviewees contacted me a day or two after their interviews: one wanted to expand on her answer to the question about what her physical appearance meant to her, while the other sent a written comment on the topic of the research by e-mail. In this way, I gave the interviewees the opportunity to manage the extent of their participation in the research. Just as I emphasised to the interviewees that they were not obliged to answer certain questions and that they could end the interview at any time, I also enabled them to make additional contributions, if they considered it important.

I believe that ethical guidelines do not consist in only informing the interviewee about the research and obtaining informed consent at the very beginning of the conversation. Ethics and respect for the interviewee need to be built into every stage of the interview, and also during the processing and the interpretation of the data (Qu & Dumay, 2011). We cannot treat the collected data as 'objective, with no strings attached' (Fontana & Frey, 1998, p. 663). To respect the ethical principles during the interview, but also during the processing and interpreting of the data in this book, I used my specific position as an 'insider' in the study matter and my ability to recognise potential vulnerability of the interviewees. I was also aware that some readers of this book might have had or might still have an eating disorder, which meant I had a responsibility towards them, as well as towards their parents and family members.

2.3 The Position of the Researcher: Advantages and Disadvantages of Previous Professional Work

In the introduction to this book, I emphasised that I am both burdened and blessed with three different professional roles: that of a scientist/researcher, counselling therapist specialising in eating disorders and activist. I work in counselling with patients every day and I know the subject extremely well, which is an advantage but also a possible disadvantage: the fact that I am too close to the research topic and the interviewees might have caused me to read meanings into the collected data which were not explicitly stated.

Also, my experience as a therapist could have made me emphasise the micro-level in my analyses while making me neglect the meso- and macro-levels. The sociological perspective in this study has certainly been heavily influenced by the psychological one, so there might be some potential difficulties in summarising the findings and reading the data through the sociological discourse.

Previous knowledge of the topic could trick one into thinking one knows everything and create preconceived notions which would close one's mind to interpretations of the data that might deviate from one's earlier experience and theoretical inclinations. There is also a danger for the researcher to treat the data as an 'illustration' of the theoretical research framework they have set.

It is possible that the socio-demographic characteristics of me as a researcher also influenced the data collection process in some way. The group identities that interviewers share with their interviewees give them an insider position (Le Gallais, 2008), and these insider identities are also associated with some outsider identities, which are also involved in negotiating power relations. Here I shall present the relationship between the possible identity positions of me as a researcher in communicating with the participants during the interviews.

As the Croatian society is racially homogenous, belonging to the Caucasian race is not relevant. The participants' experience of belonging to ethnic or religious minorities could be significant as examples of that of minority stress (Bulatao & Anderson, 2004), but the interviewees did not mention this explicitly. Other minority and regional identities were more prominent: the experience of marginalisation due to the fact that they had come from a small town or village, and self-marginalisation due to the fact that their family were war refugees.

My gender, age and sexual orientation were potentially more significant as characteristics which might have influenced the context of the interview. We can assume that my gender could contribute to us establishing a bond and trust as we shared a common experience of being a woman. I am significantly older than the interviewees, which could have reduced my understanding of them due to the generational gap and my ignorance of the subcultural identities of people who were 10 or 20 years my junior.

Furthermore, the interpersonal dynamics in a conversation between an older and a younger woman has the potential for establishing a connection and building trust, but also for making comparisons or for exclusions or pandering. The asymmetry of power inherent in the relationship between researcher and interviewee could have been additionally influenced by the halo effect (Powers & Knapp, 2010), their perception of my appearance and personality as a researcher, and the way in which I carry my femininity through visible features (my weight, clothes and shoes, hairstyle and makeup, body posture, etc.). Some interviewees probably knew that I was married and that I had three children, which defined me as a heterosexual woman who had chosen motherhood and a traditional form of partnership (marriage). These were all potential obstacles for expressing attitudes and values different from those of the majority, since I could easily be perceived as a person of so-called traditional values.

My belonging to the middle socioeconomic class and my higher education brought me closer to the participants of this research, since they mostly shared the same characteristics (or aspirations – in the case of students). Several interviewees mentioned their experience of poverty in their childhood or in the present situation, but since the research topic is not related to the socioeconomic aspect of having an eating disorder, nor have the relevant scientific studies (Mulders-Jones et al., 2017) shown the importance of SES on the development of eating disorders, we consider this aspect neutral.

What seems particularly important is self-reflexivity in the sense of recognising one's own beliefs and attitudes related to the subject of research (Finlay, 2002). I see myself as a person who leans towards feminist beliefs, but during data collection, coding and analysis, I tried to disassociate myself from my beliefs and focus on the data as much as possible in order to be able to interpret them credibly (Allmark et al., 2009).

In this study, the goal was to answer two basic research questions: 'What gender stereotypes do women with eating disorders associate with male and female gender roles?' and 'What social meanings do women with eating disorders associate with particular shapes of the female body (thin/fat) and food, eating and abstaining from food?' Searching for answers in the collected material, I singled out six basic themes and twenty-four sub-themes which shed light on the attitude of women with eating disorders towards gender roles and social meanings related to the body and food.

2.4 Specifics of Conducting a Semi-Structured In-depth Interview With Patients With Eating Disorders

In this research, I chose to conduct semi-structured in-depth interviews in order to obtain the highest quality data on the research topics, which included collecting and recording personal experiences and attitudes potentially difficult to communicate to a stranger.

Semi-structured in-depth interviews allow interviewees to communicate key information which is often hidden (Kvale & Brinkmann, 2009), in a manner characteristic of the interviewees themselves while maintaining their authentic ways of using language, styles and rhythms of speech (Qu & Dumay, 2011).

Nevertheless, I was aware of the danger of oversimplifying and idealising the method of the interview, which is based on the assumption that the interviewees are motivated and moral 'tellers of the truth', who want to serve science and reveal their experiences, feelings and values completely (Alvesson, 2003, p. 14). I bore in mind that different interviewers would elicit different answers from the same interviewee depending on the way the same questions were asked (Qu & Dumay, 2011). Therefore, I adopted a localist interview approach (Alvesson, 2003), which emphasises that both the interviewer and the interviewee participate in the interview, which becomes a complex interpersonal conversation guided by a procedure (Minichiello et al., 2008). Such a perspective is different from the neo-positivist position, which treats the interviewee as an objective truth-teller, but also from the romanticist point of view where the interviewer is an emphatic listener exploring the inner life world of the interviewee (Qu & Dumay, 2011). The collected data are also affected by the imbalance of personal power between the interviewer and the interviewee, in which the interviewee has less power and 'gifts answers' in response to the interviewer (Qu & Dumay, 2011, p. 246).

According to the localist position of conducting an interview, the data collected by the interviewer represent the interviewee's world view at a particular point in time in a certain context (Qu & Dumay, 2011); therefore, we cannot consider them as 'uncovered truths' but the result of understanding grounded in specific interactional episodes (Qu & Dumay, 2011). The already mentioned asymmetry of power is characterised by the fact that the researcher is in charge of questioning a more or less voluntary and sometimes naïve interviewee (Qu & Dumay, 2011). The possible goal of the interviewer and interviewee is to alleviate this imbalance in power and arrive at more equal footing during the interview, where it is crucial to be aware of the characteristics of the interviewer such as age, gender, race, belonging to a certain socioeconomic class, level of education, etc. (Denzin & Lincoln, 1998).

When conducting the interviews, I was aware of all these processes which influence the formation of complex interactions with the interviewees. Therefore, the first interpretation of the data took place during the interview itself, whereby I balanced between the emic insider position of the person who co-creates the dyadic situation of the conversation and the ethical outsider position, from which I reflected on how power asymmetries or other environmental factors could have affected the data collection process (Jönsson & Lukka, 2006). I was constantly reflexively 'going there and back again' in the interview itself (Jönsson & Lukka, 2006, p. 3). I wanted to achieve a balance between maintaining control over the direction of the interview, guided by the set research questions, and allowing the interviewees to redefine the research subject in order to include their authentic perspective in the collected data (Slišković, 2020).

Since a semi-structured in-depth interview combines the basic features of a structured interview (the length of the interview was limited to two hours, the fixed roles of the interviewee and the researcher were observed, and the basic agenda of the basic questions – the topics discussed – was followed) and informal conversation (the questions are open-ended and the conversation focuses on narration and experience rather than collecting objective information), I started each interview with a basic questionnaire on socio-demographic variables and I re-informed the interviewees about the research and their rights (they also signed the informed consent). Then I would start asking the pre-prepared basic questions. In order to introduce the interviewees to the research topics, I added questions about their childhoods and the very beginning of their disorders to the top of the prepared questions, and this material turned out to be extremely significant. It formed a theme which significantly contributed to clarifying their gender stereotypes, attitudes towards body size and shape and the relationship to food and eating.

During the data collection process, I was aware of the specifics related to the characteristics of the population of women with eating disorders. I would like to point out alexithymia, i.e. the inability to recognise and name one's own and/or other people's emotions, which proved to be a kind of obstacle in conducting semi-structured in-depth interviews with some of the interviewees. In interviewees who showed alexithymic tendencies, I encountered reduced verbal fluency, difficulty in expressing emotions and a lower level of abstraction in their statements. I adapted to this by asking follow-up questions and clarifying the questions additionally so that it would be easier for them to answer. In these cases, occasionally a long time would pass between the questions and answers, and pauses in the conversation were marked in the transcription. Considering my previous experience in counselling with people who have alexithymic tendencies, I did not interrupt the interviews and I patiently waited for the participants to answer the questions. The responses collected in the above manner represent very valuable data, with significant insights into the inner worlds of the interviewees.

With some participants, their accompanying psychological challenges lent a strong tone to their testimony. In the case of an interviewee who suffered from depression and took psychopharmaceuticals, her contribution was consistent with her condition. During the interview, I gently encouraged her and accepted a certain dispersion in her statements. In the case of an interviewee who had a marked borderline personality structure, the first part of the interview was conducted in a 'hyper' performance (Atkinson & Coffey, 2002) with flat, stereotypical answers: 'I had a wonderful family.', 'I was a happy child.' and 'Actually I don't have any problems in my relationship to food'. In the second part of the interview, by recounting specific situations in her life, the interviewee completely refuted the first part of the interview (her father was an alcoholic, her parents were divorced, she was overweight as a child, her peers teased her and she suffered because of it), so we included that part of the interview in the data processing.

I recorded the interviews with a mobile phone, transcribed them and then coded in the manner described in the next chapter.

Since these were semi-structured interviews, the themes of conversation were prepared, so the protocol followed the form below.

Before the interview, in a conversation with the interviewee, fill in the questionnaire with basic socio-demographic data: age, place of birth, pace of upbringing, education, employment, marital status, whether she has children, sexual orientation, when she was diagnosed with an eating disorder, where and how she was treated.

Theme: History of the Attitude Towards the Body and Food

1.   What was your attitude towards food?

     1.1   in childhood
     1.2   in puberty
     1.3   in adolescence

Theme: Current Attitude Towards the Body and Food

2.   How would you describe your current situation in relation to your body and food?

2.1 How do you see and experience your body?

2.2 How do you see and experience food?

2.3 How do you see and experience the act of eating?

2.4 Do you have allowed and forbidden foods?

2.5 How important is the number that appears on the scale when you weigh yourself to you?

Theme: Gender Stereotypes

3. When you hear the word 'woman', what comes to your mind? What are women like in general?

4. And when hear the word 'man', what comes to your mind? What are men like?

5. Have you ever wanted to be a man? Why?

6. What does being a woman mean to you personally? How do you see yourself as a woman? Examples?

7. What was growing up like for you in terms of accepting the female role? What do you remember from the period when you went from being a little girl to a girl, and later an adult woman?

8. How do you cope with the role of being a woman today?

9. Which part of the female role do you see as the most difficult?

10. Do you see any connection between the eating disorder and accepting yourself as a woman?

11. What does an attractive physical appearance mean to a woman? How important is physical attractiveness; what does it bring?

12. Do you think that women and men have an equal position in society today? Explain.

13. What do you think about the following concepts?

13.1 Marriage

13.2 Pregnancy and motherhood

13.3 Sexuality

Theme: Social Meaning Related to Food, Body and Nutrition

14. When you imagine a thin female body, what comes to your mind? What is a thin female body like?

14.1 What do you think about such bodies? Why?

14.2 How do you feel when you think about them? Why?

15. When you imagine a fat female body, what comes to your mind? What is a fat female body like?

15.1 What do you think about such bodies? Why?

15.2 How do you feel when you think about them? Why?

16. When you imagine controlled, dietary eating, what words and ideas do you associate with that kind of eating?

17. What are your experiences with dieting?

17.1 How do you feel while dieting? What are the advantages and disadvantages of dieting?

18. What are your experiences with binge-eating? Have you ever engaged in binge-eating?

18.1 How did you feel during a binge? What are the advantages and disadvantages of binge-eating?

19. When you imagine spontaneous eating, guided by the feelings of hunger and satiety, without control, what words and ideas do you associate with this form of eating?

19.1 Have you had experience with spontaneous eating? What are the advantages and disadvantages of spontaneous eating?

Theme: Healthy Food and a Healthy Lifestyle

20. What does 'healthy food' mean to you? How do you act when you 'eat healthy'?

21. How do you feel when you eat healthy?

22. What does unhealthy, poor nutrition mean to you? How do you behave when you 'eat unhealthy, bad food'?

23. How do you feel about yourself when you eat healthy food?

23.1 How do you feel about yourself when you eat unhealthy, bad food?

23. What else do you consider part of a healthy lifestyle (Exercising, other healthy lifestyle habits...)?

24. How do you feel about yourself when you 'live healthy'?

24.1 How do you feel about yourself when you do NOT live healthy?

25. What are the advantages and disadvantages of 'a healthy diet'? What are the advantages and disadvantages of 'a healthy lifestyle'?

Thank you for the conversation; you have helped me a lot with your answers.
If I didn't ask you something that you think is important, now is your chance to tell me – feel free to add anything.

Chapter 3

Development of Eating Disorders in the Socio-Historical Context

In order to understand today's forms of anorexia and bulimia, it is important to understand the socio-historical context in which they originated and were interpreted, since their origin, social construction and subjective life are directly associated with the social context of the relationship to the (female) body, the understanding of health and illness, the development of medicine and defining (female) gender roles.

Any overview of the history of anorexia will depend on which feature of the disorder we consider to be key: the physical manifestation of voluntary starvation among young girls and their firm resistance to feeding attempts, which is present to varying degrees throughout history in European and some other societies (Dell'Osso et al., 2016), or the psychological aspect – starvation that is solely motivated by the fear of gaining weight (Habermas, 2015). Therefore, we can say that there is a broader and a narrower definition of anorexia. If we define anorexia broadly as any intentional starvation without realising the health risks involved, which can lead to death, which is characteristic of young, adolescent girls, then the origins of anorexia date back to the fourth century AD. In Rome, among the group of wealthy women of high birth gathered around Saint Jerome, best known for his translation of the Bible from Hebrew into Latin, was a girl who died of starvation at the age of 20 (Bemporad, 1997; Keel & Klump, 2003). This may be the first recorded case of death from anorexia. Individual cases of voluntary starvation of women can be found in the Middle Ages as well, with the most famous representative being St. Wilgefortis ('courageous virgin'), also known as St. Liberata or St. Uncumber (Saint Liberator) (Bemporad, 1997).

The most famous phenomenon of abstinence from food in adolescent girls in history is known as *anorexia mirabilis* (or holy anorexia) and is associated with late medieval and Renaissance Italy (the period between 1200 and 1600) (Bell, 1985). Historian Rudolph Bell listed the known cases of voluntary religious fasting by 261 Italian girls or young women, who were later canonised. For about 170 of them, we have enough data to conclude that they showed signs of pathology related to eating, and about half of them meet the criteria for *holy anorexia* or *anorexia mirabilis* (Keel & Klump, 2003). Many Italian female saints of the Middle Ages wrote personal diaries to examine their souls for signs of

Eating Disorders in a Capitalist World, 23–40
Copyright © 2024 Jelena Balabanić Mavrović
Published under exclusive licence by Emerald Publishing Limited
doi:10.1108/978-1-80455-786-020231003

vainglory or the influence of Satan (Bell, 1985), and these journals were then read by their guardians and confessors. Some journals and biographies of saints later became widely read books which popularised religious fasting and other forms of suffering among girls and women in late medieval and early modern Europe. Thus, historians today have access to valuable and rare material that testifies to the inner life of these saints, their behaviour and attitudes towards the body and food (Bell, 1985).

Catherine of Siena is an example of a hundred or so religious women in Renaissance Italy who, in their asceticism and mystical ecstasy, exhibited behaviours associated with the modern concept of anorexia. In the deeply patriarchal and traditional society of the Middle Ages, the dominant life path for a woman was marriage and childbearing. In rare cases they could enter a monastery. As a female mystic who has a direct relationship with Jesus Christ, her spiritual fiancé, Catherine not only bypasses the existing church hierarchy but also violates the patriarchal structure of the Church. Because of this, the Church suspected Catherine and other Renaissance saints of heresy, often interrogated her, occasionally punished her sadistically (Bell, 1985, p. 76), and certainly kept her under strict surveillance.

Through their uniqueness, life without food and other forms of suffering, these saints proved that they were chosen, and they freed themselves from family and church bonds. They lived by their own extremely difficult, self-limiting and painful rules for which they answered only to the highest authority, Jesus Christ. Some of them succumbed to anorexia and died at an early age, while others managed to 'cure' themselves and find their place in the monastery, in the community of other sisters, where they eventually became abbesses and, naturally, continued to eat in moderation (the example of Saint Veronica; Bell, 1985).

In other parts of Europe in a later period from the seventeenth to the nineteenth centuries, we also come across 'miraculous maidens' or 'fasting girls'. Some authors link this form of female starvation to the broader concept of anorexia, proving that the concept of self-starvation has a trans-historical continuity (van Deth & Vandereycken, 1994). Other authors highlight the proven manipulation by the malnourished women themselves (the example of Ann Moore in Brumberg, 1989) or their parents (the case of Sarah Jacob, Brumberg, 1989).

The beginning of the medical understanding and description of anorexia is marked by the first physicians of the seventeenth century – the Italian Fabricius (Strober, 1986, p. 232) and Richard Morton (Malson, 1998). In his paper (1689/ 94) *Phthisiologica*, Morton described the first case of anorexia in English medical literature, calling it 'nervous atrophy' and compared the malnourished girl with 'a skeleton only clad with skin', saying she had lost her period due to 'a multitude of Cares and Passions of her Mind' (taken from Bliss & Branch, 1960, pp. 10–11; Waltos, 1986, pp. 1–2; all in Malson, 1998).

Before the official separation of anorexia as a distinctive diagnosis in European medical circles, descriptions of similar conditions of malnourished girls can be found in American authors under the terms dyspepsia, chlorotic anaemia and sitophobia or sitomania (Brumberg, 1982).

The rise of science and the bourgeoisie in Europe and the United States in the Victorian era paved the way for the medical profession to recognise the set of symptoms which physicians such as Sir William Gull (1874) and the Frenchman Lasègue (1873) called anorexia for the first time (Brumberg, 1989; Malson, 1998). Initially, anorexia was associated with hysteria and hypochondria as a form of 'hysteria of the gastric centre' (Malson, 1998). In 1873 Lasègue made a breakthrough in the understanding of anorexia, rejecting the then accepted theory that the cause of anorexic hysteria was associated with abnormalities related to the uterus (lat. *hystera*) (Sydenham in Malson, 1998, p. 62), pointing out that the cause of anorexia was to be found in the nervous system and nervous emotions instead (Malson, 1998, p. 62). A year later, Gull published an article in which he defined anorexia under the term 'anorexia nervosa', which is still used today.

In the early medical descriptions of anorexia by Gull and Lasègue, especially interesting is the fact that the signs and symptoms the patients presented with were exactly the same as today, with one exception – no fear of gaining weight was recorded (Malson, 1998). Therefore, we are talking about young girls of a higher social status who stop eating for no organic reason, who deteriorate physically, lose their periods and have accompanying physiological complications characteristic of malnutrition (cold extremities, lanugo hair growth, hair loss, low heart rate and low blood pressure). Patients are often hyperactive or depressed, they stubbornly reject all efforts of their family and doctors to feed them and they isolate themselves from the environment. However, none of the early clinicians recorded that the patients were consciously losing weight because of the desire to look thin or that they had a fear of gaining weight (Brumberg, 1989; Habermas, 2015; Malson, 1998).

The first medical interpretations of anorexia in the second half of the nineteenth century revolved around the concepts of the body, femininity and health of the time, and they testified to the new dominance of science and secular rationalism in the Western society (Brumberg, 1989). The belief that self-starvation was miraculous or divine, characteristic of the earlier historical period (the Middle Ages and the early modern period), had now come to be considered an ideology (Malson, 1998). In the Victorian era, anorexia was viewed as a female malady (despite the occasional male patient – in Gull, 1874, according to Malson, 1998), 'since women were assumed to have more delicate and sensitive nerves than men and therefore to be more prone to nervous diseases' (Wilks, 1888, according to Malson, 1998, p. 57). According to Lasègue, anorexia is associated with unfulfilled romantic or sexual desires, 'real or imagined marriage project' of adolescent girls or to 'a violence done to some sympathy' (Lasègue, 1873b, p. 265, according to Malson, 1998), and is called an 'intellectual perversion' (Lasègue, 1873b, p. 368, according to Malson, 1998). The medical construction of anorexia as 'hysterical anorexia' (French: *l'anorexie hysterique*) additionally consolidated the cultural figure of the 'nervous woman' of the nineteenth century (Showalter, 1985 according to Malson, 1998). Since femininity in early modernity was constructed as being irrational, nervous, weak and childish (Malson, 1998), anorexics required 'moral control' 'fitted for persons of unsound mind' (Gull, 1874, p. 26 according to Malson, 1998). Playfair points out that a girl with anorexia is a 'hardened neurotic sinner' (Playfair, 1888, p. 818 according to Malson, 1998). Malson concludes that in the nineteenth century 'women's nerves replaced their wombs in accounts of female pathology' (Malson, 1998, p. 76).

Although the first medical descriptions of anorexia did not record the fear of gaining weight as a direct motive for self-starvation, the historian Brumberg (1989) described the cultural climate of the Victorian era in the United States, which emphasised the desirable physical delicacy, refinement and ethereality of young girls as an expression of their fineness of spirit and incapacity for physical labour, and this was a visible sign of belonging to a higher social class. Brumberg takes over Veblen's theory (the Theory of the Leisure Class, 1899/2008) about the body as an indicator of the social status of the new leisure class, in which a thin girl testified to the wealth, education and lifestyle of her parents and was a desirable match on the 'marriage market' (Brumberg, 1989, p. 137).

Ever since the earliest description of anorexia, a paradox can be observed which continues to this day. On the one hand, anorexia can be seen as being in accordance with the expectations of an era (religious asceticism of the Middle Ages, the refined physicality of the bourgeois girl of the Victorian era, the modern ideal of female beauty mediated by the media), but on the other, it can also be viewed as a silent rebellion against these expectations, as the behaviour associated with anorexia leads to the negation of the underlying values. From this overview, we can surmise that anorexic girls indirectly boycotted entire systems, the values of which they had seemingly taken over – they rejected the ecclesiastical hierarchy and the traditional female role in the Middle Ages, they rejected the passive role of an obedient daughter in bourgeois families and prevented their future marriage and motherhood from happening. Similarly, in the contemporary globalised world of late capitalism, they withdraw from various psycho-social roles which would have been available to them as so-called attractive girls in accordance with the contemporary ideals of beauty, thus maintaining control over their body and food as the last strongholds of their threatened identities.

In the early twentieth century, in accordance with the positivist approach to science and in an effort to discover the 'real', organic cause of anorexia, the disorder was attributed to the atrophy of the anterior lobe of the pituitary gland, which was first described by the German doctor Simmond in 1914 (Bruch, 1973; Brumberg, 1982; Malson, 2009).

Meanwhile, with the development of psychoanalysis, the psychological conceptualisation of anorexia was also strengthened. In the 1940s, papers were published which interpreted anorexia through a rather 'bizarre theory' (Boskind-Lodahl, 1976) about how the affected girls refuse food due to their fear of oral impregnation – more precisely, because they were blocking their subconscious desire for oral impregnation (DellOsso et al., 2016; Gordon, 2015).

Early psychoanalytic theory focused on the difficulties in the sexual maturation of girls suffering from anorexia. The psychiatrist Hilde Bruch (1904–1984), perhaps the most significant author to make a contribution to defining and understanding eating disorders, especially anorexia, ended this practice.

Dr. Bruch dedicated her life to the study of anorexia and obesity, and in 1973 she published her book 'Eating Disorders: Obesity, Anorexia Nervosa, and the Person Within', which was followed by the bestseller 'The Golden Cage: The Enigma of Anorexia Nervosa'. Though a psychoanalyst herself, Bruch departed from the then dominant psychoanalytical interpretation of anorexia as an expression of problematic and repressed sexuality and emphasised the halt in the development of affected girls, namely their separation from parents and the construction of an autonomous personality. After a decade of clinical work with anorexia patients, Bruch singled out the distorted body image in affected girls as a specificity of anorexia (Dell'Osso et al., 2016). She described her typical patient: an obedient, well-educated girl from an affluent family ('a sparrow in a golden cage'), who felt as if she did not meet the expectations of her environment and her parents, and had low self-esteem. Such a girl fails to develop an independent sense of her own personality and cannot find her own individuality in adolescence or separate from her family (Bruch, 1978). A girl suffering from anorexia turns to her body and food and establishes extreme control over them since she believes she has no control over anything else (Dell'Osso et al., 2016). Bruch states that affected girls are overwhelmed by the vast number of potential opportunities available to them which they 'ought to fulfil' (Bruch, 1978, p. IX). They are given too many choices and are afraid that they will not make the right one. Dieting becomes a compulsive force that dominates the whole life of girls suffering from anorexia (Bruch, 1978, p. 19).

Bruch observed that there were difficulties in early bonding with a parental figure, characterised by insecure attachment patterns (Treasure & Cardi, 2017). She emphasised the role of high perfectionism and social comparison to the detriment of the affected individual, and how a patient is often in a state of 'internal confusion' (Treasure & Cardi, 2017, p. 143) associated with the misunderstanding of her own feelings and physical conditions, cognitive rigidity and poor emotional regulation (Treasure & Cardi, 2017). She directed the treatment towards a combination of physical recovery and psychotherapy, in which the patient's family is also included (Treasure & Cardi, 2017), resisting the dominant approaches of the time – the medical one, which focused on the patient's physical recovery and feeding while disregarding the psychological aspect of anorexia, as well as the psychoanalytic approach, which focused only on individual psychotherapy while ignoring the patient's malnourished condition (Treasure & Cardi, 2017).

This overview shows that there was a turning point in the conceptualisation of anorexia in the twentieth century. Even though we do not find any mention of the fear of gaining weight in the medieval or the first scientific records of anorexia, since the 1970s this fear and the desire to lose weight have been accepted as the central organisational motives of anorexia nervosa in Europe and North America (Habermas, 2015).

Even today, there is no consensus on how to define anorexia. In the Anglo-Saxon literature, a broader approach to defining anorexia is more dominant, and here the fear of gaining weight is not considered a key element (Habermas, 2015). This tendency can be seen in the criteria in DSM-V (2013), where it is acknowledged that an individual has either a 'strong fear' of gaining weight and obesity or that they take persistent actions to make it difficult to gain weight. However, proponents of conscious weight loss due to the fear of gaining weight as the central point of the anorexia nervosa disorder (Habermas, 2015) insist on a narrower definition of anorexia, which sees it as a specifically modern mental disorder fuelled by social influence and the imposition of thinness as an ideal of beauty.

3.1 The Influence of Psychoanalysis

In the second half of the twentieth century, we can see a strong influence of the psychoanalytic and other psychodynamic schools, which searched for the cause of anorexia in the first few years of the patient's life and in the dysfunctional early relationship with their mother and father.

Psychoanalysis treated the development of anorexia as being associated with an unresolved oedipal complex (Sperling, 1978). Wilson (1988) points out a fixation in the oral phase of a child's development, as well as sadomasochistic conflicts, which are supported by an overprotective mother and/or father and by the symbolic emphasis on food and feeding as an expression of love. According to object relations theory (Klein, 1930 in Lawrence, 2008), anorexia and bulimia arise from a person's unconscious attempt to kill the internalised maternal object 'within themselves' with which they are in a symbiotic relationship, as well as to control the relationship with the parents, in which the father is most often emotionally or physically unavailable (Lawrence, 2008). Anorexia can thus be defined as a developmental disorder which protects the individual from the threat of adult sexuality (Lawrence, 2008, p. 36).

A lot of controversial material has emerged from the psychoanalytic theories and clinical work, such as Birksted-Breen's hypothesis (1986) that the emaciated body of a person with anorexia represents an erect phallus with its power and potential cruelty (Lawrence, 2008, p. 84), and that exhibitionistic parental sexual and toilet behaviour was found in families of individuals with anorexia (Wilson, 1988, p. 435), or that patients with anorexia transfer their sexual and masturbation conflicts from their genitals to the mouth, equating food and eating with forbidden sexual objects and activities (Sperling, 1978, according to Wilson et al., 1983, p. 436). We can say that a consequence of the psychoanalysis-dominated period of clinical work with anorexia and bulimia patients during the 1970s and 1980s (Sperling, 1978 according to Wilson, 1988) is a distorted message that 'mothers are to blame for their daughters' eating disorders (Smalley et al., 2017), or that behind a daughter's anorexia there is always an overly domineering or controlling mother (and/or father) (Wilson et al., 1983).

Freud's legacy also includes the concept of the 'death drive' as an innate internal driving force, which is paired with libido, the creative force of life. In the behaviour of people with anorexia, the destructive death drive seems to prevail (Lawrence, 2008) as it 'operates silently' directing the individual's behaviour against themselves (Freud, 1930a, pp. 118–119, according to Lawrence, 2008).

Continuing the psychoanalytic tradition, but also building on it, the authors from the object relations school emphasise perceived and interiorised objects (internal symbols of mother and father), which may or may not correspond to reality (Lawrence, 2008). Eating disorders are perceived as relationship disorders (Lawrence, 2008, p. 20). They agree that there is a specificity of the dyadic mother–daughter relationship in anorexia, where the daughter has not established autonomy from the mother and is torn between conflicting internal needs for connecting with her internal object and for separating (Lawrence, 2008). As an individual with anorexia, neither manages to return to the infantile state of oneness with the mother nor to separate into an independent person, they consider their addictive need for protection as a weakness and blame the mother as being intrusive, too protective or too demanding, which may or may not correspond to reality (Lawrence, 2008). According to psychoanalytic theory, the anorexic girl's attack on her own body represents an attempt to resolve the high anxiety associated with the 'primitive and regressive relationship to the internal mother' (Lawrence, 2008, p. 91), to control the body that is becoming more and more mature and turning into the body of an adult female (like her mother's) and to control her own mind (Lawrence, 2008), which now thinks only about the body and food and not about its own needs. Anorexic behaviour offers the individual a semblance of identity without having resolved the relationships with the mother and father (Lawrence, 2008).

Attachment theory further emphasised the importance of the dyadic relationship, whereby anorexia is understood as an individual response to problems of attachment (Smalley et al., 2017). Ainsworth and Bowlby (Ainsworth & Bowlby, 1991 according to Bretherton, 1992) studied the early development of children, and established the ways in which they react to being separated from their mother. For these authors, the relationship with the primary caregivers (especially the mother) constitutes the basis of the model for relationships formed with other individuals in adulthood. In most children – and consequently also in adults – a secure type of attachment is observed, which allows an individual to understand and integrate pleasant and unpleasant experiences, and creates a coherent and safe relationship with the caregivers, and later ensures a stable psychological development.

Bowlby (1969) and Ainsworth (Ainsworth & Bell, 1970) also defined types of insecure attachment styles, which were operationalised into three subtypes – avoidant attachment, ambivalent or resistant attachment and disorganised attachment.

People characterised by avoidant attachment avoid close relationships in order to feel safe, they have difficulty showing emotions – especially in stressful situations – they idealise their parents, and often use work to avoid social situations.

Ambivalently or resistantly attached individuals exhibit enmeshment with their caregivers, anger and low autonomy towards them, as well as a fear of not being loved enough.

The last group, disorganised/unresolved attachment, is more recent (Main & Solomon, 1990, according to Simpson & Rholes, 1994). It does not have a clear pattern of behaviour and is characteristic of people exposed to traumatic experiences such as the loss of a parent or abuse, in which they failed to develop coping mechanisms which would help them deal with the consequences of the trauma.

Eating disorders mostly occur in adolescence, when the need for autonomy and separation from parents can come into conflict with the ways of functioning in people with insecure attachment (Gander et al., 2015). Repeated research has shown that most people with anorexia (and bulimia) exhibit insecure attachment types (Armstrong & Roth, 1989; O'Shaughnessy & Dallos, 2009; Tasca et al., 2013; Ward et al., 2000; Zachrisson & Kulbotten, 2006), where the results are not consistent for those of insecure attachment type – in some cases, the majority of patients with anorexia exhibit an avoidant attachment style (bulimia is associated with the ambivalent/resistant attachment style), while other studies highlight the presence of disorganising attachment as the most important (Gander et al., 2015). The similarity in styles between mothers and daughters with anorexia is particularly significant, where the avoidant attachment style is predominant (Ward et al., 2001), so we can talk about a transgenerational transmission of the model of insecure attachment styles (Gander et al., 2015; Smilley et al., 2017).

In the 1970s, structural family therapy was developed. It included the work of Minuchin and his associates in the United States of America and the work of Selvini-Palazzoli, who founded the Milan School (Dodge, 2016). This approach emphasised the dysfunctionality of the anorexic child's family, which led to a simplified, distorted interpretation and the idea that the parents should be blamed for the onset of anorexia (Dodge, 2016). The explanatory model of the 'psychosomatic family' (Minuchin et al., 1978) stresses harmful patterns of family functioning that lead to the development of anorexia in a vulnerable child. The concept of triangulation is based on a dysfunctional relationship between the partners in such a family, and the child is 'caught in the middle' and is responsible for creating a balance in the family system (Smalley et al., 2017). It 'takes the side' of one parent and thus intergenerational alliances and divided child loyalty are formed (Smalley et al., 2017). In families, something called intertwining can occur, i.e. an extreme form of closeness, in which the individual is overwhelmed by the influence of other family members – one family member 'knows' what the other thinks and feels, there is a lack of privacy, and children are often elevated to have a quasi-equal status with their parents, by which a clear division of roles disappears (Dodge, 2016). There is unspoken or hidden tension between the parents, where one parent is emotionally or physically unavailable, so the child assumes the role of a 'surrogate parent' as emotional support for the 'remaining parent' (Smalley et al., 2017). It was believed that children with anorexia are not aware of their own emotional needs since they equate them with the needs of their parent (Minuchin & Fishman, 1981). Therefore, children express their emotional needs indirectly, through a symptom – anorexia (Fishman, 2005). Anorexia is thus simultaneously an expression of the dysfunctionality of the family system, but also 'family glue', since caring for a sick child sometimes unites the parents and alleviates family conflicts (Dallos, 2001; Dallos & Denford, 2008).

3.2 The Influence of Society

In the late 1970s and in the 1980s, there was significant criticism of the afore-mentioned psychiatric approaches in the interpretation and treatment of anorexia. Numerous theoreticians and clinicians were faced with unprecedented high rates of anorexia (and bulimia) in Europe and North America and were not satisfied with existing explanations which treated anorexia as a result of individual or family psychopathology or the interaction of the two. At that time, feminist criticism and theoreticians of socio-cultural influences made a crucial shift and conceived anorexia and bulimia as culture-bound syndromes (Swartz, 1985) or variations of that paradigm – culture-reactive syndromes (Pike & Dunne, 2015) and culture-change syndromes (DiNicola, 1990), which I shall elaborate later on.

In this period, bulimia was clinically acknowledged as a separate symptom (Boskind-Lodahl, 1976; Russell, 1979). Therefore, I shall present a short overview of bulimic behaviour throughout history and later return to theories about the socio-cultural determinants of anorexia and bulimia.

The history of bulimia nervosa is even more complex than that of anorexia. There is no consensus about the name and the symptoms associated with the term in historical records. Medieval authors mention bulimia as excessive eating (Hufeland, 1736, according to Ziolko, 1996). Some 1980s' authors only meant binge eating, vomiting and the abuse of laxatives and diuretics by the term (Wilson, 1988), and over time it has grown into a distinctive disorder called bulimia nervosa, which in some variants doesn't even need to include vomiting or laxative abuse, but rather binge eating followed by other compensatory behaviours designed to prevent weight gain (DSM IV, 1994). Maintaining body weight within or above the normal range is crucial for bulimia, so that people with bulimia are well-nourished or slightly overweight.

When we talk about bulimia nervosa today, we talk about a mental disorder which includes episodes of overeating called bingeing and then purging through vomiting, the use of laxatives or diuretics, or compensatory behaviours – fasting or increased physical activity (DSM-V, 2013).

Bulimia, anorexia's little sister (Frey, 2020), waited a long time for its clinical recognition and differentiated diagnosis, right up until the late 1970s (Boskind-Lodahl, 1976; Russell, 1979). Bulimia nervosa is thus located on the spectrum of eating disorders between purgative anorexia on the one side and binge eating and obesity disorders on the other. It includes a series of behaviours which were only recognised in the second half of the twentieth century as a unique disorder, built around the fear of gaining weight as a central organising factor (Gordon, 2015).

Binge eating and vomiting were recorded throughout history, but they were not consistent with the contemporary idea of bulimia nervosa. Cases are relatively few (Keel & Klump, 2003) compared to historical cases of anorexia nervosa. It were mostly adult men who overate and then vomited that were recorded, while today the vast majority of bulimia sufferers are female (Witztum et al., 2008), and it is not certain whether the vomiting recorded in these historical cases was self-induced or a result of an organic cause (intestinal parasites, infections, etc.) (Witztum et al., 2008). Therefore, these could arguably be cases of what we today call binge-eating disorder (Gordon, 2015; Keel & Klump, 2003).

Even the well-known reference to Roman feasts with the characteristic group overeating and vomiting in vomitoriums, special rooms for that purpose, (Mumford, 1961), has in recent times turned out to be a mistranslation. Namely, historians today believe that 'vomitorium' is the name for a corridor under the auditorium in Roman amphitheatres (Radin, 2003).

The first cases which could indicate bulimic behaviour were recorded in the second century, and they included the Roman emperors Claudius and Vitellius (Crichton, 1996; Witztum et al., 2008). Seneca described the behaviour of the debauched Roman aristocracy: 'They eat in order to vomit and vomit in order to eat' (Gordon, 2015, p. 26). Self-induced vomiting appears in the recommendations of medieval physicians – Avicenna mentions it as a way to get relief while overeating, but he warns of harmful consequences for the stomach, oesophagus and teeth, as well as the possibility of weight loss if vomiting is excessive (Nasser, 1993 in Witztum et al., 2008), and this is actually an allusion to the disorder we know today as purgative anorexia. Arab sources also point out the dangers of making vomiting due to binge eating a habit (Witztum et al., 2008).

A minority of authors (Parry-Jones & Parry-Jones, 1991; Ziolko, 1996) claim that bulimia has a historical continuity, relying mostly on descriptions of 'ravenous hunger' (Ziolko, 1996, p. 347) in Greek and Roman medical writings, but these are most likely descriptions of the binge-eating disorder rather than of bulimic behaviour (Gordon, 2015).

In the twentieth century, Janet (1903), Linder (1955) and Stauder (1959) (all according to Ziolko, 1996) described the first 'modern' cases of bulimia – they were all of women who felt an internal compulsion towards eating, which Stauder also called 'food addiction' (Stauder, 1953 according to Ziolko, 1996, p. 355). Janet's patient would engage in binge eating continuously for 10 to 15 days, then eat normally for months and then a new period of continuous binge eating would ensue (Janet, 1903 according to Ziolko, 1996). Lindner's patient Laura 'was subject to sudden uncontrollable voracious and insatiable impulses, simultaneously occurring with episodes of depression' (Lindner, 1955 according to Ziolko, 1996, p. 355), so she would overeat until exhaustion, after which she would vomit, only to overeat again. After a series of binge eating and vomiting episodes, she would enter a state of 'utter exhaustion and total intoxication' accompanied by acute stomach pains and a need to sleep (Lindner, 1955 according to Ziolko, 1996, p. 355). Similar claims were made by Stauder (1959, according to Ziolko, 1996), who in his case descriptions introduced elements comparable to the modern diagnosis of bulimia for the first time: the patient is described as groomed and cultivated, disposed to corpulence and she consciously vomited in order to maintain a slim appearance. She compensated for her binge eating through frequent vomiting – sometimes 10 times a day, after which she would feel strong guilt and shame.

For the recognition of bulimia nervosa, two papers about a new strange form of anorexia published in the 1970s were particularly important. The first paper, written by the young psychologist Boskind-Lodahl (later Boskind-White, 1976), appeared in the American, somewhat marginal, feminist journal *Sings* (Gordon, 2015) and was unrecognised as the first clinical definition of bulimia for a very long time. Another scientific paper was published in a respectable medical journal in 1979 by a distinguished British psychiatrist G. Russell, an expert in the treatment of anorexia. The article, entitled 'Bulimia nervosa: an ominous variant of anorexia nervosa', attracted a lot of attention from the scientific community, and consequently Professor Russell has been considered the father of the modern definition of bulimia nervosa for decades (Gordon, 2015).

In her article (1976), Boskind-Lodahl compares individuals with bulimia to Cinderella's stepsisters – they desperately want to put on the glass slipper which is too small for their feet in order to win the prince's favour and social recognition. The author sees individuals with bulimia as wanting to 'enter' the socially defined beautiful female body and meet the expectations of others. As Boskind-Lodahl (1976) openly advocated the feminist perspective, she saw in the pressure towards an unrealistically thin appearance the influence of a patriarchal society and the desire of women to please others. She could not separate the individual fear of gaining weight from the social climate of idealising thinness and objectifying the female body (Gordon, 2015). Russell also pointed out (1979) that bulimic patients differ from those suffering from anorexia in that the former are much more functional, they mostly carry out their daily tasks and can hide their destructive behaviour for years (Russell, 1979).

Patients with bulimia are interested in romantic relationships and are most often sexually active (Gordon, 2015), which distinguishes them from the majority of anorexia patients. People with bulimia often have a history of periods when they were mildly overweight, followed by dieting, which in some cases escalates into anorexic episodes, only for the person to enter a cycle of binge eating and purging through vomiting or laxative/diuretic use. In some cases, binge eating alternates with periods of extreme restrictive eating or fasting, sometimes accompanied by obsessive exercising (Crow & Eckert, 2016). Fear of gaining weight is key, as well as feelings of shame and guilt after a binge (Crow & Eckert, 2016). During her professional work, Boskind-Lodahl (later Boskind-White) maintained the distinction between anorexia and bulimia, emphasising that bulimia (a disorder she called 'bulimarexia') is based on a socially created feeling of inferiority due to obesity (Gordon, 2015).

At this point, I emphasise the specific social circumstances which accompanied the recognition of bulimia in the second half of the twentieth century: bulimia arose at a time when there were two opposing trends in the affluent societies of Europe and North America – the abundance of available food and the social pressure for thinness (Gordon, 2015).

After the Second World War came a period of an economic boom, increased availability of food and the industrial production of refined and fast food (Gordon, 2015). Social changes associated with the development of the capitalist society which began in the nineteenth century, such as urbanisation, democratisation, the emancipation of women, the dominance of the nuclear family as opposed to the traditional extended family and the entry of women into the labour market led to changed eating habits. Thus food became available, cheap and highly caloric and the act of eating meals itself moved away from the family and became an independent act, unrelated to family rituals and the production and preparation of food (Pike & Dunne, 2015). Food no longer needed to be grown, processed into a semi-finished product to be stored and prepared in one's kitchen, transformed from raw materials into an edible form. Through a society organised around consumerism, ready-made and semi-ready food is available to everyone through a network of stores, and the time period from experiencing hunger to the consumption of food has shortened to mere minutes (Brumberg, 1982). With the development of mass media, the advertising industry focused on creating additional need for food, and highly processed convenience foods and sweetened beverages were equated with pleasure (Churruca et al., 2014). Processed foods with flavour enhancers and high amounts of sugar and salt are common in everyday life from early childhood (Hayes et al., 2018), and these, as we know today, can also have an addictive effect (Gearhardt et al., 2011).

It can be said that in Europe and North America in the period after the Second World War, the modern way of life dissolved the traditional ways of food consumption in the form of family meals and the so-called fast food made it possible to buy and consume ready-made food at any time of the day and away from the home. Brumberg calls this promiscuous eating (Brumberg, 1982, p. 263). All of the above has influenced the increase in the average body weight of modern men and women, which has simultaneously been marked as undesirable and unattractive.

The paper published by Christopher Fairburn and his colleagues in 2003 is crucial for understanding bulimia. From the very beginning of the clinical and scientific defining of this new type of eating disorder in the 1980s, they developed their unique approach based on cognitive behavioural therapy (Gordon, 2015). Fairburn noted that individuals with bulimia attach central importance to their appearance and body weight as a basis of their self-evaluation and that they follow a series of strict dietary rules in order to lose weight. He realised that the moment these people violate their self-imposed dietary rules, they 'lose control' over their eating and start bingeing (Fairburn, 2008). After taking in large amounts of food in a short period of time, they resort to compensatory behaviours in order to 'undo the damage they have done', i.e. expel the ingested calories in some way. Fairburn et al. (2003) observed that bulimic patients were able to break the vicious circle of binge eating, purging and dieting if they changed their rigid dietary patterns and obsession with body size and shape, which was a revolutionary departure from the practice of treating eating disorders at the time. Thus, they applied cognitive behavioural therapy to eating disorders (Fairburn et al., 2003).

Cognitive behavioural therapy based its novel view on eating disorders on the results of research on the physical and psychological effects of starvation on healthy men conducted at the University of Minnesota in 1944 under the leadership of Dr Keys. In short, in the Minnesota Starvation Experiment, some behaviours and psychological states, which were considered key characteristics of anorexia and bulimia as mental disorders, were caused by the very act of starvation (Keys et al., 1950), which is now called the Minnesota syndrome.[1] Therefore, in recovery from anorexia or atypical anorexia (a drastic loss of body mass, where the individual is not malnourished but suffers consequences similar to those of malnutrition metabolically), it is important to achieve physical recovery in order to neutralise the effects of malnutrition on the cognitive, emotional and social functions of the affected individual.

3.3 Eating Disorders and the Media

In the second half of the twentieth century, the influence of the media (film, television and print media) spread considerably. This was also a period when the position of women in society changed. They entered the labour market, which made their emancipation unstoppable, especially in the 1960s, in the circumstances of the rise of consumerism, living standards in Europe and North America, and the gradual global expansion of the capitalist way of life. Concern about body weight and shape became common in the Western post-industrial world and spread rapidly to non-Western societies as well (McRobbie, 2009; Orbach, 2009).

The media become transmitters of new ideas of thinness, imposing a thin body as the ideal of beauty (Nasser et al., 2001). Since the 1960s, through the movement of counterculture and the fight for women's rights, the new ideal of the female body has been increasingly present in the media, as can be seen in the androgynous asexual figure of the model Twiggy, who – along with the later 'heroin chic' of Kate Moss in the 1990s – became a symbol of this new form of the female body. In the twenty-first century, many members of the so-called celebrity culture promote extreme thinness as the ideal of feminine beauty in the media, and they become role models for many young girls (for example, actress Angelina Jolie).

Even Playboy playmates show a trend towards thinner bodies (Katzmarzyk & Davis, 2001). Models in the fashion industry and models in the late twentieth century became so thin that in some countries laws were passed banning the use of

---

[1]This includes a dramatic impact of malnutrition or sudden loss of body mass on the physiological, psychological, cognitive and social functioning of an individual.

unhealthy thin fashion models in the fashion industry (Seykes, 2017). Parallel to the media's idealisation of the ideally slim female body as a prototype of beauty, in the 1970s and 1980s, a cult of a healthy, thin and firm body, which must be consciously 'worked on' through dieting and exercise, was created. Since then, workouts (Jane Fonda) and jogging become part of 'taking care of one's health and appearance', which then led to the flourishing of the wellness and fitness industry with a series of sports activities aimed at burning calories and toning the body (Woitas, 2018).

The unexpected equating of thinness, beauty and health was additionally reinforced by the fight against the 'obesity epidemic' (Malson et al., 2009), which began under the auspices of the World Health Organisation in the 1990s and led to the public labelling of obesity as a disease. The creation of a social stigma against people who are overweight or obese added a moral note into the picture. People labelled as 'fat' were now social deviants, weak or even contemptible, and being fat became one of the biggest fears of adolescent girls in Western countries (Wade et al., 2011). In such an environment, being on a diet has become common practice in young girls growing up, and the development of bulimia, as well as the increased rates of all forms of eating disorders, can be interpreted as a failure to internalise this form of common social practice (Habermas, 2015).

American studies (Saguy & Gruys, 2010) show that the media are extremely biased in reporting on eating disorders and the problem of obesity. An analysis of newspaper headlines in the New York Times and Newsweek magazine over 10 years showed that thinness is associated with the wealthier strata of society and moral virtues, while obesity is mostly reported on as a problem of poor ethnic minorities, who are lazy and gluttonous. Furthermore, articles about anorexia and bulimia (eating disorders associated with low or normal body weight) highlight numerous and complex biological and cultural causes which are beyond the individual's control. People who suffer from anorexia or bulimia are presented through personal stories of middle or upper class white girls or women, thus enhancing the cultural stereotype of the young white woman as a victim. As a thin body is the ideal in Western society, trying to be too thin in print media is understood as an acceptable response to social pressure, not as a personal or irresponsible choice (Saguy & Gruys, 2010). On the other hand, when the American media talk about the problem of obesity, they do not mention the binge-eating disorder as a medical diagnosis, but treat obesity as a shameful consequence of bad decisions made by obese individuals. By emphasising that obesity is more prevalent among poorer sections of society and among Latinos and African–Americans, such reporting reinforces social stereotypes that fat people, ethnic minorities and the poor have no self-control and are lazy. In the articles analysed, African American culture is described as preferring larger women and thus representing a kind of defence against the glorification of low body weight which can lead to eating disorders, but at the same time, the very culture is blamed for obesity among African American girls and women. Saguy and Gruys (2010) conclude that biased reporting on eating disorders and obesity actually reinforces the negative stigmatisation of people of size by exposing them to discrimination based on their body weight, since they are portrayed as gluttonous, lazy and as irresponsible parents who raise their obese children in the same way. This research raises the question of the responsibility of the media, which are so influential that they strongly affect how we see and understand overweight people living in our society.

Over the last 20 years, there has been a paradigm shift in media communication. To twenty-first century adolescents, the internet and social media have become equally influential as the mainstream media (TV, radio, print), if not more so (Prinstein et al., 2020). Considering the incredible 7.5 hours that the average American teenager spends online daily (Rideout & Robb, 2018), we can conclude that social media and the internet have become the main way how messages for children and young people in Western societies are transmitted (Odgers & Jensen, 2020).

The negative influence of social media on increasing body dissatisfaction and the development of eating disorders has been shown in various studies (Park et al., 2016; Tiggemann & Slater, 2013). It would seem that social media additionally burdens adolescents in their vulnerable years since they post their photos on them and receive feedback in the form of likes and comments. Young people who search other people's profiles and comment on them more often have a greater desire to lose weight, they compare themselves more often with others and feel inferior (Ferguson et al., 2014). A longitudinal study by de Vries et al. in 2016 confirmed the harmful impact on self-image due to increased social media use.

As with the traditional media, one should take into account the pre-existence of some personality traits that mediate the association between the frequency of social media use and an increase in body dissatisfaction. It has been established that people with low self-esteem and perfectionist personality traits who seek validation online are especially vulnerable to the detrimental influence of social media (Perloff, 2014).

Gender differences can also be seen in the use of social media. Women use them more for the purpose of comparison, which confirms the traditionally greater focus on appearance in women (Haferkamp et al., 2012). Women are also more likely to edit their photos before posting them online (Fox & Vendemia, 2016), while men mostly use social media to make friends (Haferkamp et al., 2012).

Growing up with the internet and social media can be associated with the experience of body shaming. As many as 94% of adolescent girls have been shamed on social media because of their appearance (Miller, 2016) which can lead to disordered eating (Flak, 2021) and undermine self-esteem (Sugiati, 2019). If appearance shaming on social media is intentional, repetitive and carried out by the same perpetrator, it can turn into online violence (Schluter et al., 2021).

As can be expected, people with eating disorders use the internet to deepen harmful nutrition patterns, engage in sports for the purpose of losing weight, view photos of thin female bodies and gather information about ways to lose weight (Jureković, 2021). In such activities, the use of online platforms with predominantly visual content such as Instagram, Pinterest and Snapchat is especially prominent (Jureković, 2021). The existence of Pro-Ana and Pro-Mia websites that openly encourage sufferers to persevere in their eating disorders have been proven to have devastating effects on people with a disordered relationship with food. On such sites young people get advice on how to starve themselves, abuse laxatives, vomit, hide their thin bodies from their parents and the environment, use diet pills and other unhealthy practices (Mento et al., 2021). The interesting and hypocritical relationship between the pathologisation of extreme thinness in medical discourse and the celebration of thinness as an ideal of beauty in celebrity culture is best illustrated by the fact that most Pro-Ana and Pro-Mia sites post pictures of famous women with ultra-thin bodies, which inspires people to embrace anorexia as a lifestyle (Borzekowski et al., 2010).

The internet and the social media also have a potential for sending positive messages and people can join online communities that promote recovery from eating disorders, the so-called pro-recovery sites (Branley & Covey, 2017), where the motivation for recovery can be strengthened through the sharing of personal stories and where the destigmatisation of eating disorders is promoted.

We can conclude that social media, where users mostly post visual content (photos), are particularly harmful for the development of a positive self-image, and the fact that social media can be accessed via mobile devices 24/7 makes it even more difficult for young people to resist the influence of other people's comments, comparisons and appearance-based shaming. People who are dissatisfied with their appearance can find a lot of harmful content on the internet and are likely to join toxic virtual communities, which will further deepen their problems with their body and food.

3.4 Orthorexia and Clean Eating

The influence of social and traditional media can also be seen in the spread of contemporary trends of obsession with the so-called healthy diets and exercise as a form of self-care. The development of orthorexia[2], healthism and various fitness movements can be interpreted as a response to ontological insecurities resulting from the breakdown of the traditional relationship to food on the one hand and the anxiety and personal responsibility felt by individuals not being able to navigate the complex and obscure world of industrially produced food on the other.

Along with the clean eating movement, a new type of disturbed relationship to food and eating known as orthorexia emerged in the 1990s (Bratman & Knight, 2000). Orthorexia has not been included in the American Psychiatric Diagnostic Manual yet, but considering the prolific scientific literature on orthorexia, its

---

[2]Orthorexia is an unhealthy obsession with healthy food (Barthels et al., 2017).

recognition as a subtype of eating disorders can be expected in the near future (Moroze et al., 2014).[3]

Orthorexia can be defined as a pathological obsession with healthy, clean food (Bratman & Knight, 2000). In addition to the preoccupation with eating the right kind of food, orthorexia can include various 'cleanses' regarded as purifying or detoxifying (Dunn & Bratman, 2016). Some believe that orthorexia is actually a more serious and dangerous variant of clean eating (Staudacher & Harer, 2018). What brings orthorexia and clean eating together is the sense of moral superiority that an individual feels because they 'eat right' (Nevin & Vartanian, 2017), since everyone else is 'dirty' and neglecting their bodies and lives (Ambwani et al., 2019). The promises of healthy eating include more energy, glowing skin, spiritual development, cleanliness and longevity (Ambwani et al., 2019).

Certain foods are also loaded with socioeconomic implications. The poorer classes consume foods with a higher fat content (Coveney, 2006), often out of sheer economic necessity since such foods are cheaper. Social elites have the time and money to eat healthier foods and exercise regularly (Coveney, 2006). Therefore, social inequalities are continued today in the selection and quantity of food eaten in Western society (Coveney, 2006). The affluent society has eradicated the scarcity of food, but it has created new inequalities as well as new symbolic links – touching fat or being in fast food restaurants, breathing in the smell of fried oil or meat and the like can in some people create a fear of physical contact with 'dirty substances' to the extent that they feel that the mere act of touching or smelling will lead to some kind of contagion (Pittock, 2014; Warin, 2003).

---

[3]Proposed diagnostic criteria for Orthorexia (Moroze et al., 2014):
Criterion A: Obsession with healthy eating; consuming a nutritionally unbalanced diet due to preoccupying beliefs concerning food purity; worrying about eating impure or unhealthy food and the effect of food quality and composition on both physical and/or emotional health; strict avoidance of foods believed to be unhealthy, which may include foods containing any fats or preservatives, food additives, animal products or other ingredients considered by the individual to be unhealthy; excessive amounts of time (e.g. 3 hours or more per day) spent reading about, acquiring and preparing specific types of foods based on their perceived quality and composition; feeling guilty or worried after transgression in which 'unhealthy' or 'impure' foods are consumed; intolerance to others' beliefs concerning food; spending excessive amounts of money relative to one's income on foods because of their perceived quality and composition.
Criterion B: The obsession must lead to either or both of the following: decline in physical health due to nutritional imbalances (e.g. developing malnutrition because of an unbalanced diet); severe distress or impairment of social, academic or vocational functioning, stemming from obsessive thoughts and behaviours that focus on patients' beliefs about 'healthy' eating.
Criterion C: The issue is not simply a result of the symptoms of another disorder, such as OCD, AN or Schizophrenia.
Criterion D: The behaviour cannot be more accurately explained by religious ideological restrictions, professionally diagnosed food allergies or a special diet required by a presenting medical condition (diabetes, celiac disease, etc.).

Musolino et al. (2015) showed that certain lifestyles and dietary regimes have more social value attributed to them and that the so-called orthorexic lifestyle represents a source of significant power, prestige and respect, enabling individuals to increase their symbolic capital (Bourdieu, 1986). The habitus of healthism is thus created, which is associated with 'good moral character and individual worth' (Musolino et al., 2015, p. 24). Healthism is internalised through everyday practices of body care, resulting in disordered eating justified in the name of scientific hegemony (Nandy, 1988). Such a perspective fused with the public attitude towards health and diet culture, since science encouraged the pursuit of a healthy lifestyle which should be uniform and the same for everyone (Cinquegrani & Brown, 2018). The dominant cultural narrative of transformation and the search for a 'better self' is based on individualism, and it is complemented by another narrative based on resisting illness, holding on to control, insisting on personal cohesion and maintaining one's identity (Cinquegrani & Brown, 2018).

If the clean eating movement and orthorexia are seen as a lifestyle which emerged in the context of late modernity, Cinquegrani and Brown (2018) believes that the culture of hegemonic science destabilised individuals at their core and that they reached out for new, extreme forms of self-preservation by attributing moral qualities to food and eating. According to Cinquegrani and Brown (2018), individuals use the clean eating movement to manage the risks of life in late modernity, and constant self-monitoring and self-surveillance become reflexive processes. The normalisation of body-altering practices creates a new syndrome of an orthorexic lifestyle (Cinquegrani & Brown, 2018). Thus, the technology of the self offers additional positive outcomes through the body which becomes a project, such as control and management of power relations. The orthorexic lifestyle reinforces a person's position in the social hierarchy and creates narratives of pursuit through the habitus of healthism (Cinquegrani & Brown, 2018). Therefore, a person who accepts the illusion of clean eating along with shopping lists and plans for their food choices also gains social acceptance as a 'moral citizen' (Cinquegrani & Brown, 2018). Orthorexia can therefore be viewed as a possible future diagnosis of an eating disorder, but the phenomenon can also be approached more broadly, as a lifestyle which is deeply rooted and has deep social and cultural determinants (Cinquegrani & Brown, 2018).

An interesting perspective which connects healthism and high modernity comes from the research conducted by Rangel et al. (2012), who further developed Nicolosi's concept of the Orthorexic Society (Nicolosi, 2006). They showed that it is difficult for women to make informed decisions when buying and preparing food because there is a lack of reliable information about food items. Such a state creates confusion and anxiety (Rangel et al., 2012). The research (Rangel et al., 2012) showed that people are perceived as agents with a moral obligation to construct their own health, which confirms the presence of healthism in contemporary culture. Individuals are reflexive agents, encouraged to monitor and manage their health risks (Cinquegrani & Brown, 2018). They try to manage their diet as the basis for their health, but at the same time they are constrained by a system of food production, processing and sale which is becoming increasingly complex, contradictory and opaque (Rangel et al., 2012).

Chapter 4

Socio-Cultural Theories of the Development of Eating Disorders (Anorexia and Bulimia)

Modern theories on eating disorders cannot exclude the influence of the environment on the formation of attitudes about one's body. Society, the media, one's peers and parents directly and indirectly influence how we see ourselves. The most famous models of socio-cultural theories of eating disorders are: the Tripartite Model (Thompson et al., 1999), the Dual Pathway Model (Stice, 1996) and Objectification Theory (Fredrickson & Roberts, 1997). We shall briefly discuss them below.

The Tripartite Model was developed by Thompson and his colleagues in an effort to establish what external factors influence body image dissatisfaction and disordered eating. Thompson et al. (1999) proved that the pressure to be thin coming from peers, parents and the media can create a negative body image. Comments and teasing by peers and parents about body weight, appearance, clothing or eating can contribute to the internalisation of a thin appearance as a desirable ideal in a young individual and encourage comparison with images from the media or with their peers, which is regularly detrimental to the young individual. The psychological functioning of young people is thus not only impaired by bulimic symptoms, but also with the development of depression, anxiety or low self-esteem (Thompson et al., 1999).

Another approach to studying the influence of the environment on the development of disordered eating is Stice's *Dual Pathway Model* (1994). Built on an earlier socio-cultural model (Striegel-Moore et al., 1986), it takes into account various messages coming from peers, the family, and the media which propagate the thin ideal (Ferguson, 2013), the importance of good looks for women, and the importance of looks for social success (Stice, 1994, 2001). When such messages become internalised, they lead to body dissatisfaction, which consequently leads to restrictive eating in order to reduce body weight, and that can have negative consequences such as the feeling of guilt, anxiety or depression. The Dual Pathway Model was further refined by introducing the variables of a lack of interoceptive awareness and emotional eating (Van Strien et al., 2005). The authors included knowledge on key characteristics and behaviours for people with

Eating Disorders in a Capitalist World, 41–51
Copyright © 2024 Jelena Balabanić Mavrović
Published under exclusive licence by Emerald Publishing Limited
doi:10.1108/978-1-80455-786-020231004

eating disorders: having a lack of interoceptive awareness means that people cannot recognise their bodily needs, and that they ignore, suppress or misunderstand them (Khalsa et al., 2015; Oldershaw et al., 2019). If people feel discomfort or an emotion, they understand it as hunger, and want to deal with it through eating (bulimia, binge-eating disorder) or through other harmful behaviours (starvation and/or obsessive exercise in case of anorexia). Thus, emotional eating, i.e. binge eating, occurs in people with bulimia as a response to disturbing mental states, such as depression or anxiety (Van Strien et al., 2005).

What is especially noteworthy is that this model shows that in order to develop body dissatisfaction, it is not necessary to internalise the stereotypical thin ideal: if an individual is faced with the continuous repetition of the message that their body is not thin and attractive enough, this is enough for the person to develop dissatisfaction with their appearance (Stice, 2001), and to increase the risk of developing an eating disorder. This is supported by a meta-analysis of 20 studies on the influence of the amount of time spent on social media on one's body image (Holland & Tigemann, 2017), where more time spent on social media is associated with a higher prevalence of having a distorted body image and engaging in disordered eating.

The Objectification Theory was developed on the basis of a socio-cultural and feminist approach to the specific social position and objectification experience of being a woman in Western society. It shows how the cultural construction of gender can influence the development of intense body dissatisfaction, which is observed in women, as well as the wide distribution of disordered eating predominantly in the female population (Ata et al., 2015). During socialisation, girls and young women learn that their appearance and sexual attractiveness are key for their success in life (Calogero et al., 2011), and this is reinforced by hyper-sexualized media images as well as through the everyday experience of women (sexual comments, ogling and catcalling on the street, various forms of sexual harassment).

This theory was developed on the basis of a paper by Fredrickson and Roberts (1997), and it builds on the assumption that the everyday cultural practice of sexual objectification women are exposed to leads to an internalised view of oneself through the eyes of an 'outside observer', i.e. self-objectification. Women are taught to monitor themselves constantly and correct their appearance and behaviour (self-monitoring) in order to conform to expected social norms. Poorani (2012) points out that social norms for the appearance of the female body vary depending on culture and generational affiliation. In today's world, a standardisation and westernization of the ideal of beauty is taking place through globalisation, mass media and internet communication, and in addition to the predominant thin ideal (Stice, 2001), the ideal of a curvaceously thin body (Harrison, 2003; Overstreet et al., 2010) is emerging. Social norms determine not only the appearance of the body, but also the behaviour of a woman, which should stereotypically be 'ladylike' (Yap, 2016), i.e. a woman is expected to take up as little space as possible, walk with small steps, sit with her legs crossed (Young, 1980) and not be loud or aggressive (Yap, 2016).

Such practice leads to psychological damage (Calogero et al., 2011): women with high self-objectification are more often ashamed of their body, they feel anxious about their appearance, they cannot indulge in activities they enjoy or are interested in, whether it is learning, sport or sexual intercourse, which makes them suffer from a disrupted flow of consciousness (Calogero et al., 2011, p. 120). People who often view their body as an object which needs to be monitored, fixed or exposed to other people's eyes have lower interoceptive awareness – they are less able to recognise their body needs. All of this makes women a risk group for the development of mental problems such as eating disorders, depression and sexual dysfunction, and these are areas in which women are more affected than men (Calogero et al., 2011).[1]

The integration of all this knowledge about the influence of media on self-image and body satisfaction in women was carried out in the Elaborated Socio-cultural Model of Disordered Eating (Fitzsimmons-Craft, 2011), which introduces the element of choice as to which media content is accessed and how. Emphasising that women are not just passive recipients of socio-cultural messages, Fitzsimmons-Craft points out that the motivation to use media content will determine the impact these messages will have on body satisfaction and disturbed attitudes towards food. Exposure to objectifying media images will have a particularly harmful effect on women who consciously use them for the purpose of inspiration and upward comparison – comparison with (famous) people they believe look better than them (Fitzsimmons-Craft, 2011).

This is in line with the research which shows that women who already have a damaged self-image, low self-esteem and high self-objectification react particularly badly to any incentive or verbal stimulus from the environment (Ferguson, 2013): Tiggemann and Boundy (2008) showed that a compliment on their appearance does make such individuals feel good, but at the same time it increases their body shame, and thus the compliment makes them engage in self-objectification. Therefore, we can conclude that exposure to media content which promotes the thin ideal and objectifies the female body cannot *cause* an eating disorder but represents a variable risk factor (Levine & Murnen, 2009).

---

[1]The Objectification Theory has also been adapted for men. In studies conducted on sexual minorities, homosexual men showed higher levels of self-objectification and self-monitoring than heterosexual men (Boroughs & Thompson, 2002; Engeln-Maddox et al., 2011; Kozak et al., 2009; Tiggemann et al., 2007). One possible interpretation is that the 'male gaze' objectifies and sexualises women, and that the same model can be applied to the objectifying experience among homosexual men (Shaefer & Thompson, 2018). According to the same meta-study (Shaefer & Thompson, 2018), homosexual women are equally highly self-objectified as heterosexual women, while some other studies show that homosexual women are more satisfied with their bodies and have a lower internalisation of the thin ideal (Boisvert & Harrell, 2013).

4.1 Biological Medical Model of Eating Disorders

Over the last 30 years, there have been significant advances in understanding the biological basis of eating disorders (Madden, 2015). New technologies have made it possible to extend research methods of genes, brain functions and have generated large databases of genetic material (Bulik et al., 2019). Space does not permit us to present the biological medical model in more detail, so we shall only list the most important research.

The hereditary component of eating disorders is currently estimated as being between 48% and 88% for anorexia and between 28% and 83% for bulimia (Hinney et al., 2010). GWAS (genome-wide association studies) confirmed the existence of a genetic predisposition to the development of anorexia and bulimia, but the genetic influence is weaker than in schizophrenia or bipolar disorder (Bulik et al., 2019). Some genetic overlap between anorexia and obsessive compulsive disorder has been found, and it is possible that the two disorders share biological mechanisms which promote excessive repetition of certain behaviours (Yilmaz et al., 2017).

There is an interesting line of research on the influence of gut microbiota on the development of anorexia and bulimia (Bulik et al., 2019). A certain influence of intestinal microbiota on the key elements of anorexia, namely body weight regulation, metabolism, anxiety and depression, has been established (Carr et al., 2016; Kleiman et al., 2015). Now that the gut-brain axis (van de Wouw et al., 2017) has been registered, it is expected that future research will shed further light on the influence of the gut microbiota on eating disorders.

Neuroimaging has made a significant contribution, as have breakthroughs in neurophysiology, which can be grouped into studies of body image and the processing of visual stimuli of food, deviations in the reward process and the processing of emotions, as well as research on the deficient role of the insular cortex in connecting different parts of the brain (Madden, 2015).

We can speak of a breakdown in the normal processing of body images, and individuals react to their own fear of being fat instead of a realistic image of their own malnourished body (Sachdev et al., 2008).

Difficulties in processing emotions have been noted as one of the key characteristics of all eating disorders, anorexia in particular (Henderson et al., 2019). Alexithymia, which includes difficulties in recognising and describing emotions, is present in 77% of patients with anorexia (compared to 6.7% in the general population in Hatch et al., 2010, according to Madden et al., 2015). Especially interesting are experiments involving the recognition of emotions through facial expressions (Kerr-Gaffney et al., 2020), where people with anorexia and even those just at risk of developing it (Jones et al., 2008) exhibited difficulties in accurately distinguishing happy and neutral faces from faces that showed the so-called negative emotions, with a tendency of not recognising positive emotions.

The insula hypothesis (Nunn et al., 2008, 2011) aims to prove that anorexia is the result of a disconnection of different parts of the brain which process sensory stimuli, emotional responses and memory, similar to models tested in the cases of schizophrenia and dyslexia.

All these results prove the presence of disturbance in the key functions of the brain during the onset of eating disorders (Madden, 2015). However, since the interaction between genes and the environment is very complex, the biological basis of eating disorders cannot give us a clear answer to the question as to what the causal pathology underlying different types of eating disorders is.

4.2 Aetiology of Eating Disorders

The current scientific consensus about the complex aetiology of eating disorders is based on the biopsychosocial model (Vemuri & Steiner, 2006), which includes the influence of genes, biological predispositions, personality traits, the family, peer groups, and the influence of the media and the socio-cultural context.

As we have already mentioned, genetic research indicates that there is an innate predisposition to developing eating disorders. It is accepted that genetics accounts for about 50% of the variance of eating disorders (Berrettini, 2004; Murnen & Smolak, 2015). Along with the acknowledged genetic predisposition for the development of eating disorders, the question of epigenetics (the influence of the environment on gene function) arises, i.e. how gene expression changes as a result of certain external stimuli. In the case of eating disorders, it is still unclear how a gene for, for example, anorexia is activated in a person who grows up in a society in which a slender appearance is highly valued, and what the protective factors which prevent the activation of that gene (Bulik et al., 2019) might be. Yet another question arises: how the function of a gene changes in a family which has not previously had experience with eating disorders, i.e. how a gene mutation becomes hereditary after an individual develops anorexia or bulimia for the first time in a particular family.[2]

Genetic studies on twins indicate that various eating disorders have a different hereditary basis (Bulik et al., 2003; Grice et al., 2002; Yilmaz et al., 2015). According to the current findings, the restricting type of anorexia has a different genetic profile than bulimia, and the binge-eating disorder has its own genetic profile different from the two. Such a finding is in line with the personality types which are more frequently associated with certain types of symptoms: with the restricting type of anorexia we associate rigidity, perfectionism, avoidance of novelty, obsessive-compulsive personality traits, and alexithymia, while with bulimia we more often encounter impulsivity, novelty seeking, mood swings and borderline personality disorders (Bacanu et al., 2005; Fassino et al., 2004).

Such a conceptual reframing of diagnoses of eating disorders undermines the arguments of the transdiagnostic approach to eating disorders characteristic of cognitive behavioural scientists and therapists. As we have already mentioned,

---

[2]A possible genetic predisposition to eating disorders includes a tendency towards a certain type of personality, and towards psychiatric conditions such as obsessive-compulsive disorder, affective disorders or anxiety disorders, but also a predisposition to a dysfunction of serotonin, dopamine and norepinephrine – hormones which regulate eating. It is believed that this genetic predisposition can become manifest due to external triggers: keeping drastic diets or heightened emotional stress/trauma (Halmi, 2005b).

according to the transdiagnostic approach, anorexia, bulimia, other specified feeding or eating disorder and the binge-eating disorder should be covered by a single diagnosis of eating disorder for the purpose of better monitoring the patient, since patients often 'shift' from one diagnosis to another during treatment. The cognitive behavioural approach is based on the idea of common mechanisms (harmful beliefs and behaviours) which maintain all types of eating disorders, so its proponents advocate that they be diagnostically unified (Dalle Grave, 2015).

Genetic research, personality tests and comorbidity analyses in affected individuals indicate that there are reasons to separate anorexia from bulimia in a conceptual and possibly therapeutic sense, which seemingly complicates the debate about the decisive influence of nature or nurture on the development and maintenance of eating disorders.

As anorexia is a disorder with clear, visible symptoms which can lead to the death of the affected individual, this disorder was considered the 'textbook example' of all eating disorders for a long time. Anorexia was the first to have its medical diagnosis and was recognised as a characteristic set of symptoms in the second half of the nineteenth century, while the diagnosis criteria for bulimia were established almost a century later – in the late 1970s (Bemporad, 1997). Even today, the media and the general public often view anorexia as covering almost all eating disorders, from restricting type and binge-eating/purging type of anorexia, through bulimia to other specified feeding or eating disorder.

Equating anorexia with all eating disorders or grouping all eating disorders into one transdiagnostic group proves to be useful in the public health discourse for the purpose of planning preventive programs and implementing public health policies, but it seems that in a conceptual sense it makes it difficult to resolve the dilemma about the aetiology of the disorder and the nature vs. nurture clash in the field of eating disorders. Research shows that the pressure to look thin does not necessarily lead to eating disorders (Joshi et al., 2004) and that individuals are not passive recipients of socio-cultural messages.

According to Piran and Teall (2012), socio-cultural messages are received in three specific ways: through physical experience, messages about social expectations and messages about social power. While growing up, girls are exposed to media messages promoting the ideally slim female body, but also to teasing by their peers and the awareness of gender inequality (Piran & Teall, 2012). They are faced with environmental influences which emphasise one's appearance as a way to gain social power, and for some self-objectification becomes a self-preservation strategy (Piran & Teall, 2012).

Thus a question arises; if the 'cultural rain' of negative media and environmental influences (Striegel-Moore & Bulik, 2007) is so powerful, why do only some girls and women 'get wet' and develop eating disorders. According to the biopsychosocial perspective, genetic and neurobiological tendencies are activated by environmental influences. However, it should be noted that the environment also modifies the expression of the biological potential (Gottlieb, 2003). Therefore, if we accept the idea that 'genetics loads the gun, but environment pulls the trigger' (Cynthia Bulik, according to Neumark-Sztainer, 2005, p. 29), we can expand on it by saying that the environment also determines the direction of the shot. Therefore, eating disorders should be understood within a developmental and social context (Levine & Smolak, 1996).[3]

As anorexia and bulimia have been associated with the fear of gaining weight (Dell'Osso et al., 2016) in the diagnostic manuals (DSM II-V) ever since the 1970s and as the increase in the number of patients with anorexia and bulimia has been perceived as an 'epidemic' of eating disorders (Gordon, 2015), many theorists believe that eating disorders are culture-bound syndromes. As such, they are closely related to capitalist Western culture, which occurs together with modernisation, changes in the social position of women and the rise of the middle class, which would mean that the higher frequency of eating disorders is related to the media's emphasis on the ideally slim female body (Becker, 2004; Brumberg, 1989; Gordon, 2000; Habermas, 2005; Nasser et al., 2001).

For this group of authors, eating disorders emerged in the late nineteenth century in the United States and Europe, only to explode after the Second World War in a kind of epidemic of anorexia and bulimia in the 1970s and 1980s, and this trend has persisted even today. These authors believe that, together with the processes of industrialisation, urbanisation and globalisation, eating disorders spread from Western societies (North America, Europe, Australia) to non-Western societies (the process of Westernization), and they go on to prove that today, in societies which were not familiar with the concept of conscious self-starvation or the fear of being fat in the past, we encounter an increase in anorexia and bulimia (Brumberg, 1989; Habermas, 2005). Therefore, contemporary eating disorders (anorexia and bulimia based on the fear of gaining weight) peak in the context of high modernity of the late twentieth century and are equally prevalent among young women (and young men) in the early twenty-first century.

In order to understand the claim of these authors about how eating disorders are exclusively contemporary culture-bound syndromes, it is important to emphasise that this approach highlights the fear of gaining weight and the conscious refusal of food (and various purgative behaviours and obsessive exercising) in order to lose weight as a key characteristic of eating disorders. Following this argument, in places where the slim body is not socially desirable and where there is no 'dieting', there can be no eating disorders. In traditional societies where a lack of food created a risk of death from starvation and increased body weight was a sign of well-being and health, dieting did not 'make

---

[3]Forty years ago, developmental psychologists made a claim that biological heredity and the environment were in fact inseparable (Reese & Overton, 1970, according to Levine & Smolak, 2015). Therefore, the question is not whether eating disorders are determined by biology or the environment, or even how much of each or which multiplicative or additive interaction leads to a developmental result; rather their complex intertwining is implicitly understood. Not even a new-born baby is a purely biological organism (Levine & Smolak, 2015, p. 937). The prenatal and perinatal development of a child is influenced by the context in which the pregnancy occurred, and it affects the behaviours and characteristics of the new-born baby (Levine & Smolak, 2015).

sense' (Becker et al., 2002). There have been isolated cases of conscious starvation or death from malnutrition in traditional societies, or even more massive phenomena such as anorexia mirabilis in Catholic saints in medieval Italy, but these authors claim that we cannot speak of eating disorders in these cases precisely because they lack a key diagnostic characteristic: 'fear of gaining weight' (Habermas, 2015).

Bynum (1987) highlights a historicist interpretation of the behaviour of the medieval girls in Italy, who understood their starvation only as part of the general ascetic practice of physical suffering and renunciation of worldly pleasures in order to approach the divine ideal, and points out that it would be wrong to attribute today's interpretations and motives to women who lived in a different world, and who were guided by different ideas of the body, nutrition and religious ideals (Bynum, 1987). In this context, Brumberg (1989) wonders if Karen Carpenter (a popular American singer who died in 1983 as a result of anorexia) and Catherine of Siena died of the same disease.

4.3 A Universalist Approach

Another group of authors believes that a disturbed approach towards food is present in many societies and historical eras (the so-called universalist approach), and as proof they cite the practices of spiritual asceticism which include fasting in most known religions: Christian Lent, Muslim Ramadan, or living on prana in Hinduism (Keel & Klump, 2003). Religious fasting and various forms of suffering within strict spiritual orders in some individuals (mostly young girls) can take a turn into a kind of food deprivation which will lead to self-destruction, as in the case of anorexia mirabilis in medieval and Renaissance Italy (Keel & Klump, 2003). This approach is supported by the findings of psychiatrists from non-Western societies during the early modernisation of Asian societies who reported the existence of atypical anorexia in Asia (Japan, Singapore, Hong Kong) (Lee et al., 1993; Pike & Borovoy, 2004; Habermas, 2015). Researchers have proved that in these Asian countries in the late twentieth century (and to a lesser extent even today), there were cases of conscious starvation which had almost all the characteristics of anorexia: the psychiatric patients at that time were young women who talked about a 'forced' kind of starvation, which they could not control, and it was associated with feelings of disgust towards food, unspecified indigestion without an organic cause, and an inability to eat (Katzman & Lee, 1997).

This is what modern anorexia is all about except for one thing – the patients had no fear of gaining weight, i.e. their starvation was not connected with a desire for a thin appearance. In a study in Hong Kong in the early nineties, as many as 59% of Chinese individuals with anorexia had no fear of gaining weight (Lee et al., 1993). In these cases of atypical anorexia in Asia, self-starvation had a different meaning. In societies which traditionally view adult women as subordinate, in terms of social meaning, self-starvation is linked with the rejection of physical and sexual maturing (girls suffering from anorexia do not have periods and their growth and development is stunted), and thus they indirectly avoid accepting the role of a mature, adult woman who is expected to marry, give birth to children and leave the public sphere of life in which they were somewhat included during the years of their schooling (Pike & Borovoy, 2004).

A broad understanding of eating disorders, primarily anorexia, is therefore crucial for a universalist approach, since there are no significant testimonies of bulimia in non-Western societies and earlier historical periods in Europe and North America (Keel & Klump, 2003). These authors believe that any self-starvation motivated by internal conflicts by which an individual jeopardises their health and life actually constitutes anorexia. This internal conflict can be fear of obesity, religious asceticism, non-conformity to gender roles, intergenerational or family conflict, etc. (Katzman & Lee, 1997).[4]

Therefore, the universalist approach does not see eating disorders as a new syndrome or disorder specific to contemporary Western society, but believes that eating disorders have always existed in every society to a greater or lesser extent, only the contexts of the behaviour change (Ziolko, 1996). Today, we call these behaviours anorexia and bulimia, while in other societies and periods – according to the universalists – they were understood as elements of religious asceticism, a sign of obsession or some organic disease (Bell, 1985).

A possible resolution of the debate whether eating disorders are culture-bound syndromes or universally present in all societies and periods could be based on the acceptance of a universalistic broad definition of anorexia along with a conceptual separation of anorexia from bulimia. The changing prevalence of anorexia and bulimia throughout history and in different cultures points to a deep link between a disturbed relationship to the body and food and the cultural context (DiNicola, 1990; Nasser et al., 2001), as well as the key role of cultural changes related to modernisation and westernization, as a social context conducive to the spread of eating disorders.

4.4 Theory of Social Change

The next group of authors to be presented can be understood as a modification of the universalist approach. Researchers gathered around the theory of social change (Anderson-Fye, 2004; DiNicola, 1990; Katzman et al., 2004; Pike & Borovoy, 2004) argue that a disturbed relationship to food is more prevalent in periods of rapid changes in cultural identities, when new social relationships are formed, and the role of women is redefined, to which they link occasional 'historical epidemics' of anorexia (and the appearance of bulimia in the twentieth century). Proponents of this approach rely on the recorded evidence of numerous

---

[4]It is important to distinguish between internal and external conflicts – a hunger strike does not constitute anorexia since starvation is then undertaken for the purpose of a clear external goal. Anorexia also indirectly involves other people, but this relationship is not clear to the affected individuals, and they do not feel that they are in control of their thoughts and behaviour towards food, but their thoughts and behaviours seem to them as inexplicably forced and imposed.

cases of starvation in societies and social strata which had plenty of access to food, such as Renaissance Italy and Central Europe, the bourgeoisie in the United States in the mid-nineteenth century, or the middle and upper social classes in Asian countries in the twentieth century, noting that self-denial of food was not recorded in historical periods of drastically reduced resources due to disease, war or famine (Selvini Palazzoli, 1985). We can speculate that in such social circumstances starvation would be associated with self-sacrifice in order to leave food for others or as a symptom of severe depression.

The aforementioned research results which explain the presence of anorexia in many historical periods are important for the perspective which connects eating disorders and rapid social change. There are many indications that broadly defined anorexia appeared in many societies throughout history, and its prevalence increased in the second half of the twentieth century, with the cultural idealisation of thinness in Western society (Culbert et al., 2011; Hoek et al., 2005; Trace et al., 2013). However, there is no written evidence of a significant presence of bulimic behaviours in history (Keel & Klump, 2003). Thus, although there is a genetic predisposition to the development of bulimia, the development of bulimia itself is conditioned by culture (Keel & Klump, 2003).

Why is this so? Research has found that anorexia was present in different periods in many forms and with varied frequency. By this, we primarily refer to restrictive anorexia as the behaviour of conscious starvation due to an inner feeling of compulsion, which does not have to be connected with the fear of gaining weight. For this reason we can call it *anorexia multiforma* (Di Nicola, 1990)[5] and this behaviour is more widespread among girls (much less often boys) in periods of cultural change and in social strata with assured access to food. On the other hand, as research confirms, bulimic-type behaviour is closely related to the fear of gaining weight and it is a completely culturally limited syndrome characteristic of modern Western societies, which is spreading in non-Western societies through the process of westernization (Culbert et al., 2015) or modernisation (Pike & Dunne, 2015).

Based on all of the above, in this book we define the key eating disorders which we investigate as follows: bulimia as a culture-bound syndrome which arises and spreads as a consequence of the process of modernisation and westernization, while we understand restrictive anorexia as a universally present disorder, more prevalent and widespread in periods of social change, like in the Western society

---

[5]Longitudinal research by Stice et al. (2017) confirms that risk factors for the development of bulimia, binge-eating disorder and 'purging disorders' on the one hand, and risk factors for the development of anorexia on the other should be separated. The idealisation of thinness, positive expectations of thinness, body dissatisfaction, dieting, binge eating, and use of mental health services were highlighted as predictors of bulimia, binge eating, and 'purging disorders' (but not of anorexia). The research (Stice et al., 2017) confirmed that negative affect and poor psychosocial functioning also precede the appearance of eating disorders as risk factors (which is true for all subtypes of eating disorders, including anorexia).

in the second half of the twentieth century and early twenty-first century (Keel & Klump, 2003).

Through such understanding of anorexia, I maintained the epistemic incommensurability of the meanings of historical periods and the experiences of the internal conflict of young female individuals, who solve various problems typical of adolescence and their psychosocial development in different cultural and historical contexts through the same, life-threatening, behaviours that we understand today as anorexia. Considering that living in different societies and times brings different understandings of oneself and others, the same behaviours are motivated differently, but the elements that connect anorexic behaviours through different periods are as follows: voluntary starvation which is perceived as internal compulsion, female gender and the adolescent age of the patients, and rigid and obsessive behaviour with at least an ambivalent attitude towards starvation (and sometimes an open feeling of superiority due to being able to undergo starvation) (DiNicola, 1990).

Chapter 5

Research on Contemporary Social Changes and Eating Disorders

In order to study the social influence on the development of eating disorders, researchers have focused on situations in which societies, groups of people or individuals are exposed to social changes. Studies of the incidence of eating disorders due to the modernisation of non-Western societies, as well as analyses of anorexia and bulimia in migrants from non-Western to Western countries, are significant.

The processes of modernisation and globalisation are associated with a series of profound changes in values, norms and lifestyles, but also with the exposure of girls and women to media content which promotes slender and firm female bodies (Hesse-Biber et al., 2006).

The theory of there being a deep connection between social change and the incidence of eating disorders is based on findings about non-Western societies in which eating disorders are recorded only sporadically or not at all, and traditional culture stands as a protective factor against them (Pike & Dunne, 2015). Research which has followed the effects of detraditionalisation, urbanisation, industrialisation and globalisation of pre-modern societies (Becker, 2004; Nasser et al., 2001) supports this thesis. A higher incidence of eating disorders has been found among children of immigrants to Western, developed countries (Palmer, 2008) and among young people who were exposed to the influences of modern culture as migrants (Katzman et al., 2004).

In an attempt to better understand the influence of culture on the development of eating disorders and possible protective factors of certain cultures, a meta-analysis of research on American racial and ethnic minorities (women and men) has concluded that acculturation stress is positively correlated with the internalisation of the thin ideal and disordered eating (Warren & Akoury, 2020). DiNicola (1990) found a higher incidence of anorexia in girls in families of first- and second-generation immigrants to Canada (DiNicola, 1990).

We shall now list the most famous studies to come out of the theory of cultural change as the social context of the emergence of eating disorders, which studied late twentieth century social transition in previously isolated societies such as the islands of Fiji, Belize or the island state of Curacao.

Eating Disorders in a Capitalist World, 53–56
Copyright © 2024 Jelena Balabanić Mavrović
Published under exclusive licence by Emerald Publishing Limited
doi:10.1108/978-1-80455-786-020231005

As was mentioned in the previous chapter, the theory of westernisation is based on the assumption that greater exposure to Western media and culture leads to the transfer of the thin ideal to the 'recipient' culture, increasing the incidence of eating disorders among the 'host' female adolescent population (Pike & Dunne, 2015). This theory could be illustrated by the findings of the research conducted by the anthropologist Becker and her colleagues on the Fiji Islands (2002). This is one of the most famous natural experiments which strongly supports the thesis about the crucial influence of cultural change and exposure to Western media on the emergence of eating disorders (Becker et al., 2002, 2004). Before the introduction of the TV satellite signal in 1995, there were practically no cases of eating disorders in Fiji, since the traditional culture highly valued a large body as a symbol of fertility, strength and connectedness of the community which cares for the individual (Becker et al., 2002). Becker and her colleagues conducted research on the presence of eating disorders among adolescent girls in Fiji after they had been exposed to the globalised world through satellite TV channels for 3 years, and they found that bulimic behaviours (vomiting and abuse of laxatives for the purpose of losing weight) were present in Fiji in the same percentage as in an average American high school (Becker et al., 2002). The research showed that girls identified a slender appearance with success, and with the change in social values in the previously traditional community, the ideally slim female body had also been adopted as a symbol of prestige. After 3 years of exposure to Western media content in this media-naive community, 74% of the girls stated that they felt too big or too fat, and 12% used purgative behaviours to control their body weight. In 2007, the percentage of disordered eating increased to 45% of the adolescent female population (Becker et al., 2011).

The case of Fiji exemplifies the impact of acculturation and modernisation in traditional societies, which is an area of interest for many researchers who study the rise of eating disorders in non-Western societies (Pike & Dunne, 2015).

When only a small number of individuals are exposed to Western influences due to migration, such a group is also at a greater risk of developing eating disorders. The research conducted on the island of Curacao supports the conceptualisation of eating disorders partly as a 'migratory disease'. In this Caribbean island with a predominantly black population, there were no eating disorders in the black population (Katzman et al., 2004). Cases of anorexia were recorded in girls of mixed race, who belonged to a higher socioeconomic class and who had spent some time in other Western countries. Katzman et al. (2004) observed that anorexia patients considered themselves different from other girls and wanted to belong to the social elite, which was predominantly white. Furthermore, girls suffering from anorexia were better educated and more travelled while growing up and were thus torn between modern and traditional models of femininity as they were exposed to Western culture and media on their trips abroad.

The example of Belize shows how culture can resist the harmful consequences of modernisation and rely on the existing protective factors that strengthen women's identity and perception of their bodies. Anderson-Fye (2004) studied Belize, a small country in Central America, whose culture proved to be extremely resistant to eating disorders. Although Belize was a developing nation going through a rapid social transition entering the global market and undergoing strong exposure to Western media, its number of patients with anorexia and bulimia did not increase significantly. As reasons for this, Anderson-Fye (2004) cites protective factors such as the traditional ideal of female beauty, which includes emphasised curves, and their ethnopsychology, which strengthens the female identity.

These examples show that the complex process of exposure to Western culture can never be one-sided in the sense of simple adoption of Western culture by the traditional community. A complex definition of culture, which questions its monolithic nature as well as its connection with other social processes – modernisation, industrialisation, urbanisation, democratisation, the strengthening of civil rights and the emancipation of women – will determine the unique opportunities in each community.

Researchers who study eating disorders in Asian countries point out that their development is different in Japan, rural and urban China, Hong Kong, India or Korea, which reflects the cultural specificities of each society when they faced the challenges of modernisation and participation in the globalised media world (Pike & Dunne, 2015).

In the twenty-first century, eating disorders have spread to almost all non-Western countries, and we find the highest rates of anorexia and bulimia in the fastest growing economies in Asia, which have reached the averages we find in the Western world (Pike & Dunne, 2015). The fact that traditional societies of Asia went through modernisation at a later period provides an opportunity to research the modernisation of the disorder itself (Pike & Dunne, 2015). In the 1990s, a significant percentage of anorexia patients in Hong Kong (Lee et al., 1993) showed similarity to the first medically described cases of anorexia in France and Great Britain in the nineteenth century – anorexia without the fear of gaining weight. Today, the clinical picture of patients with anorexia and bulimia in Asian countries is the same as in Europe or North America, where the fear of gaining weight and the idealisation of a thin body are key characteristics (Pike & Dunne, 2015).

We can also talk about possible local specificities in the development of eating disorders. For example, in South Korea we find a stronger idealisation of a thin body in young girls than in Korean women who immigrated to the United States or their American peers, which disproves the hypothesis about the acculturation stress as a trigger for anorexia and/or bulimia (Jackson et al., 2006). In urban areas of China, disordered eating and fear of gaining weight are significantly more prevalent than in rural areas (Lee & Lee, 2000), although on average girls in urban areas were significantly thinner than in rural areas.

Trends of modernisation in Asia, which include urbanisation and industrialisation, are also accompanied by changes in people's lifestyles (a transition to a sedentary lifestyle) and an increased consumption of fast food, which is rich in fat, sugar and salt, which in turn results in an increase in obesity, high blood pressure, diabetes and other non-communicable chronic diseases (Kelly, 2016). The already mentioned deep and significant change in gender roles is combined with the fact that a significant number of women are entering the labour market and are exposed to the consumer culture of the globalised fashion and cosmetics industry through the media (Witcomb et al., 2013). In this new and competitive culture, women are expected to develop new skills and are being judged externally, which encourages them to self-evaluate increasingly, and physical appearance becomes one of the domains in which they can 'measure' their success according to the desired ideal.

Women get caught between two worlds, which may include the bridge between the traditional and modern society, a generation gap, or the tension between business and private lives (family vs. work). They can then use starvation as a way of negotiating the transition, the loss of relationships or the oppression they are going through (Katzman et al., 2004). A feminist/transcultural perspective suggests that if we define anorexia exclusively as a body image disorder (based on the desire to be thin) and as a syndrome bounded by Western culture, we will miss the broader context and meanings behind food refusal (Katzman & Lee, 1997; Katzman et al., 2004).

Chapter 6

Gender Roles and the Body

From the very beginnings of the feminist discourse on eating disorders, gender has been a key category for understanding anorexia and bulimia. We can say that gender has been identified as a 'persistent risk factor' for the development of eating disorders (Striegel-Moore & Bulik, 2007).

The traditional definition of femininity rests on identifying women with qualities such as tenderness, humility, self-sacrifice, empathy, selflessness (Murray, 2001), which is in contrast to the traditional masculine qualities such as action taking, being courageous, ambitious and rational (Murray, 2001). The changes in gender stereotypes in modern Western society have been explored in various studies (Haines et al., 2016; Hentschel et al., 2019), which indicate the general resistance of these stereotypes and their 'lagging' behind social changes which include the entry of women into the labour market and greater equality in housework (Diekman et al., 2010; according to Haines et al., 2016).

Gender stereotypes also affect the way women perceive themselves: self-stereotyping generally makes women rate themselves as less active and become more community-oriented. Although, in some aspects a visible social change is taking place: women are increasingly perceived as independent and practical, just like men are (Hentschel et al., 2019).

Stereotypically, a woman is necessarily also a mother, and her reproductive status determines her social role, which some feminist theorists have called the 'tyranny of reproduction' (de Beauvoir, 1949; Firestone, 1970; according to MacKay, 2020). Biological sex also creates social pressure towards compulsory motherhood, and a stereotype of normative femininity is imposed.

If a woman resists this compulsory motherhood, which in the traditional stereotype implies taking on the role of a mother who is focused primarily on caring for children and the home (Gorman & Fritzsche, 2002), she may feel as if she is questioning dominant social values and violating norms of her gender, and she may risk negative social sanctions (Rudman & Glick, 2001; according to Haines et al., 2016).

Girls whose attitudes and behaviour deviate from normative traditional femininity may feel discomfort during the developmental period of growing into a woman and assuming the female role. Women's gender role implies acceptance of a predetermined place in society, which is burdened by the legacy of patriarchy and submissiveness, the imperative of motherhood, with the home and family as

Eating Disorders in a Capitalist World, 57–61
Copyright © 2024 Jelena Balabanić Mavrović
Published under exclusive licence by Emerald Publishing Limited
doi:10.1108/978-1-80455-786-020231006

the primary place where their femininity is realised. They are expected to self-silence their needs, while the needs of others are emphasised, as is the need to maintain an attractive appearance as a key aspect of female identity.

The experience of being a woman in modern Western society is burdened with normative dissatisfaction with one's appearance (Silberstein et al., 1988), which has led to the fact that the vast majority of the female population is dissatisfied with their appearance. This is why they want to lose weight (Green, 2001), and dieting becomes a common socialisation experience of adolescent girls (Habermas, 2015). Therefore, the image of normative femininity is closely related to self-monitoring, abstaining from food, correcting one's appearance and behaviour in order to achieve the unattainable ideal of an unrealistically thin and firm fit body (Calogero et al., 2011; Tiggemann & Williams, 2012).

In terms of traditional stereotypical femininity, investing in beauty is investing in the social capital of every woman – namely her sex appeal, good looks, and desirability (Green et al., 2008). Therefore, in feminist terms, disordered eating can be interpreted as a practice of subjugated femininity and an expression of the oppression that men have exercised over women for centuries (Orbach, 1986; Smolak & Piran, 2012). By investing in practices of correcting and beautifying their bodies, women participate in a patriarchal society and waste their energy, time and money on shaping their appearance to conform to the imposed standards of beauty, rather than addressing more important issues of political and economic power relations (Wolf, 2002). More radical feminist authors have gone so far as to see the media's promotion of unrealistic thinness as the beauty ideal in the second half of the twentieth century as a conscious attempt by men to blunt the edge of female emancipation and further subjugate women (Wolf, 2002). Therefore, Wolf calls dieting 'the most potent political sedative in women's history' (Wolf, 2002, p. 187).

Other authors believe that the fact that the key milestones of improving the status of women in society (the right to vote, equal opportunities in education, women's entry into the labour market, control over their own reproductive potential and sexuality, etc.) were followed by the media-promoted ideal of thinness to be a coincidence (Green et al., 2008) or that this relationship is much more complex, and that the increased prevalence of eating disorders in Western society is precisely the result of the changed role of women (Nasser et al., 2001). In this sense, belonging to a traditional society provides women with a protective factor for the development of eating disorders (Miller & Pumariega, 2001).

The relationship between gender and eating disorders can also be interpreted as the complete opposite of submitting to social standards of beauty. Through practices of suppressing the natural feeling of hunger and exerting maximum control of their own bodies, women can also reject their own gender, i.e. deny their traditional femininity, and thus distance themselves from the expected social role and possible unpleasant experiences associated with the sexual objectification of the body (Piran & Teall, 2012).

For some women with eating disorders, resistance to the discourses of normative femininity constitutes a key issue, and this is a topic that feminist authors explore extensively (Bordo, 2012; Holmes, 2018; Malson, 1998). MacSween (1993, p. 252, according to Moulding, 2016) suggests that body management in anorexia can be understood as 'an attempt to resolve at the level of the individual body the irreconcilability of individuality and femininity'.

The fact that a history of sexual abuse represents a non-specific risk for eating disorders, especially those of a bulimic type (Thompson & Wonderlich, 2004), once again indicates a complex relationship to the body and the acceptance of one's sexuality.

The study of recovery from eating disorders has revealed a change at the level of personality and behaviour in interpersonal relationships (Moulding, 2016), from which a problematic aspect of gender experience can be inferred. Afflicted girls and women point out that the only important thing to them is their appearance (D'Abundo & Chally, 2004) and that they are caught up in meeting other people's expectations (Björk & Ahlström, 2008; Weaver et al., 2005). Abusive relationships (Lamoureux & Bottorff, 2005) and excessive control by parents and partners (Patching & Lawler, 2009) are highlighted.

When the socio-cultural context of the development of eating disorders is interpreted through the lenses of gender, an opposition between the values behind the socialisation of women and men emerges. In the traditional understanding of the male role, men realise their sense of personal worth through concrete achievements, while for women and girls the ability to create and maintain relationships is important (Gilligan et al., 1990). Jack and Dill (1992) singled out four cognitive patterns used by women to maintain their focus on maintaining relationships with other people (Jack & Dill, 1992 according to Moulding, 2016): girls and women are more influenced by peer pressure or externalised self-perception than boys and men; they are also more likely to 'silence' and 'hold back' their thoughts, needs, feelings or opinions in order to avoid conflicts with the environment; women tend to strengthen their relationships by putting other people's needs before their own; girls and women suppress anger and aggression more often, and present themselves as nurturing, caring and obedient. These four patterns of functioning are associated with symptoms of depression which often occur with eating disorders (Jack & Dill, 1992), and higher scores in all four of them were also found in patients with anorexia (Buchholz et al., 2007; Forbush & Watson, 2006; Geller et al., 2000, 2008) and bulimia (Striegel-Moore et al., 1993).

6.1 Third-Wave Feminism and 'Self-Care' Through Disordered Eating

Third-wave feminists focused on affirming sexual self-objectification as hedonistic or ludic participation of women themselves in consumerist culture (Maclaran & Kravets, 2018; Thorpe et al., 2017) in which 'girl power' is complemented by playing with symbols of normative sexiness (high heels, makeup, fashion trends, emphasised sexual attributes, enjoyment of shopping, just like the characters in the 'Sex and the City' show, McRobbie, 2015). According to this reading of the female appearance, in the age of social equality of the sexes, a woman becomes truly liberated through the consumerist creation of her own appearance. The construction of her personal style can include her voluntary acceptance of sexual self-objectification as a source of personal and social power (Thorpe et al., 2017) since a sexualised appearance is no longer an indicator of social oppression, but a sign of freedom and power, and the acceptance of one's body and sexuality, in a society where a woman is no longer economically dependent on a man and is allowed to be 'single and sexy' (Thorpe et al., 2017).

With such a view of the female body, even eating disorders can be thought of as an expression of a healthy lifestyle, and as a type of 'self-care' (Lavis, 2014; Musolino et al., 2018). Gill (2007) emphasises that in post-feminist culture the key themes are ownership of one's body and, accordingly, the transition from objectification to subjectivisation, with an emphasis on self-surveillance, self-monitoring and self-discipline. Individualism, freedom of choice and girl power of late capitalism are also connected with consumerism and commodification of what makes us special. These are concepts which will help us in understanding the meaning that patients with eating disorders attach to gender roles and how they eat, i.e. abstain from food.

This is supported by the global estimate that 70% of people with eating disorders do not receive treatment, since they understand their relationship to their body and food as a legitimate choice (Musolino et al., 2015). Anorexia can then be understood as a protective shield from emotions, which helps a vulnerable person cope with unpleasant interactions with other people and the world (Lavis, 2018). Since anorexia gives patients a sense of control and achievement (Fox & Diab, 2013; Hipple Walters et al., 2016; Lavis, 2018), many of them start basing their identity on their relationship to the body and food. Recovery can only be achieved when the individual adopts new ways of expressing psychological discomfort which are not physical (but verbal), thereby overcoming the body-spirit dichotomy (D'Abundo & Chally, 2004; Jenkins & Ogden, 2011; Weaver et al., 2005).

Over the last two decades, the concepts created by the second-wave feminists based on the media's sexual objectification of women have faced a lot of criticism (Halmi, 2005a; Holmes, 2014; Musolino et al., 2015; Warin, 2010). The authentic perspective of the affected women themselves and their narratives have been stressed. Qualitative research into the mental world of people with eating disorders, their construction of the self and the narratives related to the disorder and recovery (Conti et al., 2016; D'Abundo & Chally, 2004; Ross & Green, 2011; Weaver et al., 2005; Williams & Reid, 2012) no longer present people with eating disorders as individually pathologised (the biomedical perspective) or as powerless victims of the media, social influence or gender inequality (the socio-cultural and feminist perspectives), but as agents who construct (and reconstruct) their personal identities through their experiences of eating disorders (Conti et al., 2016, p. 166) and reflect on the meanings of their own experience of living with (and recovering from) the disorder. Studies dealing with virtual Pro-Ana communities[1] show the existence of a sense of control and superiority in

---

[1]Pro-Ana (short for pro-anorexia) are websites which promote anorexia as a lifestyle, not a disease; also, Pro-Mia (short for pro-bulimia) are websites which promote bulimia as a lifestyle.

individuals with anorexia (Giles, 2006) and affirm the interpretation of anorexia being 'a lifestyle, not a disease' (Musolino et al., 2015; O'Connor & van Esterik, 2008).

Latest research in the field of eating disorders seeks to consolidate various 'contradictory, ambivalent and shifting meanings embedded in anorexic "bodies and practices"' integrating the experiences of LGBT women and ethnic minorities (Malson & Burns, 2009, p. 4).

This is where the psychological, individual dimension, based on the individual's genetic and biological predispositions, can meet the socio-cultural context of the development of eating disorders: the way in which the female gender is embodied includes a certain regulation of emotions, behaviour and understanding of oneself in relation to others. Gender identity is thus linked to the macro-social dimension, but also to the immediate experiences of growing up and constructing one's personality (Piran, 2010). The complex interplay of prodromal, risk and maintenance factors of eating disorders (Stice et al., 2017) encouraged researchers to see one dimension as key and more important than the others, which resulted in permanent conflicts within the scientific and clinical community, which could be summarised in the 'nature vs nurture' dilemma of the past (Levine & Smolak, 1992). With the emergence of postfeminist or postmodern researchers, who brought their own past or present experience of eating disorders to the table, a new depathologising perspective of eating disorders as a lifestyle (Musolino et al., 2015; O'Connor & van Esterik, 2008) and a legitimate choice of any individual was affirmed.

Closely linked to bioethical issues surrounding the right to live and die (Carney et al., 2006), dilemmas related to understanding eating disorders continue to exist (Clough, 2016). In most European countries, there is a legal basis for force-feeding adults within the framework of national legislature on the treatment of mental patients (for the United Kingdom, consult NICE, 2017), which is used very cautiously and only in extremely severe cases (Carney et al., 2007).

Chapter 7

Thematic Analysis

The key advantage of thematic analysis is its exceptional flexibility, applicability and ease of application (Braun & Clarke, 2013). Unencumbered by theoretical concepts, a thematic analysis provides the possibility of detailed and deep insight into the collected data, which can lead to complex reports and establishing links with broad theoretical concepts (Braun & Clarke, 2013). In the data analysis, I took a phenomenological position – I believe that the experience of an individual participating in the research is a product of interpretation and is thus constructed and flexible, but it is real for the individual who experiences it (Slišković, 2020). Therefore, I wanted to identify the categories of meaning which the interviewees assigned to their life experiences, and connect them with existing discourses on gender stereotypes, the body and food.

The disadvantage of thematic analysis is the risk of imprecise and arbitrary use of the method if it is not conducted according to its scientific principles, which is summed up in the phrase 'anything goes' used as criticism of qualitative research (Antaki et al., 2003). Even the approach of 'giving voice' to members of a certain neglected social group involves selecting, editing and arranging data to support one's arguments (Fine, 2002, p. 218) and in some way affects the results of the research. I am aware that the collected data do not 'produce' codes and themes on their own, but that conducting a thematic analysis involves making a series of decisions which shape the results (Braun & Clarke, 2013).

In order to overcome this problem, I conducted all phases of the research consistently according to professional protocols (Braun & Clarke, 2013; Saldana, 2013), and I paid special attention to personal and epistemological reflexivity, which are reflected in the initial definition and perception of the phenomenon being studied, as well as in research design and data interpretation. I defined the key terms of the research subject carefully, and I presented an exhaustive historical overview of eating disorders and their link to gender issues, as well as a wider social definition of the notions of body shape, food, eating and abstinence from food.

Therefore, I took a contextual approach (Braun & Clarke, 2013), which lies between the poles of essentialism and constructionism. A contextual approach recognises the ways in which individuals attach meaning to their experiences, but also reveals the influence of a wider social context on those meanings, including material and other constraints of 'the real world'. In this way, thematic analysis

Eating Disorders in a Capitalist World, 63–68
Copyright © 2024 Jelena Balabanić Mavrović
Published under exclusive licence by Emerald Publishing Limited
doi:10.1108/978-1-80455-786-020231007

becomes a method that simultaneously reflects reality but also deconstructs the appearance of 'reality' (Braun & Clarke, 2013).

7.1 Coding Strategy

Working with the collected data includes making choices between different alternative lines of interpretation and alternative 'exit points', i.e. levels at which we will stop the reinterpretation (Alvesson, 2003, p. 14).

In this research, I used a deductive approach. The research direction, areas of interest and the themes were determined in advance. The basis for the semi-structured interview questions were research questions about the nature of gender stereotypes which women with eating disorders associate with male and female gender roles, and what social meanings women with eating disorders associate with thin and fat female bodies, food, eating and abstaining from food.

During the data collection process, I also collected a significant amount of data that do not contribute to the clarification of the research questions. These data were also processed through a thematic analysis and grouped into residual themes and the 'Other' category.

As I have already mentioned, the areas of research were determined in advance. However, they were determined as 'neutral' (Attitude towards food/ Attitude towards body/Attitude towards gender roles, etc.), which Braun and Clarke (2013) call a domain summary since they represent the basic description of the theme in a descriptive, 'shallow' way.

It was during the data processing that these themes were given meaningful names, determined by insights into the coded material (Magical food/Body as the basis of identity/Insecure femininity, etc.), which will be explained in later chapters.

At the beginning of each interview, I engaged in some 'small talk' with the interviewees, which served as a kind of introduction and 'breaking the ice'. I asked them about their childhoods and about their relationships to food in their early years in order to prepare them for the basic topic of the interview (Mellon, 1990). This is how a separate theme emerged on its own, so to speak, and – enriched by the contribution from the later stages of the interview – it became 'Different ways of growing up'. I had not assumed that childhood experiences and the description of the beginning of the disorder would be important for elucidating the inter-viewees' understanding of gender roles or their current relationship to the body and food.

During the data collection process, I implemented the recommended strategies for 'the single researcher' (Miles et al., 2019, p. 28), which includes taking notes through a reflective journal and conducting initial pre-coding.

The material was coded in its entirety for the first time after all 30 interviews had been conducted, recorded and transcribed. The transcription method was almost verbatim verbal transcription (Sližković, 2020). I also recorded some more important non-verbal events: pauses in speech were marked with three dots, and if an interviewee paused for a longer period of time, I marked this as 'longer pause'.

Also, the transcript recorded when the interviewee laughed or cried. Intonation, volume and other features were not recorded.

The transcriptions were entered into the MAXQDA software programme for data processing, which was also used for the coding.

The coding was carried out by one person, me, in two stages with a 2-month break in between, so that I would be able have to study the first coding with the benefit of coming back to it with a fresh pair of eyes. Then I once again carried out a thorough recoding and interpreted the material the way I presented it in this book, with certain refinements.

Carrying out the coding by one person has its advantages and disadvantages: in this case it is not possible to perform a reliability calculation (Cohen's kappa, according to Joffe, 2011) between different coders in order to prove that the coding is 'correct'. We acknowledge the arguments of reflexive thematic analysis (Braun & Clarke, 2019) which indicate that there is no single correct way of coding the data, and that coding is an active and reflexive process which inevitably bears the mark of the researcher. On the other hand, through reflective thematic analysis, it is possible to provide a deep analysis of the data and offer interpretations which reveal new meanings of the analysed phenomenon and their relationships with existing discourses.

The data were coded using mixed coding methods (Saldana, 2013), which relied on the latent meaning of the analysed sections of the text, rather than semantic coding. The following was carried out: descriptive coding – words or phrases which succinctly describe what was said in the analysed section of the text were selected; in vivo coding – words or short phrases from the text being analysed were used as codes; and affective coding – the code expresses emotions or values, attitudes and beliefs of the interviewee. For the answers to certain questions from the semi-structured in-depth interviews, which refer to questions whose answers vary within a predetermined range (e.g. Have you ever wanted to be a man?), I used hypothetical coding, which was partly anticipated and partly derived from the content of the interviewees' answers themselves (I wanted to be a man/I never wanted to be a man/I never wanted to be a man but…).

For the section of the text which deals with the relationship with one's body and food, I mostly decided on process coding, since it emphasises temporality, change in time and the dynamic aspect of the action.

When describing the experience having to do with specific very complex attitudes, values and emotional statements, such as attitudes towards menstruation and marriage, for the sake of easier monitoring and insight into the obtained findings, I grouped the codes into opposing categories using the versus coding method (e.g. Positive attitude towards menstruation/Negative attitude towards menstruation) which later, at the next level of coding, describe the different content of the analysed text.

The grouping of codes into subthemes or categories and the formation of themes themselves was based on an assessment of which content significantly answers the research questions. As I have already mentioned, I am aware that the obtained themes do not contain 'the truth' hidden somewhere in the collected data, nor can we rely on the percentages of representation of a certain code, category or theme, since this is a realistic perspective and it ignores the role of the researcher in the interpretation of the material.

As we are dealing with qualitative methodology and a purposive sample in this analysis, the frequency of occurrence of a code, category or theme cannot influence the ranking of statements by importance or the conclusion about a more frequent presence of a certain content in the general population.

7.2 Features of the Sample

Thirty interviewees, who make up the purposive sample in this research, filled out a questionnaire with questions covering the socio-demographic characteristics of the sample before participating in the interview.

Age	Range	Average Age		
$N = 30$	19 to 36	26		
Sexual Orientation	**Heteorsexual**	**Homosexual**	**Bisexual**	
$N = 30$	26	2	2	
Population	**>700,000**	**30,000–700,000**	**10,000–30,000**	**10–10,000**
Place of birth	17	11	2	0
Place where they grew up	15	9	3	3
Education	**High School**	**In College**	**College Degree**	**PhD**
$N = 30$	11	9	9	1
Employment	**Unemployed**	**Employed**		
$N = 30$	20	10		

Marital status: 24 interviewees (80%) stated that they were not married, 2 that their status was that of cohabitation and 2 were in a registered partnership. One interviewee defined her status as 'engaged' and one as 'divorced'. Of the 30 respondents, only one person had a child (one).

The age when they were first diagnosed with an eating disorder: the lowest age was 14 (three participants) and the highest was 30 (one participant). The average age was 20.

Five interviewees had previously been treated only at the Sveti Ivan Psychiatric Hospital, a further six interviewees had private therapy in addition to their treatment at the Sveti Ivan Hospital.[1]

As for how long participants had been treated at the Day Hospital for Eating Disorders at the Sveti Ivan Psychiatric Hospital, this varied from 2 weeks to 2.5 years. The average length of participation in the Day Hospital programme was 9 months.

As for the participants' self-assessment of the state of their disorder at the time of the interview, 24 of them stated that they had the disorder, of which 10 reported some progress. Three interviewees assessed themselves as having recovered. Three interviewees testified to significant progress, but did not state that they had recovered (for the purposes of sample analysis, qualitative data were here converted into quantitative data). In the cases of interviewees who assessed themselves as having recovered from their eating disorder, or those who saw their current way of thinking as significantly different from that during the acute period of their eating disorder, the questions were reformulated in such a way that they answered as if they were 'speaking from the disordered mindset', i.e. what they would have said while they were still suffering from the disorder (Table 4).[2]

7.3 The Overview of Residual Themes

According to Braun and Clarke (2013), the collected data consist of data relevant to the objective of the project, which are grouped into codes, categories and themes corresponding to the research questions, and residual, coded material irrelevant to the said research. In addition to the themes just mentioned, a certain number of residual themes cropped up in the analysis, and I will only list them in this chapter and not deal with them further.

The residual themes are *the beginning of treatment, the current state of the disorder*, and *after psychotherapy*.

---

[1]Other participants were treated at the University Hospital Centre Sestre Milosrdnice in Zagreb, University Hospital Centre Zagreb, University Psychiatric Hospital Vrapče in Zagreb, Psychiatric Hospital for Children and the Youth in Zagreb, University Hospital Centre Split, General Hospital Dubrovnik, Children's Hospital Zagreb, Centre for Eating Disorders BEA in Zagreb and with psychotherapists in private practice.

[2]At the time of the interview, the participants had been treated in the Day Hospital for Eating Disorders programme at the Sveti Ivan Psychiatric Hospital in Zagreb (Jankomir). Cognitive behavioural psychotherapy adapted for eating disorders (CBT-E) is part of the programme, and this is one of the best practice psychotherapy approaches. In the CBT-E modules, as well as in other psychotherapy techniques, so-called externalisation is used, which is consciously recognising the voice of the eating disorder and separating that voice from the 'healthy' self of the person having the disease (Chua, 2020; Williams & Reid, 2012). Therefore, the interviewees were already familiar with 'speaking from the disordered mindset' since this approach is used in therapy.

Table 4. Overview of Research Themes and Subthemes.

Themes	Subthemes
Insecure femininity	There is a link between the eating disorder and the acceptance of the female role The superwoman and the woman as a victim – the discomfort of being a woman Complex male-female relationships
The despised vs. the idealised man	I have wanted to be a man – I have behaved like a man I have never wanted to be a man The strong, the weak and the privileged – male roles
Magical food	Dieting – proof of self-control Binge-eating as a forbidden pleasure Vomiting brings on emotional discharge The promised land of spontaneous eating Multiple meanings of food
The body as the basis for identity	The body as the centre of the world The thin ideal Negating one's body Repulsively fat Menstruation – mixed feelings
The slippery road of the healthy life	Healthy food – the way in and out of the disorder Exercise abuse
Different ways of growing up	Different relationships towards food in the early childhood The experience of oneself as a child Birth family – focus on food and appearance Messages from the environment – appearance matters The beginning of the disorder – the overlapping of influences

Also, I introduced the 'Other' category, which covers low-occurring independent codes that do not fit into any other theme.

I will present the main themes identified in the thematic analysis according to the research questions; firstly, two themes related to the perception of gender roles in girls and women with eating disorders, and then four themes which shed light on the issue of social meanings assigned to food, eating/abstaining from food and the shape of the female body.

Chapter 8

Insecure Femininity

Gender roles include a set of behaviours and attitudes which are socially acceptable, appropriate and desirable for a man or a woman (Levesque, 2011). In their answers, the interviewees explained how they view their own gender role and society's expectations of women. Their answers are categorised under the theme *Insecure Femininity*, which points to highly problematic notions of one's own gender role in girls and women with eating disorders. The interviewees perceive their gender role primarily through two basic stereotypes: the superwoman and the woman as a victim. Those, completely opposite stereotypes reflect the interviewee's conflicting ideas about what it means to be a woman.

The stereotype of the woman as a victim is linked to the traditional, patriarchal worldview and the role of the woman who is there only to be a wife and mother, who can achieve self-actualisation only by serving others. *The woman as a victim* is submissive, vulnerable and focused on taking care of the needs of other family members, primarily her husband and children. Her main goal is to give birth to children. She is weak, shows emotions, is dependent on her man and is less valuable than a man. Her body is round and large, with visible female attributes. This is the normative view of femininity in traditional societies. In the view of our interviewees, a traditional woman is a victim of her female gender, without many life choices and focused on serving others.

> What are women like? Um... Oh, wait a second, what's the word? Subordinated to men. So they are worth less than men. They have to meet certain stereotypes. Certain rules imposed by society, or whoever. Religion or whatever. I come from a Christian family, so religion too. She can achieve much less in life than a man. There is quite a number of limitations from a business point of view. The weaker sex. Physically. Um... As far as physical appearance is concerned, she's been blessed with more fat, quote unquote. It means she is destined to be fat. (R 24)

Traditional role here is viewed as a model for female victimisation, not as a culturally conditioned, neutral form of participation in traditional gender segregation. In patriarchal societies, men and women have a precisely defined position in society and segregated areas of activity: men are focused on the public sphere, the

Eating Disorders in a Capitalist World, 69–82
Copyright © 2024 Jelena Balabanić Mavrović
Published under exclusive licence by Emerald Publishing Limited
doi:10.1108/978-1-80455-786-020231009

area of work, professional advancement and making important decisions, while women's primary focus is the family, taking care of children and the home. What is the social division of roles and segregation of gender roles for conservative theorists (Parsons, 1959), for feminist criticism is a form of hegemony and dominance of the male gender over the female (Maine & Bunnell, 2010). It seems that growing up in a society that still (openly or covertly) transmits traditional values and the patriarchal division of gender roles left a significant imprint on the formation of gender identity in the women suffering from eating disorders in this study.

The woman as a victim stereotype corresponds to the perspective of Mahalik et al. (2005), who emphasised the traditional female role as important for patients with eating disorders – with one important difference: in our study, the interviewees do not consciously identify with the traditional female role, but reject it and distance themselves from it. One of the possible interpretations of this significant difference in our findings is social change towards greater equality for women and a shift in general social values towards a detraditionalisation of gender roles which is taking place in Western societies. Following Green et al. (2008), from the set of social norms associated with the traditional female role, the interviewees bring up only the physical aspect of femininity as still important and desirable (the thin ideal).

Thus, the desired thin appearance simultaneously represents the achievement of the modern ideal of female beauty, but it is also a remnant of a stereotypical expectation transferred from the traditional view of femininity. Therefore, the interviewees acknowledge that a woman is still expected to be beautiful to catch a man's eye, busy trying out numerous beautification practices, with the main goal of getting and keeping a man (Smolak & Piran, 2012). Although the interviewees reject the traditional view of femininity, they still recognise such expectations in society through the stereotype of women as being obedient, passive, gentle and fragile.

How strong the influence of the traditional woman as a victim stereotype is can be seen when the interviewees say how they view the link between eating disorders, the acceptance of the female role and the desirability of the male gender role. Although they reject the normative image of femininity, patients with eating disorders often identify femininity with something weak and negative. For the interviewees, femininity is still partly perceived through the traditional model and is associated with suppressing one's own needs and submitting to the needs of others. Such findings are consistent with research on greater presence of self-silencing in people with anorexia and other eating disorders (Geller et al., 2000; Waller et al., 2003; Wechselblatt et al., 2000) and on self-silencing one's own needs as a predictor of appearance of eating disorders in the general adolescent population (Zaitsoff et al., 2002).

This line of research was supplemented by a study on pathological altruism (Bachler & Oakley, 2016), which confirms that people with anorexia want to please and be validated by others, and that they more frequently try to avoid criticism and rejection by other people. According to Bachner-Melman and Oakley (2016), such pathological altruistic behaviour stems from a weak sense of self and is based on reading, predicting or guessing other people's needs and putting other people's needs before one's own. Similarly, Mahalik et al. (2005)

found that a negative self-image in women is associated with greater modesty, which creates a feeling of inadequacy since such a woman dismisses her own achievements. Furthermore, in a study by Williams and Ricciardelli (2003), girls with binge-eating disorders (including bulimia) identified more strongly with negative stereotypical aspects of femininity, such as shyness or needing approval from others. A similar result was found in a study by Clay (2015) in which all participants distanced themselves from the traditional female gender role as negative, limiting and undervalued in society.

Similarly, my interviewees considered the traditional stereotype of the woman as a victim to be a negative female identity, the loss or negating of the self, possibly in accordance with the transgenerational view of women as the other, weaker and inadequate, as one of them put it in the next statement.

> Some stereotypes, being a good housewife and so on. I've heard things like that. I think it's so retarded and sick. That she has to be... I can't even explain it. My grandmother's, like, really into these things. That you have to be a good housewife, good to your husband, good... I don't even know what not. It's so retarded (laughs). (R 18)

As the complete opposite of the traditional stereotype of the woman as a victim, the interviewees bring up the modern stereotype of the superwoman. If the traditional woman was perceived as submissive and flawed, *the superwoman* is a woman who is successful in all areas: she has both a family and a career, she is attractive and confident. There is no area in which the imaginary superwoman is not superior. She is highly educated and makes a lot of money, but at the same time she is a caring mother and a good wife, has a rich social life, and she takes care of her appearance, health and nutrition. The superwoman has everything: a family and a career, and – most importantly – an attractive, slender appearance.

> ... I had always thought, until now, that I should be what is expected of me. A woman who is going to give birth to children, who is going to take care of the children, who is going to... I don't know... finish all those studies, who will be able to do everything around the house and go to work and take care of everything and who won't complain about any of it, but will do it all with ease, and won't complain about it. Because it's her job and nothing is difficult for her. (R 1)

While the patriarchal stereotype of the female gender role has been analysed in detail in feminist literature (Malson, 1998; Orbach, 1986), the stereotype of the superwoman is a product of the women's liberation movement where women enter the labour market of the capitalist society and compete professionally on an equal footing with men, retaining the imperative of family life: motherhood and partnership. The ideal representation of the superwoman is seemingly empowering, suggesting the idea of independence, freedom and limitless choices, but in fact it is another harmful stereotype that sets unrealistically high criteria for success and a 'must have it all' mentality.

What connects the old rejected stereotype of *the woman as a victim* and the new stereotype of *the superwoman* is the idea that a woman must be beautiful, which is in line with the focus on appearance and body in girls and women with eating disorders. Whichever stereotype they choose, physical appearance becomes the basis of gender identity for people with eating disorders. Later in the analysis, this will be further complicated with the rejection of an attractive body as a key determinant of femininity.

At this point, we can say that the superwoman embodies the characteristics of the neoliberal ideal of femininity described by McRobbie (2015): an educated, working and successful woman who also has a family and children and looks 'perfect'. McRobbie (2015) points to a new form of self-surveillance and self-subordination of women to the never-attainable ideal of a perfect life in which they will 'achieve everything' through their own effort and commitment, and continuous control of their own needs and weaknesses. At the same time, apparent emancipation has become a new form of subjugation and self-alienation, enslavement to the uniform and internalised ideals and goals, which are now understood as 'one's own choice' and a form of 'self-care' (McRobbie, 2015). Harman calls such social expectations of women a composition made up of 'good life, good health and good looks' (Harman, 2016, p. 22), where *good* means *right*. For Harman (2016), the good life of the superwoman is epitomised by the concept of a perfect balance between work and private life, where a woman is expected to take care of her family physically and emotionally (Lois, 2010), to be a good parent, an organised and creative homemaker, and a conscientious and productive employee/worker (Harman, 2016). It seems that the participants in this study also recognised this new social stereotype which has taken root in the late neoliberal society and which represents a hegemonic image of a new, superior femininity.

When they compare themselves to the requirements of such an ideal image of a modern successful woman, patients with eating disorders often feel inadequate. On the one hand, our interviewees looked for strategies to get closer to the stated ideal through a thin appearance, and on the other, by using other strategies (primarily eating disorders), they tried to delay their growing up or to bypass the competition and comparison with such a perfect image of a woman.

I find something similar in Fullagar (2009, p. 397), who also uses the term superwoman, like our interviewees, to denote a modern woman who evaluates herself as not 'good enough' since she fails to 'perform consistently, effortlessly and tirelessly as a superwoman – working, shopping, caring, cooking and being attractive', all in accordance with the expectations of contemporary normative femininity.[1] As one of the interviewees says in her own words:

---

[1] McRobbie (2015, p. 15): Various technologies bring the perfect into life or vitalise it as an everyday form of self-measurement. How well did I do today? Did I manage to eat fewer calories? Did I eat more healthily? Did I get to the gym? Did I achieve what I aimed to achieve at work? Did I look after the children with the right kind of attention? Did I cook well after the day's work? Did I ensure that my family returned from school and work to a well-appointed and well-regulated home? Did I maintain my good looks and my sexually attractive and well-groomed body?

That's what my mum told me. I didn't come to that conclusion myself. But when my mum told me that, I realized that it was true. She asked me once – why do I look and why do I persistently want to look like a child and not like a woman? I was around 24 or 25 at the time... Then I stopped... like, what do you mean, well no... But yes, basically I guess... I was ... I didn't want to accept this adulthood and this femininity... This... I'm not strong enough... Should I have said "was" (laughs) was... to be now... all that I can be. (R 25)

So in addition to having a career and a family, a superwoman is expected to realise herself in the area of 'self-care' as well. She is expected to exercise regularly and eat properly, which results in a well-groomed and attractive slim appearance. The concept of a woman's 'third shift' devoted to beautification was elaborated by Naomi Wolf (2002), who also uses the term superwoman[2] to describe a modern woman who, after a paid first shift (professional work) and an unpaid second shift (taking care of the children and the household), also accepts the responsibilities of the third shift, and that is maintaining an attractive appearance through exercise, cosmetic treatments and diet regimes.

We point out that within this neoliberal stereotypical femininity, the female body is once again understood as a passive object or 'resource' which is controlled, refined and improved through proper nutrition, exercise and beautification practices (Gremillion, 2002; Harman, 2016; Malson, 2008).

The ideal of femininity which links the heteronormative ideal of consumerism with the discourses of beauty, success, individuality, the imperative of having a slim body and self-control has already been established in patients with bulimia (Burns & Gavey, 2004), and the results of our study expand these findings.

Feminist literature has already dealt with the superwoman phenomenon, both in the media – film, comics (Cocca, 2016) – and in public discourse (Martino & Lauriano, 2013). Martino and Lauriano (2013) associate the ideal of the superwoman with the women's liberation movement of the 1960s, and – like our interviewees – define it as an ideal woman who 'can do it all and have it all' (Martino & Lauriano, 2013, p. 167). Social messages about the need to approach the desirable ideal of the superwoman create pressure and greater social isolation in women, since they feel incompetent to respond to these unrealistic demands. Just as the interviewees in this study believe that it is necessary for a superwoman to be physically attractive, women in the general population express the need to be independent, successful and beautiful (Hart & Kenny, 1997, p. 36, according to Martino & Lauriano, 2013).

The findings of this research are in line with earlier studies which have linked the ideal of the superwoman with symptoms of eating disorders, such as Hart and

---

[2]Naomi Wolf (2002, pp. 26–27): "The beauty myth is the last, best training technique to create such a work force (obedient)... Superwoman... had to add serious 'beauty' labour to her *professional* agenda."

Kenny (1997), Mensinger et al. (2007), and Dour and Theran (2011). We can say that there is certain continuity of this perspective in feminist research, and that it is important to study how the superwoman ideal is connected to the development and maintenance of eating disorders.

> In today's society, she is expected to be all of the things I have listed. But also to be very, very successful. To be strong. Of course, in our society, she has to be the mother of two, three children at least, and four would be ideal, I guess (...). She's simply has to be flawless. To be perfect, of course. Um, God forbid she gains a few pounds with age. Because with all that, she has to go to the gym. Yes, I said that she has to have a good salary, she has to travel. Absolutely everything. I don't know if there's anything that's not expected. (R 19)

In addition to the two dominant stereotypes mentioned, the interviewees also brought up the stereotypes of *the beautiful woman*, *the archetypal mother*, and *the overwhelmed woman*. These emphasise certain features which are not exclusively linked to one of the two basic stereotypes. In these additional stereotypes, physical beauty is once again understood as a key part of femininity. A woman's tenderness and warmth stand out as positive qualities separate from the stereotypes of the woman as a victim and of the superwomen, but they are key and inherent to the female role. Being overwhelmed with responsibilities and obligations is seen as an inevitable aspect of being a woman in this society, whether within the patriarchal or the emancipated stereotype.

At this point, I would like to offer an additional analysis of the interviewees' answers to the question if they see any connection between eating disorders and accepting themselves as women. As I have already pointed out, the majority of patients with eating disorders believe that there is a connection, and this connection is very complex. The interviewees accepted different positioning strategies in relation to the aforementioned stereotypes as models of normative femininity, and the dominant strategy is a complete rejection of femininity or its delay. That is why I called this theme Insecure Femininity, as it indicates ambivalence towards, questioning of and caution towards ways of living one's gender identity.

The vast majority of the interviewees pointed out that they do not accept their femininity and that they do not know how to be adults/women. The interviewees claimed that while they had an eating disorder, they did not have to grow up (and accept an adult female role). In such cases, the interviewees wanted to remain 'little girls', they used the disorder in their conflict with their parents, or they wanted to lose their (female) body because they had experienced sexual traumas. Note that the research included adult women, mostly in their twenties or older, who perceive the issues of growing up, maturing and accepting the female role as highly problematic.

> No, I don't want to grow up. I definitely don't want to. I want to remain a child. Not an incompetent five-year-old, but I still don't

want to take on the responsibility of becoming a woman. I don't know if I might be afraid of that kind of responsibility and loneliness, because when you're an adolescent, you know that there's somebody there, that is, your parents who have your back and help you, and this way you're on your own. Well, like... I'm not really ready to do it. I don't think anyone with a disorder, I think most of us with a disorder don't want to grow up, that's why all of this is happening. (R 9)

The interviewees testified to their own discomfort regarding the female gender role, whether they affirmed the role of a child as desirable (Sadeh-Sharvit et al., 2016) or whether they associate themselves with socially desirable masculine traits such as success and self-discipline (Ravaldi et al., 2006). In the context of gender roles, these findings confirm the thesis that the majority of patients with eating disorders belong to the group of so-called undefined according to Bem's (1974)[3] gender role questionnaire (Hepp et al., 2005), i.e. individuals who show low identification with either a feminine or a masculine gender role. This is in contrast to the research which links more pronounced femininity with eating disorders, and lists androgyny and masculinity as protective factors (Behar et al., 2002; Sarner-Levin et al., 2018).

The meanings that the interviewees attribute to their eating disorder in relation to the (non-)acceptance of the female role are partly in line with the study by Nordsbo et al. (2006). In the case of women with anorexia who were asked to describe their understanding of anorexic behaviours, this study has also established the existence of a need to control oneself and be confident (Nordsbo et al., 2006, p. 559). As for our study, this would correspond to the desirable aspects of the masculine gender role. Further, women with anorexia nervosa expressed the need for more attention, care and tenderness (Nordsbo et al., 2006, p. 560) which corresponds to findings on need for psychological regression and a certain infantilisation in relation to one's biological age, as well as communicating internal difficulties to the environment (Nordsbo et al., 2006, p. 561).

It (anorexia) is full of rules, but it is basically... an escape... from everything that I wanted to go through but I didn't know how. So I preferred to run away. (R 25)

This ubiquitous feeling of inadequacy and incompetence has been highlighted over and over again, from the most influential work of Hilda Bruch (1973) to the

---

[3]Masculine traits: Defends one's own beliefs, independent, assertive, strong personality, forceful, has leadership abilities, willing to take risks, dominant, aggressive, self-reliant, athletic, analytical, makes decisions easily, self-sufficient, individualistic, masculine, competitive, ambitious. Female traits: affectionate, sympathetic, sensitive to others' needs, understanding, compassionate, eager to soothe feelings, warm, loves children, yielding, cheerful, shy, flatterable, loyal, soft-spoken, gullible, childlike, does not use harsh language, feminine (Hoffman & Borders, 2001).

present-day studies of personality traits of girls and women with eating disorders (Henderson et al., 2019). This feeling of inadequacy is most often imagined and completely contrary to reality since patients with eating disorders are often very successful in school, and people around them perceive them as promising above-average capable individuals. What is important to point out is that, since these girls did very well in school, both the environment and the girls themselves have extremely high expectations of themselves. Therefore, in addition to having low self-esteem, patients also feel the need to prove themselves to the world, to meet very high expectations of others (their parents, the environment) and to compensate for the subjective and deeply hurtful feeling of inadequacy through external success (Nordbo et al., 2006).

Unfortunately, for many women in today's society the realisation of self-worth leads through self-control and getting a thin body (Calogero et al., 2011), which 'sets the stage' for the possible development of eating disorders. Let us not forget that the risk of developing an eating disorder in adolescent girls increases as much as 18 times after following a drastic diet (Patton et al., 1999). Therefore, equating personal efficiency and losing weight is a dangerous road that many vulnerable adolescent girls walk down, additionally burdened with gender-related feelings such as shame, guilt or even responsibility for sexual abuse (Moulding, 2016). Thus, in patients with eating disorders, the conflicting theme of trying to build one's identity with the risk of disappointment or rejection from the environment is supplemented with a sense of duty towards the wishes and needs of other people, which are perceived as more important than one's own (Moulding, 2016). Despite a very complex inner world characterised by feelings of powerlessness and lack of control, together with attempts to fulfil one's own and other people's unrealistically high expectations, people with eating disorders maintain a utopian idea of the ultimate solution to all psychological struggles: getting a thin body and abstaining from food. At the same time, there is an unconscious simplification and somatization of multi-layered conflicts within the personality itself and difficulties in relationships with the environment, and so the painful search for a personal or gender identity is ignored. Patients are preoccupied with the illusory solution that the environment will accept them only if they are thin enough, and they neglect other personality traits and important relationships (in accordance with the findings of Moulding, 2016).

> I have this feeling of inferiority, as a woman in a relationship, a feeling of guilt, a feeling that nothing I say is good enough, that I will be misunderstood. The feeling that I'm not enough, that I don't give enough of myself in relationships. Or that... it's never enough, no matter how much I give, it's never enough. With my partner, with my friends, and with my parents. And that they are never satisfied. (R 10)

We can thus summarise that the interviewees clearly reject the traditional role of the woman as a victim, and that they feel ambivalence towards the stereotype of the superwoman. On the one hand, some of the interviewees idealised beauty and an attractive thin appearance, and automatically associated a number of social gains with a thin body – success, recognition, acceptance from the environment (Heinberg et al., 2008). On the other hand, they also find the hard-to-reach and unrealistic image of the superwoman who 'can do it all' repulsive, and they prefer to stay in the 'waiting room of femininity and adulthood'. As the interviewees in the study of Swedish adolescent girls with eating disorders (Lindstedt et al., 2018) say: an eating disorder arrests life for a while.

> I don't allow myself to be a woman. And that's it. To get to that
> goal I need my eating disorder and that's what I need. (R 18)

Some interviewees delay their entry into the adult world because they do not accept the available forms of normative femininity – the repulsive woman as a victim and the too perfect superwoman – to such an extent that they start problematizing femininity itself. Getting an extremely thin body or regressing towards a childish/androgynous body which lacks feminine features such as breasts, hips and menstruation is described by Bordo (1993) and by many affected women as a form of freedom (Saukko, 2008; Tully, 2015) and as erasing the 'unwanted femininity' (Malson & Ussher, 1996, p. 512). These contemporary feminist theorists with first-hand experience in eating disorders point to an indirect rebellion against the expectations of the environment, which patients with anorexia and bulimia (usually unconsciously) join (Holmes, 2018). For some patients, the desire of having a thin body in a society where femininity is often reduced to 'negative femininity' and encourages 'self-silencing' (Piran & Cormier, 2005; Smolak & Munsterteiger, 2002) and an inauthentic existence in women can represent a kind of liberation from gender-imposed bonds. In a society which reduces women to 'sexy bodies', eating disorders can represent a rebellion against the traditional female role and a search for a different kind of identity (Squire, 2003). The androgynous body embodies prominent cultural values of the Western society such as success, control or restraint (Bordo, 1993; Holmes, 2019), which some people with eating disorders feel are incompatible with female physicality, since the female body is perceived as extremely fleshy, fat and repulsive (Fournier, 2002).

> I think it's, um, like a girl. That's... I think I may have even
> realized it before, but I only really understood it here, like, I have
> to be that child, my parents' child, something like that. I don't
> know... And, like, when I'm a little girl, everything is somehow
> innocent and... I don't know. Just... you see. I don't know, like
> innocent and pure maybe. Everything is innocent and pure. (R 4)

Some patients get the idea that having a small body means going through life unnoticed, like a shadow, not leaving a mark in other people's lives (Lavis, 2014). Also, gaining weight is associated with selfishness and overindulgence since the person is taking up more space (the same as in Lavis, 2014). While anorexia protects a person through a thin body, gaining weight breaks the boundaries towards others and makes a person vulnerable to other people's influence, their words and emotions (Lavis, 2014). Therefore, the expression 'I feel fat' is characteristic of people with an eating disorder (and perhaps also of undiagnosed women who share the same normative body dissatisfaction): it speaks about breaking through the boundaries towards a world which is now all too present through the feelings and actions of other people, and also about the increased vulnerability and exposure of the individual (as confirmed in Lavis, 2014). In patients with eating disorders, the strategies of self-silencing, disappearing or withdrawing are associated with breaking the ties with the environment which the person cannot control. Therefore, anorexia creates a safe identity, a cocoon and a zone of control, and a thin body is proof of having the right to such an identity (as already noted in Lavis, 2014).

Thus, a traditionally understood woman has no right to an authentic existence, her own voice or her place in the world, and her feelings of self-worth and self-concept are articulated through the body (similar to Lavis, 2014). If a thin body is the basis of identity, gaining weight would mean 'breaking the boundaries', those that set the person apart from the world and other people (Colls, 2007).

The body becomes a site of resistance in which the typically female social roles are examined. This can be seen in the statements of the interviewees where they re-examine the sexual body, which is the basis of a woman's role as a partner and wife according to the normative female role, and the reproductive body, which leads to pregnancy and motherhood. Numerous studies show that women with eating disorders have difficulties in accepting pregnancy and motherhood (Koubaa et al., 2008; Vandereycken & Dekerf, 2010). They feel discomfort or even disgust towards menstruation and experience relief in periods of amenorrhea (Holmes, 2018; Malson & Ussher, 1996). They even consider their curves contemptible (Fuchs, 2021; Nordbo et al., 2006).

> I always knew, somehow, if I lost all my curves and what attracted them to me, no one would be fucking with me. I wouldn't exist. And really, in that period, I didn't exist for the male world, for the other sex (. . .) I'd walk down the street, nobody would notice me. (. . .) I didn't even put any make-up on, or anything, so, you know, it was all, like, completely bland. (R 15)

In the themes which include attitudes towards sexuality, the reproductive role and partnership/marriage, the interviewees put forward highly polarised answers: extreme rejection and negation of these topics, or acceptance and open desire for motherhood and partnership in the future.

> I was totally asexual. So. . . I didn't have my period for years, so I was really. . . I wasn't producing hormones, nothing. (R 20)

> . . . I was basically by. . . through these sexual, right, these sexual experiences, I was looking for love. Looking for love, looking for attention. That was proof to me. If he wanted to sleep with me, that means that I am loved. (R 22)

Even in earlier research, sexual dysfunction in adult patients with eating disorders was observed to be more present than in control groups (Castellini et al., 2019; Kravvariti & Gonidakis, 2016). Girls and women with anorexia often have no interest in sex so they abstain from it, and the majority of women with all types of eating disorders are dissatisfied with their sex life even when they are sexually active, which in some people (more often with bulimia) can also take forms of promiscuous behaviour.

As was already mentioned, for women with anorexia and bulimia, getting thin and controlling their body constitutes delaying maturity, but it is also an indicator of their success and worth. By adopting a restrictive attitude towards food and overcoming the natural urge of hunger (and related states of fatigue, as well as physical and psychological pain and discomfort), people with eating disorders prove to themselves and others that they are self-disciplined and that they can achieve a socially accepted goal: implementing an extreme dietary regime. In this way, the eating disorder indirectly empowers these women, moving them away from the stereotype of the woman as a victim and bringing them closer not only to the stereotype of the superwoman, but also to masculine qualities of efficiency, dominance of mind over matter, and the victory of reason over emotion.

> Basically, the disorder gave me that power and strength that I did not associate with the female gender, but with the male gender. So that too, power, control, strength, will, whatever, that... That's what was happening to me when I was in restriction, while I was rejecting food, while I was exercising, while I was doing this and that, shedding pounds, that was, basically, bringing me closer to the male gender. That, some kind of strength and values in society, recognition. (R 24)

As can be seen in the analysis thus far, the world of meaning of patients with eating disorders is characterised by pervading ambiguity and contradiction (Fuchs, 2022). In order to convey as faithfully as possible the complexity of meanings with which the interviewees interpret their behaviour, I use the metaphors of peeling an onion or the Russian babushka dolls, which best illustrate the attempt to map the meanings that the interviewees attach to gender roles, the body and food. This paradox can be confusing to a person encountering eating disorders for the first time, but it seems to me that reaching a single conclusion which would negate this internal contradiction would be the wrong way of interpreting the findings. For example, the interviewees reject traditional gender role of a woman, but still suffer because they are not accepted and loved by the environment. They want to approach the ideal of the superwoman, but at the same time they find this ideal is very off-putting because it is unattainable and unnatural. A thin body is their path towards fulfilling social gender expectations, but also, paradoxically, a sort of boycott of that same gender role. Toning down female curves and amenorrhea represent a return to the innocence of childhood, to purity and protection, but this also affirms self-discipline, strength and superiority, normally attributed to the male gender role. Sometimes these contrary meanings can be found in a single person, creating internal conflicts which 'pull' the person in several directions, while in other cases there is grouping in the sample and a tendency towards the creation of subtypes, which could be further investigated in some future research.

What is particularly important to point out is that only a small number of the interviewees saw eating disorders as a way to achieve an attractive body which would help them compete for men's attention. In this strategy, the body is seen as an object which needs to be shaped a certain way in order to win and keep a partner. This strategy brings the interviewees closer to the stereotype of the woman as a victim since the woman is perceived as inadequate and having to belong to a man. The aforementioned group of statements is consistent with early interpretations of bulimia as the result of excess femininity (Boskind-White & White, 1986) and with trying to attain external recognition and confidence through a thin appearance. Some evolutionary psychologists explain eating disorders through the theory of intrasexual competition (competition with other members of their own sex), whereby harmful body weight regulation behaviours are used to make a person more desirable in the competition for a man's attention (Li et al., 2014).

> For me personally, it (physical attractiveness) is very important, it is important to me because I think that then I will be more desirable in the eyes of my partner. I can't believe I'm going to say this now, I had never thought this before... I don't think he's going to cheat on me or leave me if I'm physically more attractive. That he won't want another woman. (R 10)

The study by Davis et al. (2000) indicates that physical attractiveness (rather than deviation from the standard ideals of beauty) is actually an additional risk factor for the development of eating disorders. Likewise, the subjective feeling of unattractiveness also contributes to the appearance of eating disorders, and clearly both criteria can be present in the same person (Davis et al., 2000).

In the third sub-theme *Complex male-female relations*, most interviewees described inequality in male-female relations. They pointed out that even in today's society, women have it worse. They offered examples from their own families, where there was a traditional division of roles in which the man was the decision-maker and he did the physical work, while the woman was preoccupied with her household duties and raising children.

> I think men have more of it (influence). And like, at least in my case, I know from my own family, that dad always had the last say. Mum would just nod her head, "Yes." (R 13)

They point out the limiting aspects of marriage, which subjugates and enslaves women, and – after freeing themselves from the influence of their parents – they have to answer to someone again.

As a woman, when she becomes a woman, she becomes independent from her parents. And from her family. And then she hangs out with her friends, and so on. And then when she gets a husband, then she is in some kind of family again, she is once again in some community she can't get out of, and then it's all like... I don't know. (R 5)

In order to make their attitudes towards marriage better understood, the interviewees described in more detail their behaviour in love relationships as well as the role of their disorder. While the eating disorder often represented an obstacle to the realisation of a romantic relationship, they also stated that the partner provided them with great support and motivation for the treatment.

Let us first consider the idea that eating disorders prevent intimate closeness and the realisation of romantic relationships. One of the interviewees pointed out her fear of rejection and her emotional distance in romantic relationships, which persisted even in the so-called thin phases, in anorexia, when the interviewee, perfect by her standards, could not achieve a romantic relationship.

I have never given myself so completely to anyone. I have never fully surrendered myself. I have always kept my distance. And it's always been, like, with some kind of fear that I would be rejected, that I would be abandoned. It's always been like that. Not really consciously. I can only understand that now. However... But it's been like that, yes. And yes, that's how it would start. I would suffer terribly in those thin phases because even though it wasn't as important to me as college and my thinness, I still wanted it. It was even incomprehensible to me that I, so perfect at the time, couldn't be with someone... (R 20)

Another interviewee compared food intake and receiving emotions, and concluded that during the period of restrictive eating, she did not want to exchange emotions with her partner, but was attracted to the feeling of emotional emptiness.

Sometimes I would like to, but I can't receive some feelings that my partner wants to give me, I don't accept them at all. I try... It's like I want to tell myself that they are, like, fake. That it's not the real thing because I can't accept it. It's like I want this sort of emptiness. And this is restriction in eating and with the feelings of other people. (R 10)

Difficulties in romantic relationships in women with eating disorders were also observed in earlier research (Bussoloti et al., according to Arcelus et al., 2012) in the sense of reduced intimacy and dissatisfaction with existing romantic relationships. It was also observed that patients with eating disorders have a poorer social life and tend keep to themselves.

We can conclude that most of the interviewees had real difficulties in accepting the female gender role and that they defined it through the stereotypes of the traditional woman as a victim or the successful superwoman. The traditional woman as a victim was perceived as a negative stereotype which the interviewees wanted to avoid at all costs. The superwoman was perceived as a perfect, unattainable ideal, to which the interviewees simultaneously strove but they also rejected it, feeling that it was unfairly imposed by society and the media. As a strategy to resolve the conflict with their own femininity, some interviewees reached for the values and behaviours attributed to the male gender role. These were girls and women who emphasised success and social recognition as desirable, while others preferred to maintain the status of a child so that they wouldn't have to grow up, take responsibility and accept their sexuality. The interviewees who had accepted this as a strategy for dealing with the excessive demands of the gender role used the eating disorder in order to achieve an androgynous childlike appearance, to hold on to parental care and prevent themselves from becoming mothers.

We can also see tension between the traditional values of belonging to the family and community, where personal needs are neglected for the greater good (a woman's care for children and husband), and the neoliberal, individualistic aspirations of a professionally accomplished, attractive, well-groomed woman who becomes successful in her career and is a wife and a mother at the same time. Through the superwoman stereotype, the interviewees integrated masculine traits (assertiveness, independence, individual success) with traditionally feminine ones (concern for others, silencing one's own needs, emphasis on physical appearance) and combined them into an idealised representation of contemporary socially desirable femininity.

Similar results were found in an Israeli study of the socio-cultural influence on the emergence of eating disorders (Eli, 2018), which pointed to a rebellious individuality of anorexia and bulimia patients, expressing the tension between the collectivist values of the Israeli society and neoliberal, capitalist influences.

A similar internal conflict between male and female principles was described by one of our interviewees:

> Yes, yes, really big. That eating disorder, I could feel it inside me like some man. And health could be like a woman. So, yes... As if both the male principle and the female principle are... like it's... the disorder seems to have more of that male, masculine part in it.
> (R 28)

Chapter 9

The Despised Versus the Idealised Man

The second set of answers has to do with the perception of the male gender role. The interviewees offered contradictory statements in this theme as well, so that normative masculinity was both idealised and despised.

Since I have not found similar studies on stereotypes of male gender roles in patients with eating disorders, I will link my findings with research on male gender roles in the general population.

The traditional male gender role is based on expectations related to hegemonic masculinity (Connell, 2005) about a man who is dominant, active and takes care of his wife and children. The stereotype of traditional, hegemonic masculinity is based on three imperatives of the male role: provide, protect and procreate (Connel & Messerschmidt, 2005). Studies (Haines et al., 2016; Hentschel et al., 2019) show that the stereotypical conception of the male gender role is maintained despite significant changes in the labour market, education and sports, and there is a cultural delay of gender stereotypes in relation to these social changes (Diekman et al., 2010).

We called the stereotypes of the male gender role in this research the strong privileged man, the modern emotional man, the sissy, the sexual predator and the narcissist. The traits that the interviewees associated with the traditional profile of the strong privileged man are the same that the general population associates with the stereotypical understanding of the male gender role (Hentschel et al., 2019), namely assertiveness, independence and efficiency, with the critical assessment of the male social status as privileged.

> Everybody always said that life was easier for them. My late grandmother was sad that my mother's children were girls because women have a much harder time in life. And so, more during my childhood. Maybe like that "if I were a man, I could do this or that" thing. In puberty, they were able to get away with more stuff. I wasn't allowed to go out because my dad wouldn't let me, I wasn't allowed to go out much at night, if I was a man, I could do whatever I wanted now. I'd have my own car already, I wouldn't give a damn about my father and mother at all, I could do my own thing, but I'm a woman, so I have to listen to them. Well, in that context of sorts, the relationship with my parents...

Eating Disorders in a Capitalist World, 83–87
Copyright © 2024 Jelena Balabanić Mavrović
Published under exclusive licence by Emerald Publishing Limited
doi:10.1108/978-1-80455-786-020231010

> Or if I was hurt, in a relationship, then sometimes I would wish
> that I was a guy so that he would feel it, and that I was a guy, and
> that it was the other way around, then he would feel what he did to
> me... (R 10)

This stereotype combines the traits and behaviours traditionally attributed to
the patriarchal man: he is physically stronger than the woman, does not show his
emotions and is in charge of his family's financial security. Some interviewees
reacted to this stereotype with extremely negative feelings such as repulsion or
fear, and they described it with the words 'male pig'. Other interviewees admired
this stereotype and envied such a male gender role – 'good for them' – and they
also expected that they would be protected if they had such a man.

> So why did I want to be in those stages, that is, why did I think
> that it would have been easier to be a man. Because I felt that my
> role as a woman was limiting or insufficiently free. As if I couldn't
> do all the things I could if I were a man. (R 20)

The understanding of men through traditional masculine traits is in accordance
with the study of the dynamic nature of gender stereotypes, which shows that in the
general population of the Western society, the female stereotype is changing in the
sense of incorporating more masculine traits, such as enterprise and assertiveness.
However, the male stereotype remains more or less the same, and it includes fewer
of the feminine properties of caring for others (Wilde & Diekman, 2005).

> That they (men) are firm, that they are rocks, that they never admit
> what they're feeling. That they pretend when... That they are
> completely separated from themselves. That they are something
> they are not. That they are superhuman. Something like that. (R 28)

In addition to the traditional stereotype of the dominant, privileged man, a
more modern model of masculinity also appears in the statements of the interviewees: the modern emotional man. It is a possible stereotype which involves a
departure from the traditional male role of someone who does not show emotions
(MacArthur, 2019) and includes the man helping with the care for the children
(Banchefsky & Park, 2016). Therefore, the modern emotional man is open, gentle,
supportive and also witty and charming. Such a stereotype is an idealised representation of the desirable qualities which some interviewees looked for (and
found) in a male partner. It is associated with the expectation of equality in a
relationship, sharing the parenting load (parental leave for fathers) and financial
equality (the woman's and the man's earnings are equal).

> I don't care who does what and how much money they have. To
> me, I want to be a person who... I don't want to be dependent.
> For me, a man is not someone who is going to support me. He has
> to be my partner. A partner in our growing up together. That's

> how I see it. Of course, I would like my partner to make a lot of money, but not to support me. Oh, no. I don't expect that and I'm not looking for that. (R 21)

Other male stereotypes that the interviewees identified included *the sissy* based on the belief that women are more capable than such men and that they are useless, which on a social level may reflect a shift in the perception of women as the more competent gender (Eagly et al., 2020). Furthermore, there is a stereotype of the man as *the sexual predator*. Here, it is important to bear in mind that as many as 20–30% of patients with eating disorders have experienced some form of sexual abuse (Tagay et al., 2014), which is a hidden trauma that can contribute to this stereotype.

The sexual predator is a stereotype of a sex-obsessed man who views women as sexual objects and separates sex from love. Such a man focuses on a series of sexual encounters with different partners with whom he does not establish a deeper emotional connection. Living in a world of a male dominance, with potential sexual predators all around, was (and still is) a very disturbing experience for some interviewees:

> ...(I was) seen exclusively as a sex symbol. I had the feeling that I was just that. And every man who ever started talking to me, that this was all they ever wanted from me. (R 15)

The third stereotype is the male narcissist, in the sense that more and more men pay attention to their physical appearance, which was traditionally a female domain (Weltzin et al., 2005). The narcissist is a stereotype of a "new man" who is focused on maintaining an attractive appearance 'almost like a woman'. He works out in the gym to get a muscular physique, waxes his body and implements special diet regimes. He is perceived as a victim of the media and the media-mediated image of the ideal male body.

The forth male model mentioned by the interviewees is a *sissy* – that is a stereotypical representation of an incompetent, weak and lazy man who does not take responsibility, is unable to take care of his family and his wife has to carry the burden of everyday life. *The sissy* attaches himself to a capable woman who takes care of both work and family, which makes *the sissy* useless – except for enabling procreation. In the words of our interviewees:

> And before I used to think that they (men) were useless. They're fine for making babies and the like, but for the rest... I don't know... they don't know how to do their work properly. Like, the role of a father or a husband who should be some kind of support, and provide understanding, but they are not like that. These are rare, I mean, but somehow they are... like unnecessary... (laughs)... (R 1)

The interviewees were also asked whether they had ever wanted to change their gender role. More than half of the interviewees claimed that they had wanted to be a man because men have it easier in life than women. They do not need to worry about their physical appearance, and they are not exposed to sexual aggression. Some interviewees claimed that they had never wanted to be a man, while others stated that they had never consciously wanted to be a man, but that they would wear 'men's clothes' (which they had bought at the men's department or borrowed from their brothers). In this sample, we did not come across any individuals who openly expressed gender fluidity or transgender tendencies in the interview.

As I stated in the description of the sample, two participants out of 30 stated they were homosexual and two bisexual, which is too small a number for a comparison of the findings according to the criterion of sexual orientation.

This ambivalence towards one's gender role and the desire to (temporarily or permanently) assume the role of a child or a man is elaborated in the chapter Insecure Femininity and will be further elucidated in the following theme of *Body as a Fundamental Determinant of Female Identity*.

If we compare the codes having to do with the rejection of the female gender role in favour of that of the male, the codes explaining the link between eating disorders and (not) accepting the female gender role, and the codes on how sexuality is perceived, they formed clusters which can provide additional insights.

Interviewees who had never wanted to be a man understand their eating disorder more as a way of prolonging their childhood and delaying growing up ('I want to be a little girl'). At the same time, this group more frequently reported sexual trauma and the desire to 'lose' the female body. We can assume that people who have been sexually traumatised (by a man) retain a negative attitude towards men in general. Their rejection of the female gender role is then not accompanied by the identification with the male gender role, but rather by retaining the role of a child, a kind of infantilisation which protects them against sexual matters.

The interviewees who did say that there had been times they wanted to be a man because men are not exposed to sexual aggression often also said that they had engaged in promiscuity and self-punishment through promiscuous behaviour. For them, eating disorders were linked to the conflict with their parents and the issues of not accepting the role of an adult woman. However, they still exhibited ambivalence regarding sexuality (for them problematic), which they could live out more safely if they were male.

The interviewees who had wanted to be a man because men are privileged by their social status and do not need to worry about their appearance see their eating disorder as an attempt to prove their own worth and to be successful. Here, we can see that they view the masculine role as a desired status through which they would be able to achieve social power and dominance and feel more valuable as a person. As was mentioned in earlier chapters, people with anorexia often perceive themselves as inefficient, and anorexic behaviour becomes an instrument for testing self-discipline (Batista, 2019).

There are clusters which do not contain a code about the (un)desirability of the male gender role and which show an interesting link between the interviewees' attitudes towards sexuality and the meaning of eating disorders. These are statements of interviewees who developed the eating disorder in order to have a more desirable body and be more attractive to men. They treated sexuality as something natural and positive and connected love and physical pleasure. Finally, in this group of clusters again we have items pointing out at eating disorder as a temporary delay in entering the adult world ('when I have the disorder, I don't have to grow up to be a woman'). Once more, in the cluster analysis, it is confirmed that infantilisation and rejection of adulthood are combined with an extremely negative attitude towards sexuality which this group of interviewees find repulsive.

From all of this, it is evident that the interviewees' understanding of female and male gender roles is linked to the meanings attached to eating disorders, as well as to their understanding of sexuality.

An additional analysis of the simultaneous occurrence of the codes of female stereotypes under the theme *Insecure Femininity* and the meaning codes associated with eating disorders and (not) accepting the female role mostly confirmed the above explanations and expanded on them.

Women who express deep insecurity about the female gender role, who do not accept their own femininity and do not know how to be an adult woman often also express insecurity about their own motherhood. Such individuals mostly accept the traditional patriarchal stereotype of a woman who is obedient and submissive and who sacrifices herself for others. Therefore, we can conclude that by rejecting their femininity the interviewees are actually rejecting traditional femininity. They associate negative feelings and fear with sexuality and believe that, when they have the eating disorder, they don't have to grow up (into a woman).

The second cluster connects opposing stereotypes: the interviewees believe that women are the weaker sex, and that they are vulnerable and less valuable, but also that they should overcome such a stereotype through the role of the superwoman and a beautiful exterior. In that cluster, there are also codes which speak about rebelling against the two stereotypes ('I have the right to live the life I want') and about the women being gentle and warm.

The third cluster includes statements having to do with the experience of sexual trauma, the desire to 'lose' one's body and reading marriage as something that brings uncertainty and problems.

The cluster opposite to that one contains codes about marriage as something beautiful based on love and expresses a positive attitude towards motherhood. Sexuality is perceived as something natural, something that provides pleasure and is related to love. Along with this positive stereotyping of the woman's role, there is also a code saying that women bear too big of a burden – the stereotype of the burdened woman.

The cluster which includes the largest number of codes with relatively low frequencies and incoherent, sometimes conflicting, meanings is built around the most represented code 'I want to be a little girl'. Here, a multitude of codes are included, from positive stereotyping of the female gender role ('I like being a woman', 'The charismatic and powerful woman' or 'A woman does what men want'), through emphasising the flaws of female attractiveness and the belief that a woman must have a husband and children, to the emphasised need to prove one's worth through the disorder. This cluster is difficult to interpret unambiguously, but it shows us that the relationship between eating disorders and stereotyping of the female gender role is complex and in many cases contradictory.

Chapter 10

The Body Is the Fundamental Determinant of a Female Identity

As the title of the theme *Body as the basis of identity* suggests, people with eating disorders see their body as the basis of their self-concept. Their primary goal in the interviewees' lives was to get a thin female body, which patients with anorexia and bulimia interpret in three different ways: as a sign of success, as a path to physical beauty and attractiveness and thinness as a protection against sexual attraction. If a thin body is interpreted as an indicator of success, control and power, for the interviewees it becomes a source of confidence, positive self-determination, pride and a sense of personal achievement. The remaining two reasons are completely mutually exclusive – the interviewees once again fell into two groups: those who associate the aesthetic criteria of beauty and sexual attractiveness with a thin female body and those who also strive for a thin female body, but do not think that they will achieve beauty and attractiveness through being thin. On the contrary, for them being thin is actually an escape from female beauty and sexual attractiveness. In this sense, there is denial and rejection of one's body or even hatred towards it, especially towards secondary sexual characteristics (body curves).

The complex, emotionally charged relationship towards one's own body is illustrated by the following two statements:

> On the other hand, I did not accept myself. Simply put, I used to wear baggy clothes, they were black, so I had these phases of "I just want a Harry Potter cloak so that absolutely no one would see me, touch me, or anything." No, I definitely didn't love myself. No way, no way. (R 22)

> ... this here is disgusting to me (*breasts*). I hate my breasts. I wear a sports bra just so you can't see them as much because I find them so disgusting. Then this thing here that is always hanging here, I don't know, when I see it, I want to, like, I don't know, chop it off. (R 4)

Body image as the basis of the interviewees' identity is in accordance with the basic diagnostic criteria for eating disorders (APA, 2013). Attaching too much

Eating Disorders in a Capitalist World, 89–100
Copyright © 2024 Jelena Balabanić Mavrović
Published under exclusive licence by Emerald Publishing Limited
doi:10.1108/978-1-80455-786-020231011

importance to body shape and weight is a transdiagnostic criterion for eating disorders (Fairburn et al., 2003) and has been confirmed through the meanings of the body as a key determinant of the experience of one's own existence. It is further elaborated in the codes *The body is the centre of the world* and *Kilograms define my whole life*, which is in effect a continuation of the results of earlier studies (Cascino et al., 2019; Stein & Corte, 2007). Making the body the basis of identity is paradoxically related to the feeling of alienation from one's body and self-objectification (same as in D'Abundo & Chally, 2004; Stanghellini et al., 2015). Therefore, changing one's body is also a way of forging a new identity (according to Nordbø et al., 2006; Skarderud, 2007a). Eating disorders are associated with efforts to create a façade of perfection, to hide imagined weaknesses and to avoid any kind of criticism (already confirmed in research by Gustafsson et al., 2011; McGee et al., 2005).

Being thin is mostly perceived as an absolute, internalized social ideal, just like in earlier studies (Heinberg et al., 2008; Stice et al., 2017), and there is continuous comparison with other thin female bodies in the real and virtual world (same in the study of Jones & Buckingham, 2005). The interviewees perceive their own body primarily as an object which others observe, i.e. the individual herself applies the external perspective of the observer to her own body and defines herself primarily through the ability to control the weight and shape of her body (in accordance with the findings of Stanghellini et al., 2012).

When it came to their own body, as well as to food, the interviewees felt they were not good enough or not successful enough. A reduced ability to accept one's own mistakes or imperfections points to perfectionism,[1] which can be seen in doubts about one's worth, concern about one's mistakes and expressed sensitivity to real or imagined expectations of the environment (Simonich, 2007). Perfectionist tendencies can drive a person towards external, objective indicators of evaluation, such as grades, kilograms, calories, kilometres run or abs exercises preformed. Measurable indicators serve as orientation for individuals who have not (yet) built a solid sense of identity, such as adolescent girls. Relying on numerical indicators, a girl with perfectionist tendencies can more easily rank herself or evaluate how she compares to others. Perfectionism thus appears more often in adolescent girls who compare the appearance of their body with others, and it is associated with the variables of shame, submissive behaviour and social comparison to one's own detriment (Wyatt & Gilbert, 1998, according to Simonich, 2007). Here, we once again interpret the behaviours of girls over 18 and women with anorexia and bulimia through the context of adolescent

---

[1]Perfectionism is a visible and measurable phenotypic manifestation of one's personality, but I also have to point out that perfectionism and related traits are hereditary (Tozzi et al., 2004, according to Simonich, 2007). These are proven to be more present in patients with eating disorders and their family members (Lilenfeld et al., 2000; Woodside et al., 2002 according to Simonich, 2007). Some research indicates the existence of more pronounced perfectionistic tendencies in girls before the development of eating disorders (Fairburn et al., 1999, according to Simonich, 2007), which are present to a high degree even after recovery (Bardone-Cone et al., 2010).

developmental processes since unresolved issues of individualisation continue to affect their self-concept.

> R: How important was the number on the scale for you?

> I: Hugely important. It had the greatest importance. Like, absolute importance. "I'm good enough" or "I'm worthless" importance. Yes. (R 20)

Therefore, measuring practices (of oneself, calories, food) are very important, almost ritualistic, because they represent solid, measurable points of reference for self-evaluation. The interviewees testified to various practices related to weighing: some used the scale repetitively up to 10 times a day to control the effect of food and water consumption and exercise, while others avoided weighing at all costs because they assumed that they had gained weight. Such results are in line with previous research, where over half of outpatients with eating disorders used scales two or more times a day (Shafran et al., 2004), while other patients preferred 'blind weighing' even in the hospital environment (Pacanowski et al., 2016) – a practice in which the medical staff does not share the information about the patient's body weight with the patient. Both practices – obsessive weighing multiple times a day and panicked avoidance of weighing – speak of the patient's focus on the number on the scale as a key indicator of their worth. Since kilograms determine the patients' rank and status for them, the decision about whether to be aware of that number or not is a constant source of stress and tension.

> ... I think the biggest problem is that, like... the number on the scale is equal to me existing, and I would like to get away from that, so I don't really want to know, and then when I have to know, I want it to be as small as possible... (R 3)

In this case, a thin female body embodies patients' striving towards the ideal of thinness and beauty, and they score high on the Thinness Expectancy Scale (Stice et al., 2017). The individual believes that achieving the thin ideal of beauty will significantly improve the general quality of their life, and that they will be more popular in society, accepted by their peers, successful and happy, just because they have hit a certain number on the scale (Stice et al., 2017).

> When I achieve this, then it's over. Then the disorder will be gone... It's like that is... Like, now I need to get down to... I don't know... 45 kilos and then that's it, then I can do whatever I want. Like hell it is, then you come up with another goal – then it's 43. (R 20)

Such expectations are consistent with the thin appearance of women gla-mourised on social media, the internet and in mainstream media, where a thin body is portrayed as attractive, sexy and desirable.

Regardless of actual body mass, the interviewees see their body as fat (the same as in Carey & Preston, 2019), and losing weight is perceived both as a way of achieving control and a visible indicator of that achievement, metaphorically expressed in the name of a code I took over from one of the participants: *weight loss is like getting yet another A in school*, which is consistent with previous studies (Gustafsson et al., 2011; McGee et al., 2005). The interviewees associate a thin body with qualities such as success, confidence and control, which can be seen in their statements over and over again (consistent with Burgard, 2010).

> Thin people are identified with success. I think it was more, yes. Simply... If you can't control yourself, how can you be successful in any other areas? This was the main conundrum... which partly continues even today. (R 30)

Along with the understanding of thinness as an indicator of success and the desire for the patient to 'join' the world and respond to society's unrealistic demands for self-discipline and a perfect appearance, a thin body can also offer a sense of identity to the individual through anorexia since the disease and a malnourished body represent a safe way of being in the world but also with-drawing from the world (Lavis, 2014). In a way, it is a way of 'being disappeared' (Lavis, 2014, p. 5). When eating disorders (especially anorexia) are viewed in the way in which there is no emphasis on getting thin as an ideal of beauty, the thin body is more of a reminder of one's own identity, of the constant presence of anorexia as a protective shell in contrast to the destructive force of eating (Lavis, 2014).

> I loved that you could see all my bones. That was great for me. So I really enjoyed the fact that I didn't have any sexual... Any feminine features on my body. And in my fat phase I really felt terrible that I had them. So, that was disgusting to me. (R 20)

This way the interviewees affirm hatred of their own body (as in the study by Nordbø et al., 2006). They reject their breasts and any curves (similar to Fuchs, 2021); they engage in self-injury (described in Koutek et al., 2016) and use clothing as a shield for the purpose of hiding their body. Non-suicidal self-injury is a relatively frequent companion of eating disorders (Ernhout et al., 2015) in people who show high impulsivity, body dissatisfaction and difficulties in dealing with their emotions. Additionally, cognitive distortions encourage them to adopt a negative thinking style, so they frequently think in extremes (black-and-white thinking), apply excessive generalisations and focus on the negative aspects of the situation while ignoring the positive ones and the like (Coelho et al., 2015).

Self-injury is most often carried out in the form of cutting the skin with a sharp object, but people also hit or burn themselves, swallow objects and also scratch themselves (Peebles et al., 2011).[2]

Self-injury is a way for the patient to alleviate unpleasant thoughts and feelings and replace mental pain with physical pain. Sometimes an individual feels nothing, so physical pain serves as a way for them to feel 'at least something' and to get rid of the feeling of emptiness. Furthermore, people who injure themselves in this way can attract attention to themselves and express the inner suffering they cannot express in words (Whitlock, 2010). They also list self-injury as punishment for when they make what they feel is some kind of mistake.

> ... (long pause)... I don't know (*how I perceived my body*). I mean, like some big dissatisfaction and I don't know... I don't know... something, like, what I would punish if I didn't do something right. (R 27)

In addition to self-injury, with eating disorders there is also a high risk of suicide (Smith et al., 2018), which is the second cause of death in anorexia patients, and the suicide rate is also higher in people with bulimia compared to the general population.

> I really didn't accept myself. And there was also self-injury and self-destruction because you simply want to get out of that body, but you can't. (R 22)

Findings (Bell et al., 2017; Marques et al., 2021) about the presence of self-disgust in patients with eating disorders, as well as initial confidence and pride related to weight loss, were confirmed (Faija et al., 2017).

A common feature of women who experienced sexual trauma and those with eating disorders is that they suppress their own sexual urges more often, trying to 'forget' about their bodies. They also practice self-punishment when they feel emotionally overwhelmed (Levitt, 2007). Women diagnosed with eating disorders develop sexual dysfunctions more frequently (Price et al., 2020), but certain differences between the types of eating disorders can be seen.

Thus, it has been observed that patients with anorexia exhibit the weakest sexual desire and have difficulties achieving an orgasm (Price et al., 2020). Reasons for losing interest in sex or the absence of normal sexual development in anorexia patients can be a direct consequence of malnutrition (the Minnesota Starvation Experiment, Kalm & Semba, 2005), but also deep dissatisfaction with one's physical appearance (Stephens, 2019). Exposing your body to another person's gaze can be so stressful that it leads to reduced sexual desire. Naturally,

---

[2]Self-injury occurs more often in patients with eating disorders who engage in binge eating and purging, than in individuals who only engage in restrictive forms of the disorder (anorexia) or only binge eating (without vomiting or laxative use) or only engage in purgatory practices (Peebles et al., 2011).

the impact of sexual trauma is potentially devastating for patients with eating disorders (Madowitz et al., 2015), which is also evident in the sample of this study. The experience of sexual trauma in some interviewees strongly influenced their attitudes about gender roles as well as their attitude towards their bodies.

> Because if I really have to live in this body, I don't know how I'm going to do it, to live like this because I'm too disgusted with myself to. . . I don't want to continue living like this, I really don't. (R 4)

A meta-study on the relationship between eating disorders and sexual trauma (Madowitz et al., 2015) proved that sexual trauma can precede the onset of eating disorders and it contributes to the development of a disturbed relationship to food and the body in two ways. A distorted, negative body image after the trauma can lead to body dissatisfaction, shame, sexual dysfunction and fear of future sexual trauma (Madowitz et al., 2015). A person may want to become unattractive, hide signs of physical maturity and through extreme malnutrition lose feminine curves as a form of defence strategy (Berge et al., 2012). Also, an individual can start binge eating and develop a large body, which also deviates from what is considered attractive. Additionally, a person of size can be potentially more dangerous and threatening to a future attacker (Berge et al., 2012).

Moreover, psychological difficulties may occur as a result of sexual trauma, such as the need to control and regulate emotions (Madowitz et al., 2015) through a disturbed relationship with food.

> . . . but when I had my first boyfriend at the age of thirteen, I had a very unpleasant, let's call it, a traumatic experience, and that's where my problems basically started. So when I got my period at thirteen, after that loss, that is, let's call it some kind of abuse, rape or whatever, I lost my period. And that's why somehow I even started holding my breath and all kinds of things happened. Because I guess. . . when that happened, that was my neighbour. So we knew each other, we lived in the same street. He never spoke to me again, so that left quite a mark on me. (R 14)

We can extend the analysis of the relationship with one's sexuality to the influence of religion on the perception of the female body.

Grenfell (2006) points out the gap between the Christian understanding of the female role and the one characteristic of Western culture, which emphasises the sensual appearance of a woman. The analysis of the statements of women with eating disorders contributes to the discussion about the influence of traditional religiosity, which associates the female body with shame, sex and something impure, while the male body is 'the sacramental body' (Grenfell, 2006). Tully (2015) summarises: the thin ideal has become such an established part of the cultural hegemony of the Western society that it is also reflected in the symbolic reading of the disorder itself, whereby anorexia embodies all the social expectations of a woman – to be clean, in control – while bulimia represents the 'bad' or non-feminine qualities: licentiousness, exaggeration, untidiness, emotionality, rebelliousness.[3] Anorexia was perceived as a purer disorder, associated with biblical saints and their extreme thinness was often associated with asceticism and holiness (Squire, 2003).

In line with their challenging of their bodies as 'female', the interviewees have deeply divided opinions about menstruation, as one of the key biological signs of growing up and femininity. In some cases, a positive acceptance of menstruation has been established, while in most cases, menstruation is perceived as something negative and unpleasant, even dirty, disgusting and imposed.

> For a while I used to be disgusted by menstruation, then I just, like, wanted to be a guy or I didn't want to have periods. (R 12)

These findings are in line with previous research (Fuchs, 2021; Holmes, 2018), which highlights the problematic and tense relationship many women with eating disorders have with the normative femininity based on motherhood. Menstruation is described as a crucial part of being a woman physically, and a woman who does not menstruate is thus removed from her femininity. According to this interpretation, menstruation is biologically and symbolically associated with fertility and motherhood, and amenorrhoea with the rejection or at least modification of the female role (Holmes, 2018).

> ... I didn't like those big breasts of mine that I had, um, I just hated them, I always, like, hated them. What I want to say is that they really bothered me, they annoyed me. Why are those things here? I wanted to get rid of them. I had such an attitude, they were ugly, really ugly. And all those things that seemed to be feminine, like, and some kind of indicator of femininity, of a woman's body, to put it like that, I didn't like them. (R 19)

These findings complement the research of Beck et al. (2017), who studied the feelings and attitudes of girls when getting their first period and the subsequent development of eating disorders. It was found that girls who later develop eating disorders feel fear, sadness and disgust towards their first period more strongly. Another study (Boyd et al., 2009) indicates that, for the vast majority of girls with eating disorders, the interest in losing weight and dieting did not develop before the first period. Boyd et al. (2009) emphasise that the time of a girl's first period is a time of physical maturation, which is accompanied by growth, an increase in body weight and the proportion of fat in the body.

---

[3]In this imaginary hierarchical structure of types of eating disorders, binge-eating disorder is at the bottom of the scale, since it is often accompanied by obesity, a highly stigmatised body shape among people with eating disorder (Orsini, 2017).

The statements of the interviewees also link puberty and body changes to two potentially problematic processes: gaining curves perceived as 'getting fat' in a society that highly stigmatises obesity and becoming a woman in a society where femininity is burdened with numerous conflicting expectations. We can conclude that for most of our interviewees, growing into a woman was not perceived as 'good news'.

When coding statements related to the dichotomy fat[4] – thin, it is necessary to keep in mind the development of the public discourse around the thin female body characteristic of Western society since the 1960s. The media-mediated idealisation of thinness as a standard of female beauty is characteristic of the late twentieth century, and it was joined by the tabooing of obesity for health reasons in the twenty-first century. For the last 20 years, a 'war against obesity' has been waged: on a global level, it has been encouraged by the efforts of the World Health Organization and national health guidelines and actions (Branca et al., 2007) in raising awareness about health risks related to obesity. Terms like 'globesity' (O'Hara & Taylor, 2018) or 'the obesity epidemic' (Branca et al., 2007) are often immersed in the context of pathologising and moralising about obesity (Long-hurst, 2012). This reinforces the social stigma related to it, which is based on the belief that thin is good and fat is bad (Davison & Birch, 2004), and our research also confirms this. Emphasis on dieting in overweight people can lead to the so-called atypical anorexia, a condition when a person has an apparently healthy body weight, but is actually metabolically compromised as if they were malnourished (Eiring et al., 2021). The risks of drastic dieting for overweight people are most often ignored in public discourse, and the media broadcast various challenges and reality shows with competitions in rapid weight loss, which deepen stereotypes towards obesity and promote unhealthy ways of losing weight (Karsay & Schmuck, 2019). People who are not malnourished often think that they are 'not sick enough' to seek help or even qualify as someone with an eating disorder (Eiring et al., 2021). Such obstacles are encountered by people with atypical anorexia but also those with bulimia and other specified feeding or eating disorder, who often experience minoritisation and trivialisation of their struggles by their environment (parents, peers) (Eiring et al., 2021).

While reading the statements of girls and women with anorexia and bulimia, we are faced with the toxic potential of the stigmatisation of obesity. Since obesity is marked as deviant or rejected in contemporary Western culture (Forth, 2013), a fat body is read as the corporeal presence of 'incorporeal' characteristics (LeBesco

---

[4]In this book, we use the term 'fat' without a pejorative meaning, but instead continue the tradition of fat-studies, a scientific-activist movement which arose as a reaction to the bio-medical discourse of the fight against the obesity epidemic and which, through the use of the term 'fat' wants to restore 'pride and identity' to people with large bodies (Cooper, 2010, p. 1021).

& Braziel, 2001), ranging from laziness to lasciviousness (LeBesco & Braziel, 2001), and from excess to gluttony (Farrell, 2011; Gilman, 2010; LeBesco, 2004; Rasmussen, 2012; Throsby, 2012).[5]

> (*A fat body is*) Disgusting. Worthless. Without any control in life. Neglected. Um... Lonely... Ugly. (R 24)

> To me it's not attractive (*a fat body*). It's definitely, like... it reminds me of something dirty, untidy, I don't know... and so, and it's repulsive. (R 8)

The above findings are in line with the already established prejudices about obesity, where fat people are perceived as lazy, untidy, undisciplined, self-indulgent and of poor personal hygiene (Puhl & Latner, 2007). Therefore, the need to lose weight does not only come from possible health risks, but it is presented as an urgent matter of self-control, often accompanied by strong emotions both on a personal level and in public discourse (Lavis, 2014). Obesity is presented as a public health problem and as a crisis (Saguy, 2013) and fat people are widely represented as being 'disgusting' (Campos, 2004, p. 67).

Therefore, the interviewees perceived a fat female body as generally repulsive, and mostly associate negative ideas with it – it is ugly, unattractive and lazy, and fat women are weak.

> R: And if you imagine a fat female body... What ideas come to your mind? If you can go back to the time before entering the program?

> I: Carelessness, laziness, sloppiness, ugly, neglected... incompetent. (R 9)

Since obesity is mostly seen as extremely negative and undesirable (in accordance with the findings of Korn et al., 2020; Mortimer, 2019), the interviewees had a strong fear of their own obesity (Wilson, 2020). The comparison with obese female bodies, as well as the physical proximity of such bodies, created an additional fear of their own weight gain in most of the participants, which confirms the findings of Rancourt et al. (2016). Most interviewees felt discomfort, contempt or disgust around obese women.

> ... just when I was in the ana phase, I couldn't have anyone around me who was fat. I insulted all the people. When I ended up in hospital, the doctor in the paediatrics emergency room was a

---

[5]As an example of an alternative reading of obesity, Colls (2007) also offers testimonies of subjective positive experiences which view fat enveloping or gathering on a large body, and fat hanging, flowing or dancing in a pleasant and attractive way, and not as a sign of shame or degradation.

chubby resident, I now regret so much that I said so many disgusting things to that woman. That she would never marry, that she was ugly and all that. I mean, because, realistically, I wasn't thinking for myself then, I mean, who can think for themselves when they weigh 36 kilos? Nobody, aliens. And then I was just, like... she wasn't allowed to get near me, she wasn't even allowed to listen to my heart just because she looked like that. That's sick now. And I know it's stupid, but yes. Now I'm trying to tone it down a bit. (R 5)

In addition to the denigration of obesity and constant mistrust of one's ability to exercise self-control, in some patients with eating disorders, the fear of gaining weight is more dominant than the idealisation of thinness (similar as in Warin, 2010). We can say that patients with eating disorders take over the dominant discourses about the danger of obesity and then model, reshape and integrate them into the perception of their own body and identity (Puhl et al., 2007a). For people with eating disorders, obesity can represent the idea of physicality as such, which is linked to the idea of impurity and the feeling of disgust (Warin, 2010). The ideal body is perceived as something light, clean and quiet (Durif-Bruckert & Armand, 2007), the body as a non-body. Here, we encounter the duality of spirit and body once more, a concept which has been present in the Christian tradition of the West throughout the centuries (Lavis, 2014).

As an interviewee summarises:

That fear of being fat, which for me meant "you're worthless, you're stupid, you're not worthy of love or anything." (R 20)

Continuing the understanding of the body as matter which restrains the spirit, we shall refer to a study on Pro-Ana websites (Tully, 2015), which analyses statements of girls with eating disorders and reveals the idea that the female body is a cage and that anorexia is the way to freedom.

According to this interpretation, anorexia and bulimia allow women to free themselves from the physical and social constraints of femininity (Tully, 2015). Through an eating disorder a woman is able to bodily express the rejection of the ideal femininity, surpassing what it means to be feminine in the social sphere by embodying essentially an un-gendered physique (Tully, 2015). The Pro-Ana pages actually talk about how anorexia will eventually kill a person, ending the constant battle of femininity and physicality (Tully, 2015).

Similarly as our study has shown, here too, eating disorders develop as a by-product of striving for the ideal female body, i.e. practicing femininity in modern Western society (Tully, 2015). Since a woman can never achieve a perfect body and the ideal femininity exists as an unattainable cultural myth, a woman is caught in a constant and futile effort to produce perfect femininity (Tully, 2015). If the eating disorder progresses to malnutrition, a woman loses almost every aspect of her physical femininity – the breasts, hips and thighs disappear, the menstruation stops and the woman gets downy hair all over her body (Tully, 2015). In this way, a girl or woman with anorexia rejects the ideal femininity on a physical level, which is perceived as conflicting, imposed and prescribed.

> To me, this is now as if I was trapped. I don't know, I feel trapped. All these curves, it's too much for me. When I see myself with these breasts, I hate my breasts terribly, I really don't like them at all, and if I could cover them, I will find any way to cover them so that they can't be seen. But when I see how huge my butt is, ugh, I don't know... so... I can't... I just can't bear it. So... yeah. (R 4)

We can conclude that the statements of the interviewees do not unequivocally point to eating disorders representing a 'silent rebellion' against the oppression of the patriarchal regime and the fight against dominant ideals of femininity, as stated in the classic feminist interpretations of anorexia and bulimia (Orbach, 1986). On the contrary, the interviewees express an internalisation of the ideal of thinness, which is highly conflicting and a source of personal suffering (similar as in Orsini, 2017). In reference to the ideal of thinness as a stereotype of 'being a woman' in contemporary Western society, the interviewees take different and contradictory positions, at the same time agreeing to interpret thinness in women as a sign of self-control and success (Burns, 2004), but also denying their own physicality and femininity through that thinness.

How can these contradictions be explained? We can recall the various theoretical approaches to anorexia and bulimia from the introduction of this book according to the seminal paper by Keel and Klump (2003), which defines purgative forms of eating disorders as culture bound syndromes. This means that they are, therefore, more influenced by cultural pressure towards a thin female body, while restrictive anorexia is considered a specific form of eating disorder which is more universal in its aetiology and prevalence (Keel & Klump, 2003; Stice et al., 2017).[6] The confusing contradiction of seemingly incompatible meanings of the practice of losing weight in women indicates an objectifying attitude towards one's body for the purpose of monitoring and perfecting the body (Ata et al., 2015) and also alienating from it and negating it (Fuchs, 2021). Eating disorders are both the desire for a perfect, attractive body, but also hatred, contempt for one's body and the desire for it to be asexual, androgynous or childlike. As I have already stated in other places, when I came across paradoxical, incompatible statements, the stratification of the sample was evident. However, what was particularly interesting were internal contradictions within the statements of a single interviewee. Therefore, when analysing key topics related to eating disorders, ambivalence should be maintained in the interpretation of the results and the internal conflict should be presented as characteristic of this population.

---

[6]Thus, Wildes et al. (2013) find a higher number of patients with restrictive anorexia without significant concern for their physical appearance.

Can the inner contradiction in girls and women with eating disorders provide insights into the specifics of the experience of being a woman in Western society in the twenty-first century, or are these extremes limited to women diagnosed with anorexia and bulimia? I believe that the experience of women with eating disorders can tell us a lot about the dilemmas of today's girls growing up, and that the conclusions of this and other studies are relevant for gender theory.

To continue with the binary reading of male and female stereotypes, a thin female body shows that a girl or woman is in control, that she is a master of her own life, her natural urges, and demonstrates personal competence in self-discipline (she ignores hunger, and as for obsessive exercise, she doesn't even allow fatigue or physical pain to distract her from accomplishing her goals) (Malson, 2009). Such determination towards achieving goals, overcoming the limitations of nature, and a certain heroic component to her lifestyle are traditionally associated with men, whereby the thin female body transcends or overcomes the limitations of its gender (Malson, 1998). Physicality lived in this way prepares a woman for success in the competitive capitalist labour market, and a thin body is proof of the superiority of will and intellect over nature and instincts, which are perceived as weak. Building on the feminist school of thought, we can say that the relentless pursuit of excessive thinness represents an attempt to embody certain values; it expresses an effort to create a body that will speak for the self in a meaningful and powerful way (Bordo, 1993, p. 67). Therefore, in our culture, a thin body can be used to express (sometimes contradictory) anxieties, aspirations and dilemmas (Bordo, 1993, p. 67). For feminist theorists, the interpretation of the anorexic thin body implies an awareness of many layers of cultural signification that are crystallised in the disorder (Bordo, 1993, p. 67).

> Yes, I see more and more how the process goes in my mind, why I don't like this display of femininity so much because I really associate it with the fact that in men's eyes I will be just an ordinary body. With no mind, no intelligence, no thinking of any kind. Just a sex object with breasts, with a bottom and that's it. Nothing more. (R 9)

We can conclude that the theme *Body as the basis of identity* unites the conflicting ideas of a thin body – on the one hand, it is an attempt to approach the thin ideal (Stice et al., 2017), but on the other, it also represents the rejection or negation of one's body. As Anna Lavis (2014) found: anorexia is a safe way of being, but it is also clearly a way of disappearing or 'being disappeared', which we associate with the rejection of corporeality and normative femininity.

Chapter 11

Magical Food – The Morality of Food Consumption

In the content covered by the theme *Magical food*, the previous knowledge about how patients with eating disorders associate medical and ethical values with food consumption was further elaborated (Musolino et al., 2015). The collected data confirm that people with eating disorders attach numerous intimate, emotional, ethical and social meanings to food and eating.

The statements of the interviewees show that patients with eating disorders experience food as *magical* since they believe that it has the ability to transform their life completely. For the interviewees, dieting is proof of self-control, while food causes fear and guilt and is felt as a burden. There are permitted and prohibited foods, as well as a permitted caloric intake, and when the interviewees eat restrictively or when they fast, they feel clean and powerful.

> For me, that was, um... totally, like... And that's when I felt that I could really do anything. Something like "I don't need anything from food except for those few foodstuffs of mine that I know won't make me fat. And that's all I'm going to eat, and that's why I'm great and good and losing weight and the best in the world." And all sorts of things. And it gave me a huge sense of complacency. And it gave me strength. Like, I can only eat that. You all eat some crap, and I can only eat that. (R 11)

From the point of view of the patients themselves, abstinence from food has the highest ethical value, followed by binge eating and vomiting and binge eating on its own as having the least (the same as in Mortimer, 2019). Restrictive behaviours are associated with meanings of personal power, confidence and a sense of purity and self-control (in accordance with Nordbø et al., 2006).

Therefore, for the interviewees, controlling food constitutes an attempt to control life. Many interviewees associate the idea of chaos with themselves and their lives, which can only be controlled by rigid rules and restrictive eating. The order-chaos dichotomy is also visible in their relationship to food, which is also divided into opposing all-or-nothing categories: either fasting, i.e. drastic dieting,

Eating Disorders in a Capitalist World, 101–114

Copyright © 2024 Jelena Balabanić Mavrović

Published under exclusive licence by Emerald Publishing Limited

doi:10.1108/978-1-80455-786-020231012

or exposure to the danger of binge eating, chaos and complete loss of control. The interviewees' attitude towards food is a reflection of their personal values and identity (which confirms the findings of Aarnio & Lindeman, 2004). An extremely thin appearance, restrictive eating and obsessive exercise become interconnected determinants of personal identity (O'Connor & Van Esterik, 2008).

> (...) it's absurd how many rules you set for yourself in anorexia, and how much you become just some kind of... simply a slave, who has to follow all those rules... and that was a total distraction. That was a distraction from any real life and any real roles. Then you only have to be anorexic and that's it. You then have this bunch of rules, but it's actually quite easy. From the point of view of an anorexic, it is much easier to have (*rules*)... what I have to do in the morning, what I have to eat that day. What I have to do, how much and when I need to walk... this and that. Rather than... live and let go of control and see where it takes you. That is very difficult. (R 25)

People who have difficulty identifying and describing their emotions often have difficulty recognising other body signals. In patients with eating disorders, damage to some aspects of interoceptive awareness (Phillipou et al., 2022) has been found – for example, the inability to feel hunger and satiety. However, it is not yet clear whether such difficulties are the cause or consequence of eating disorders. The very core of eating disorders has to do with ignoring the signals of the body, which makes it easier for the individual to starve or overeat. On the other hand, it is possible that some people are more vulnerable to developing eating disorders since they have difficulty 'reading' their body's needs, such as hunger and satiety, which leads to disturbed eating habits during adolescence (Jacquemot & Park, 2020).

In anorexia, we can most clearly establish the meaning of abstinence from food, which is also present in other forms of eating disorders (bulimia, other specified feeding or eating disorder). If we apply the principle of continuity (Tylka & Subich, 1999), from these findings we can conclude something about the attitudes towards food and eating among women in the general population, and how the manner in which we eat is connected with the expectations of the female gender role. In today's Western society, dieting or abstaining from food is part of the daily disciplinary practices through which normative femininity is lived. Women are expected to regulate what they wear, how they act and feel and the most fundamental of all biological needs: 'the innocent need of the organism for food' (Bartky, 1988, p. 96). To be a woman means to be beyond needs (Tully, 2015), so the need for food should be curbed or even eliminated.

The desire for food, as the drive of all desires, undermines the illusion of complete self-control and omnipotence, and reminds us that we are not self-sufficient, that we need the world, food, other people and relationships. By suppressing hunger, a person also suppresses all other needs, including those of sexual nature.

I mean, I'd be happiest if I didn't have to eat at all. That would be the easiest for me. And I functioned like that for a while, so I wouldn't eat anything for five, six days, then one day I would eat something and then the same thing all over again. And I drank water in abnormal amounts and it worked great for a while. Of course, that also has its consequences, but... (R 4)

The sub-theme *Dieting – proof of self-control* once again confirms that patients with eating disorders attach meanings of power, confidence and self-discipline to abstaining from food (which is in accordance with O'Connor & Van Esterik, 2008; Warin, 2010). These are principles highly valued in Western society, and are associated with a traditionally masculine role. Through the practice of fasting and cleansing, they promote asceticism, rectitude and purity (O'Connor & Van Esterik, 2008; Warin, 2010).

For me, the disorder definitely helped me... It helped, I mean... It was a mechanism for me to control myself. And to discipline myself. It was just right for me. So, whenever I started a project, whatever. I was always on some projects. Let's say it was a project, I don't know, to be the best at the entrance exam or... Those kinds of things, let's say, I'm thinking of things like that. Then I would always start with greater food control because it helped me to do other things as well. (R 20)

Through the restrictive practices of fasting and abstaining from food, the interviewees created a sense of control and avoided emotions (*I feel clean and controlled*) (confirmed earlier in Espeset et al., 2012; Gustafsson et al., 2011). The interviewees were afraid of food, they struggled with it (as in Nordbø et al., 2006), they felt guilty and hated themselves when they ate and rigid rules provided them with a sense of security and achievement (similar to Godier & Park, 2015).

So, if I was productive, in the sense - if I studied enough, if I was good. If I've been naughty, no, I can't eat. It's been like that since I was little, if I'm naughty and show my true emotions, I can't eat. If I'm sad, I can't eat. You don't eat when you're sad. I would have to satisfy these... I had to be a certain kind of person to get food. Or it was, like, that I had to study enough. Or if I'm going to eat, I have to go jogging with my dad that evening. That's normal to me. I have to exercise, jog. (R 28)

This striving for absolute self-control which leads to self-negation and, ultimately, death can also be seen on Pro-Ana blogs in sentences like 'I trained myself to enjoy feeling hungry' (Dear Ana, 2006, according to Tully, 2015, p. 41) or 'blessed are the starving, for they shall teach us not to want' (Dear Ana, 2006, according to Tully, 2015, p. 41). If women are taught not to want anything, the absolute not wanting or not needing is a form of perfection: 'thin is perfection, I'll die trying to achieve it' (Pro-Ana Lifestyle, 2007, according to Tully, 2015, p. 41).

> I expected that... that then somehow everything would be a little bit more orderly in my life. There was always some chaos around me... I'm chaotic by nature and then there was chaos with my family that never stopped... and I needed some order... desperately... so I expected to get it with that (*weight loss*)... so that was the main thing. (R 25)

When we interpret restriction or starvation in the statements of our interviewees, we also come across a basic motive which appears in other themes as well: the paradox of anorexia can be seen in the fact that abstaining from food is a form of self-monitoring which is a practice of normative femininity in Western society, and at the same time it represents a rejection of that same femininity (Tully, 2015). A woman with anorexia has transcended the ideal of femininity and gone beyond it: beyond desire, beyond need, beyond the feminine, beyond the body (Tully, 2015). 'When your body is your cage, [Pro] Ana can be the key to your freedom' (Miss Ana Mia, 2011, according to Tully, 2015, p. 46).

For people with eating disorders, anorexia is often not a disease nor is it a game. 'Anorexia is a skill, perfected by a few: the chosen, the pure, the flawless' (Dear, Ana, 2006, according to Tully, 2015, p. 21). In order to put the participants' statements into the context of striving for purity and perfection found in anorexia patients, we should once again remind ourselves of the dichotomy of indulging in the pleasures of the body (food), which often causes self-disgust in girls and women with anorexia (Glashouwer & de Jong, 2021). Through starvation or reduced eating, progress is made towards purity and asceticism which filled the interviewees (at least in the initial stage of the disorder) with pride and superiority (O'Connor & Van Esterik, 2008; Warin, 2010). We can conclude that anorexia emerges as a desired ideal, since abstinence from food in patients with eating disorders represents a moral victory and an 'excess of self-discipline', highly valued in Western society (Orsini, 2017).

> R: Are there any periods when you are satisfied with yourself and the way you eat?
>
> I: When I manage to beat others and myself. When I beat myself.
>
> R: And that is...? How do you eat then?
>
> I: Well, I generally don't eat then. (*laughs*) (R 23)

In addition to overcoming natural bodily needs, the cultural construction of the concept of a woman is also associated with the internalisation of anger. Women are taught that the aggression they feel should be suppressed (Norwood et al., 2011). Therefore, eating disorders can also be interpreted as extremely violent acts towards oneself, as a misdirected anger which originates from the unattainable cultural ideals of femininity felt by most women, not only those with eating disorders (Lavis, 2014).

> While I was eating and while I was performing that act, that- I am worthy, I'm rebelling... I'm rebelling against all that nonsense, those rules, and after that food I would have a lot of confidence. The next day, if I did the same thing, the next day I would feel ashamed or I would hear my dad in my dream, my dad's voice, something that haunts me – now I will be punished, I am always waiting for that punishment – when will I be punished. (R 28)

Along with anger, Brown (2010) highlights the fundamental role of shame that arises in the encounter with the contradictory, impossible expectations of the female role. So Brown claims that perfectionism is not striving for excellence, but a cognitive-behavioural process of a person who believes that if they can look, live and work perfectly, then they can avoid or reduce the shame and disapproval of their environment. Shame is the belief 'I'm bad' which is amplified by hiding, silencing and judging, and is directly related to eating disorders (Brown, 2010).

The following statements of the interviewees speak about the deep and inextricable connection between emotions and attitudes towards food:

> I have some kind of anger in me. Let's say it's more connected with food, I find something unspoken in food. (R 6)

> Before, food was my comfort, when I had unpleasant emotions, when I didn't have friends. So, like, food was everything to me. (R 13)

> Most often it's this anxiety. It's not even sadness, it's anxiety. Where I simply have to... I have to give my body pleasure and fill it up so that it calms down. (R 14)

The connection between emotions and eating disorders has been confirmed in several places in the results of the study, especially in the meanings related to eating. The codes *I feel clean and in control during restrictive feeding; emotional need for food/tension is resolved by eating/suppressing emotions through eating; vomiting brings on emotional discharge/I'll throw out emotions together with the food* are in accordance with the findings of Bekker and Boselie (2002) and Geller et al. (2000), who found that emotional eating and dietary behaviours represent a specific way of dealing with the so-called negative emotions, and that affected women had more repressed anger than the control group (measurement of self-silencing).

Earlier research has already shown that anorexia is characterised by extremely negative attitudes towards the expression of emotions. People with anorexia often hide their inner feelings of anger and dissatisfaction through visible behaviours of obedience and cooperation (Schmidt & Treasure, 2006). People with anorexia consider 'negative emotions' unacceptable and rarely express them in order not to be criticised or rejected (Schmidt & Treasure, 2006). In this way, patients want to prevent conflicts and preserve important relationships (Schmidt & Treasure, 2006).

People with anorexia are excessively worried about possible distress and discomfort. They also have a heightened sensitivity to the reactions of others and a preference for long-lasting relationships and emotionally stable environments (Jack & Dill, 1992, according to Hambrook et al., 2011). We can assume that people with anorexia would rather sacrifice their own interests and suppress their needs than actively oppose and stand up for themselves. This was confirmed in the research of Hambrook et al. (2011), where patients with anorexia scored highly on the self-sacrificing scale. In the words of Rieger et al. (2010, p. 402), 'engagement in eating disorder behaviours comes increasingly to replace healthy engagement with the social world in the individual's efforts to attain positive self-esteem and affect.'

> What was at the beginning, what was before that? Then I wanted (*by vomiting*) just to silence these... um... these emotions of some kind, all of these things I didn't understand... it was all too strong for me to deal with. (R 25)

The interviewees stated that they were less able to deal with emotions (similar to Corstorphine et al., 2007) and they more often avoided situations which could trigger the so-called negative emotions. They preferred to suppress anxiety by harmful behaviours (starvation, binge eating, vomiting) in order to reduce the intensity of emotions which were difficult for them to bear (in accordance with the findings of Corstorphine et al., 2007; Haynos & Fruzzetti, 2011). Such an approach results in emotional confusion, the desire to completely control emotions and the use of eating disorder symptoms to suppress these emotions or express them through the symptoms (Fox, 2009). When a person feels strong emotions, this translates into 'feeling fat', a term used to describe the psychologically distressing conditions characteristic of eating disorder patients.

> With anorexia, you eat, your stomach hurts because it's all small, puny, tiny, God knows when the last time it got any food was. Then you overeat so much that your stomach hurts from the amount of food. So we have those links. The same goes for emotions. With binge eating, you eat, that is, you consume too much food just to dull those emotions, while in anorexia you do not eat in order to dull your emotions. (R 22)

Apart from restriction, the key symptoms of eating disorders are binge eating and compensatory behaviours, such as vomiting. Binge eating and vomiting can also be associated with anorexia, in which case this constitutes purgative anorexia, but in fact these behaviours are typical for bulimia.

The interviewees associated the idea of loss of control with binge eating (in line with the findings of Churruca et al., 2014), which on the one hand brings pleasure and freedom from self-imposed restrictions but at the same time arouses feelings of self-disgust and guilt because of a moment of indulging in weakness (the same as in Burns, 2004).

> The danger lies in the fear that I will totally lose control. So maybe it's not as being afraid of one, two or three kilos more so much. Although it is, but in essence it isn't because I felt in the hospital that I'm not really afraid of those one, two or three kilos, but I'm afraid that I'll have some food in front of me and that I won't be able to stop. That it will be something stronger than me. That I simply won't be able to hit the brakes. And that I will get fat and that I will only get fatter, fatter and fatter and that I will never be able to lose weight ever again in my life. Fear. Sometimes it's stronger, sometimes weaker. (R 19)

One's attitude towards food can be determined by self-regulating emotions and proving one's worth through self-discipline, and also by the internalisation of the thin ideal and the belief that an attractive physical appearance and thinness are necessary for success (Heinberg et al., 2008). More about this branch of meanings has already been said in the themes *Insecure Femininity* and *Body as the Basis of Identity*. Time and time again, we see how in patients with eating disorders there is a link between the concepts of identity, food and body. These create potentially different psychological profiles positioned differently according to the key issues of growing up, social success, female attractiveness and sexuality. Therefore, the relationship with food also finds a place within three different sets of meanings which also appear in earlier themes: Girls and women with eating disorders are torn between conflicting aspirations. On the one hand, there is the need for regression, disappearance and self-silencing of their own needs, then there is the striving for perfection and success achieved through fulfilling social ideals and finally pursuing masculine values, asceticism and self-discipline. Different ways of eating perform a function within these motivational circuits, intertwining with ways one can deal with emotions, self-perception and attitudes towards one's body.

As for the moral interpretations of food and abstaining from food, obesity is marked as something bad and the so-called correct, healthy food and fasting acquire the moral value of something good and clean (O'Connor & Van Esterik, 2008). Therefore, it can be said that some of our interviewees are focused on 'virtue and not beauty' (O'Connor & Van Esterik, 2008, p. 6).

> Something that is dirty, like how I feel for example now or whenever I eat normally and things like that. For example, now that I'm eating normally and I'm not on a restriction and then I feel dirty and awful and disgusting and so on, I don't want to go into it anymore. (R 5)

The interviewees divided food into two categories: permitted and forbidden, which represents one of the key mechanisms of maintaining eating disorders (Dalle, 2015). Judging which food is good or bad was based on the nutritional properties of foods they have learned, the calories individual foods contained and health guidelines on desirable and undesirable foods. However, the key thing was the subjective interpretation of this information, which determined how extreme an individual would be in applying advice on a healthy diet or avoiding 'forbidden ingredients', such as carbohydrates, sugar or fat. We must not forget that for people with eating disorders, all food is inherently bad, and the ideal lifestyle would be fasting, i.e. complete avoidance of food (already pointed out by Lavis, 2014). For many of the interviewees, food was directly constructed as obesity (in accordance with the findings of Churruca et al., 2016). Since one must eat in order to survive, the division of food into prohibited and permitted, strict rules regarding preparation, quantity, caloric value and schedule for food intake can create a feeling of some kind of security when exposed to the risk of eating (in accordance with Nordbø et al., 2006). Certain food is perceived as particularly 'bad', and when people eat that type of food, they become bad and worthless themselves (as in Churruca et al., 2016). Eating 'bad food' is perceived as an immoral act, like lying, and it creates the feeling of guilt (Churruca et al., 2016, p. 6). Consuming 'good', i.e. permitted food, makes our interviewees better people, and they feel clean and in control (in accordance with Churruca et al., 2016).

> Yes, it's as if I'm not a good person and considering that I've already taken the first step towards sin, so let's go all the way now, because, well, why not since you've already been so stupid to get into that in the first place. And that's why it's easier. It's easier for me not to eat. Because for me any kind of food, for example today we ate pizza and my stomach hurts so much because I'm just thinking about how I'm going to survive this day now. Will I go into restriction or will I go into vomiting? I don't know. Because I've already eaten that forbidden thing and now I feel guilty, uh. Really a lot. (R 4)

Hunger and eating are burdened with dense meanings, and they are key criteria in how the interviewees evaluate themselves. The relationship to food shows what kind of person they are, and changing eating practices transforms their identity completely. Degrassi (2006, according to Tully, 2015, p. 24) reports 'Hunger is a feeling, thin is a skill'. In this designation of anorexic abstinence from food as a method of self-improvement, we encounter echoes of religious fasting, surrendering oneself to a higher goal, and elevating anorexia to the form of a deity (Pittock, 2014). Desired asceticism present in anorexia, and to some extent also in bulimia (Orsini, 2017), can be linked to the Christian tradition and the seven deadly sins of pride, greed, wrath, envy, lust, gluttony and sloth. People with anorexia often think in religious terms of 'temptation' and 'purity' (Griffin & Berry, 2003), where food is equated with sin (Stammers, 2020). Apart from the view of food as a battlefield where a war with one's urges is waged, there is also the relationship to the body, which is a parallel line of meaning in the interpretation of eating disorders (more in the theme *Body as the basis of identity*).

Binge eating is a forbidden pleasure, and it is perceived as yielding to an internal compulsion – it resembles addictive behaviour. The emotional need for food is linked to the suppression of emotions as well as to the resolution of inner tensions through eating. In this way, people with eating disorders use self-destructive behaviours related to the body and food as a way of regulating their emotions by directing them towards the body (Aldao et al., 2010; Danner et al., 2012), i.e. what occurs is a somatisation of an emotional state.

The interviewees described their binges as moments when they had no control or limitations, which for some created feelings of pleasure, relaxation and freedom, while others felt dirty, fat and ugly, and even punished themselves through binge eating. Therefore, some of the interviewees preferred an extremely restrictive way of eating because they were afraid they would otherwise overeat. Binge eating usually took place in solitude. It was most often performed with 'bad' or forbidden food, which was not only perceived as unhealthy, but also as a threat to the interviewees' self-control (Churruca et al., 2016).

> But... there is something else there. I mean it's not just "I'm having a good time and I'm enjoying the food." There's this feeling, you know, like, I fucked up, like, I'm stuffing my face, let's go all the way. I will undo it all in the end. You also get that feeling. Because bulimia is essentially a kind of purge. You first get very dirty and that is very comorbid with my OCD. Because when I binge-eat, I can eat off the floor, you know. And otherwise, I'm terribly clean. Like, I wouldn't... If my apple isn't really thoroughly washed, I won't eat it. So there is this feeling like "and now there's nothing to stop me." (R 21)

Therefore, we conclude that the concept of *Binge eating as a forbidden pleasure* is formed in a binary opposition to the superhuman control of abstaining from food, as a behaviour related to pleasure, freedom from restrictive rules (already present in Eli, 2015), but at the same time as a moment of self-punishment and indulgence in a shameful (and solitary) practice. Experiences of relaxation and pleasure during the binge are complemented by the 'addictive character' (following the findings of Leslie et al., 2019) of this behaviour as an insurmountable need for the individual to 'stuff' themselves with food.

Thus, the need for binge eating appeared in most of the interviewees as a feeling of internal compulsion, similar to an addictive need for food. They felt that they 'had to do it'. The tension before the binge resembles an anxiety attack before the consumption of an intoxicant.

In the words of one of the interviewees:

> I see only that (*food*), I see nothing else. It's like I'm hypnotized or something. I can be terribly nice if that'll help me get to my goal. I can be terribly rude. So I become a typical addict who will do

anything to reach his goal. I can lie, I can make stuff up, I can...
(R 21)

Although they understood that giving in to binge eating would lead to a type of self-destruction and bring suffering, most of the interviewees described moments of giving in to an inner compulsion as cathartic. Therefore, binges also had an intense 'liberating' effect.

While it was addictive, it was a thrill, I couldn't wait. But depending on the situation, sometimes there was this tension, basically, like, you want to get rid of that tension quickly and when you eat, it's like you've got your drug and you calm down, your brain calms down. Yes, I would compare it with that. (R 30)

Such an interpretation is in line with Eli (2015), who pointed out the need to fill the existential void people with bulimia nervosa or purgative anorexia feel, whereby their emotions and bodily sensations overlap in a concrete way. Churruca et al. (2016) also come to a similar conclusion. They link binge eating and vomiting to the patients' desire to improve their mood, to experience excitement or to escape from various problems in their lives.

Hm... it's still the same for me. I like to say that I love that vomiting now. Because when I... I don't know. I had that when my folks came. That's a great example because it was recently, about two weeks ago. Um... I have this food in my house, which was forbidden to me before, but it didn't... I just need that fullness in my stomach that I will throw up later. And that happens exactly at that moment when... when things get to be too much for me and when I feel very insecure. And when I totally lose control. Not over things, but over my thoughts and emotions in general, and I don't know what to do with myself anymore. So it's not the same as before, but for me that vomiting is now better than binge eating, but I need the eating, because I can't throw up otherwise. And then that's it, yeah. (R 11)

The division of food into good and bad and labelling abstinence from food and/or controlled eating as desirable, and eating, especially food marked as bad, and eating 'without control' as undesirable is connected with the concept of food as the basis of health. This is further strengthened through public health campaigns on the dangers of the obesity epidemic (Malson, 2008).

Defining obesity as a disease and thinness as health opened the door to the perception of food as either healthy and good or toxic and bad.

And the allowed (food)... and things like oats, flakes, rye bread, buckwheat, and such cereals. Fruits, vegetables. (R 12)

The division of food into good and bad is also frequently used in the advertising industry: some types of food are associated with concepts such as 'temptation', 'decadence' and on the other hand 'heavenly' and 'pure' (Pittock, 2014), all in order to the established links between types of food and moral values. Also, the advertising industry and the media use certain types of food as the proverbial forbidden fruit, relying on the fact that people most often binge on the foods they consider forbidden. Advertising encourages indulging in sinful pleasures – for example, chocolate. However, if a person has already sinned and eaten the forbidden food, then they must fix it (or atone for it) through exercising or dieting, which is, in turn, promoted by thin and happy-looking models (Pittock, 2014). It should be noted here that binge eating is perceived differently – both as a punishment and as a sin. For some interviewees, binge eating is a punishment through the painful act of 'conscious sin' of excessive food consumption for the previous mistake of 'taking the wrong bite'. Vomiting is also sometimes perceived as 'redemption' in the sense of cleansing from 'bad and excessive' food and as such brings emptiness and peace, while in other cases it is a punishment for binge eating, since the experience of vomiting is unpleasant and for some of the interviewees embarrassing. This dynamics and the adoption of the religious model: sin-punishment-redemption through behaviours related to food are present in many of the statements of the interviewees:

> And as soon as I go into binge eating, that is a sign that I have sinned. And now I have to punish myself if I ate something other than fruits and vegetables. I will punish myself by eating too much and then get it all out. It's exclusively a form of punishment for me. (R 4)

The division of food into good and bad also includes subjective experiences of certain types of food as particularly dangerous or repulsive. Many of the interviewees singled out sugars and carbohydrates as forbidden, while for some fatty foods were unacceptable. The experience of animal fat as heavy, rotten and potentially dangerous for patients with eating disorders was already mentioned in Durif (1992), according to Forth and Leitch (2014).

In contrast to forbidden food, desirable food is perceived as light, useful and fat-free, which reflects the desire for the body to be light and almost immaterial. Research by Lupton (1996, p. 82) showed that participants described 'good food' as clean, light and healthy in contrast to unhealthy food which was seen as repulsive and slimy, and also heavy, dirty, greasy and sticky.

> Basically, I'm more concerned about calories, fat. I don't like fat. So the sensation if I eat something and I feel that it. . . feels like oil, like when you eat some kind of fish with olive oil, I can't stand it. I can't stand that. But let's say I know that olive oil is healthy and I consider it healthy and I love olives and that, but the sensation of that oil as such, any oil, it terrifies me. (R 19)

Warin (2010, p. 106) pointed out that the properties of fatty foods are particularly disturbing for women with eating disorders 'not simply because of their fat content, but because of their form, their ability to move and seep into the cracks of one's body'. Thus, patients with eating disorders associate fat with terms like dirt, pollution, even excrement (Forth, 2014). However, it is not possible to completely 'get away' from fat in food, since it is to some extent an integral part of a large number of foods, but also of the body itself. Therefore, fat is perceived at the same time as something expelled from the body (Kent, 2001), as a danger lurking in one's identity itself (Kristeva, 1982, p. 71) and also as something external, unnecessary, like an ulcer, as a corruption of the body (Klein, 2001, p. 27 according to Forth & Leitch, 2014).

Despite the negative associations that fat can evoke, Miller (1997, p. 121 according to Forth & Leitch, 2014) points out that 'the greasy and the sweet continue to allure us with their taste.' Such foods have the ability to 'make' us eat more of them than we wish, so we can see fatty and sweet foods as will-weakening or will-deviating (Miller, 1997 according to Forth & Leitch, 2014). Fatty acids in certain foods are proven to change one's mood, reduce anxiety and increase feelings of happiness and relaxation, which is why they are called 'comfort foods' (in Oudenhove et al., 2011).

> I was obsessed with food in the sense that I loved eating snacks, all the forbidden food, sweets, I would eat all the time at school also. Because at home it was supposed to be... my folks paid attention to what was eaten, so I would overeat at school and so on. And because I wasn't eating enough healthy food, I was scared that I would get sick and all that, but somehow the desire for that junk food was much much greater than anything else, and that was my world and that was my only pleasure. When I overate. So that I would often overeat such food... (R 28)

Such irrational reactions to certain types of food are especially visible in people with eating disorders, who divide food into clean and dirty based on their specific, material qualities and their ability to produce a reaction of disgust (Warin, 2003). Sometimes such a subjective attitude towards certain foods has no basis in the objective quality of the food and the actual fat or calorie content (Warin, 2003). Such findings were also confirmed in a qualitative study by Lavis (2014), which describes how the material properties of fatty foods in patients at an eating disorder residential treatment centre aroused fear and rejection of such foods (like eating a doughnut, Lavis, 2014, p. 9).

> Disgust, self-disgust. Although maybe it's not the act of eating itself, but disgust at the fact that I won't be clean, and unfortunately that's food. (R 3)

People with eating disorders do not see only the consumption of fatty or high-calorie foods as problematic – they often experience any kind of eating as a personal failure (Lavis, 2014). Therefore, qualitative research often describes experiences such as 'When I eat I feel fat, disgusting, dirty and a failure' (Lavis, 2014, p. 6) and the feeling that through eating the person becomes contaminated, gets fat and expands during the intake of food itself (Lavis, 2014).[1]

> Repulsion. Fear. Disgust. Anger. Anger especially after eating. "Why did I even eat that? What was I thinking anyway? Now I have this pain in my stomach again." So, I had such thoughts on a daily basis. In my head, after eating. (R 22)

Pittock (2014) links the reasons why eating is stigmatised in patients with eating disorders to the legacy of Christianity, which lists gluttony (intemperance in eating and drinking) as one of the seven deadly sins. If satisfying lower, even animalistic, urges leads to further weakening of the will and readiness to sin (Pittock, 2014), then controlling one's own desires is important so that our spirit is more connected to God. In traditional societies, the purity of women is held in very high regard. In the Catholic Church, women entering a religious order accept celibacy so that they would not succumb to lust (Pittock, 2014). Fasting is also a way for a person not to give in to the sin of gluttony (Pittock, 2014). The connection between the desire for food and lust is evident in this statement of an interviewee:

> It can create lust for me, fear – that's usually when I see a lot of food at parties I attend. Fear, lust, maybe confusion about what of it all I can have, how can I make something normal for myself so that I don't go into a binge without being restricted, so that something normal can come out of it all. (R 10)

Another interviewee explicitly stated that what happened was placing libidinous energy into food, instead of sexuality.

> I: But my libido is still directed in the wrong direction.
>
> R: How? In what way?
>
> I: In buli... Still... I figured it out, I even told (*last name of a doctor*) that. When a bulimic goes to binge, you feel some excitement. Almost sexual excitement. That's what I told (*last name of a doctor*). It's... I think girls can hardly explain it, but

---

[1]Therefore, it is particularly important to understand the experience of forced eating or un-agential eating (Lavis, 2014, p. 8), which is carried out in most treatment centres for anorexia and bulimia, during which patients have no information about the nutritional composition of their meals (Long et al., 2011) and thus are unable to control food. Since eating control in patients with eating disorders is related to a sense of control over their lives and personal identity (Nordbø et al., 2006), taking away this balancing tool has strong psychotherapeutic potential that may (but does not have to be) be used as part of therapy.

it's literally like... (*sigh*) It's a similar feeling. Libido is simply directed in the wrong direction. I think. That's how I explain it to myself. (R 21)

In line with the connection between binge eating and sexual excitement, another interviewee verbalised purity in restriction and defilement through binge eating – when there is nothing stopping her and she goes all the way, only to finally re-establish control and purity through vomiting.

I used to have that rational realization about it, "it's not good, why am I doing this" or "come on, stop it already." But I would simply... I would suppress it. There would simply be only, "I want it! I want it! I want it!" And if I resisted that, then I would fight with that, "I want it! I don't want it! I want it! I don't want it!" That is, like, my greatest suffering. Because I literally don't know. I would go take a shower. I would go for a walk. And I couldn't get rid of that thought "Destroy yourself!" Destroy yourself! Destroy yourself! Destroy yourself!" It seemed to be getting louder and louder and it would only calm down when I'd start eating. (R 20)

Chapter 12

Independent Meanings of Binge Eating and Vomiting

In studies conducted on bulimia so far, as well as in the conceptualisation of bulimia, binge eating has commonly been viewed as a consequence of excessive abstinence from food (Fairburn et al., 2003, p. 510). However, judging by some of the interviewees, the opposite interpretation could also be put forward. Considering the significant emotional investment of the interviewees while engaging in binging practices (combined in the codes – *emotional need for food, pleasure, relaxation during binges*), I am inclined to accept the interpretation of Eli (2015) that binge eating as 'relaxation' and 'fulfilment' was actually for some of the interviewees the initial basic practice of a disturbed relationship with food, and that dietary practices were a reaction to the fear of gaining weight due to binge eating.

Following on from the already mentioned moralisation of food and behaviours related to eating, bulimic behaviours were interpreted by many of the interviewees as a sign of weak will, moral failure and as a form of 'failed anorexia' (Orsini, 2017). Bulimic behaviours include binge eating and some form of purging (vomiting, laxative abuse) or compensatory behaviours (intense exercise or extreme dieting).

> And then the binge eating begins where there is peace and where I am happy. I mean, I'm already happy when I start planning that I will go on a binge. And then peace, happiness, comfort, some kind of fulfilment, freedom, I've finally let go of control, so there's freedom. And then I eat like that and then, like, rest a bit to stay in that moment. So I'm not exactly like the rest of them, who as soon as they eat they go to vomit, I stay in that moment because I obviously like it very much. (R 9)

The subversive meaning of binge eating as a rebellion against restrictive dehumanising dietary regimes (Eli, 2015) was also partially confirmed in the findings of this study (there is *no control and no restrictions* in binge eating), but the interviewees in this study also had a strong fear of binge eating as yielding to an internal compulsion which they could not control. Therefore, some interviewees concluded

Eating Disorders in a Capitalist World, 115–118
Copyright © 2024 Jelena Balabanić Mavrović
Published under exclusive licence by Emerald Publishing Limited
doi:10.1108/978-1-80455-786-020231013

that 'it is easier to be anorexic'. Thus, the interviewees form their subjectivity somewhere between two poles: self-control of the natural drive of hunger and giving in to the desire for food (Burns, 2004).

> I honestly don't even know why I sometimes binge because I feel disgusting during the whole process, especially in (*name of the city*) where I know that when I feel like doing it, I know I have to do it, but I don't know why I have to do it. (R 4)

Orsini (2017) emphasised the hierarchical structure of anorexia, bulimia and the binge-eating disorder as different forms of moral conversion. By achieving self-discipline, control and abstinence from food, people with anorexia 'become better people' (Orsini, 2017, p. 137), while people with bulimia nervosa in this study identify themselves as lapsed, failed anorexics (Orsini, 2017, p. 132). I do not fully agree with such an interpretation, since most of the interviewees associated strong meanings of liberation, rebellion and pleasure, breaking down boundaries and inner fulfilment, as well as emotional release through vomiting with binge eating and purging. At one point, an interviewee used the phrase 'eating your emotions' as the best description of what happens to her during her binges.

> I don't think I have any thoughts at that moment, just "give me more" and then I eat my emotions. (R 27)

> Maybe as excitement and relief because I deny myself some of these things all the time, and then I allow myself not to think about it anymore and I can do what I want, but later I feel guilty. (R 27)

Therefore, the behaviours of binge eating and purging have separate meanings and sometimes occupy a central place in the experience of eating disorders. Consequently, they cannot be interpreted solely as a result of 'failing to starve oneself'. As a central mechanism in emotional self-regulation in some interviewees, binge eating and vomiting become difficult to replace, and they persist in the form of purgative anorexia. Vomiting takes place in solitude and there is a feeling of compulsion, of *having to*, which links purgative behaviours with addictive patterns (Leslie et al., 2019).

> Well, for me, it (*binge eating*) is the only method that helps me when I can't stand something, some emotional state or something like that. (R 7)

> ...actually it depends on which emotion it is, but there is an emotion in the background and then it depends on what you want to do with it... Well, yes, either dulling the emotion if it is too strong... mostly just... like you're not dealing with that emotion, you deal with food. (R 3)

Contradictory feelings and interpretations of binge eating and vomiting as a simultaneous source of pleasure and freedom, but also self-blame and shame, open up the possibility of understanding such forms of eating disorders as dynamically determined by the meanings of starvation, binge eating and vomiting. These are, in some cases, directed primarily towards binge eating and vomiting as the key points of one's experience.[1]

> ... but then it's either vomiting or laxatives and there's purity again. And it even isn't... I used to binge many times just so I could throw up. It wasn't even binge eating, it was the normal amount, but I needed purity, that's what it was. (R 3)

Therefore, planned binges and vomiting introduce elements of rebellion, daring and risk-taking (Eli, 2018), and some interviewees testified that they binged so that they could vomit and *expel their emotions with food*. In addition to the positive labelling of vomiting, the interviewees also presented negative meanings of *shame and guilt, self-disgust* (Burns, 2004), as well as *physical pain* during the vomiting.

The multi-layered understanding of vomiting as a 'disgusting' act (R 24), but also as punishment and self-purification after eating 'bad' food is in line with the findings of Churruca et al. (2016), whose qualitative study additionally interprets bulimic vomiting as maintaining a clean and healthy body after eating bad or dirty food (Churruca et al., 2016, p. 7).

> What was in the beginning, what came first? Then I wanted (*by vomiting*) just to silence some... um... some emotions, all that I didn't understand... all that was too strong for me to deal with. (R 25)

We can, thus, conclude that the interviewees emphasised the understanding of vomiting as an important act rich in meanings which go beyond the usual definition of vomiting as 'reversing the effects of a binge' for the purpose of preventing weight gain (Churruca et al., 2014). The interviewees attributed meanings such as *pleasure, excitement and relief* to vomiting, which makes this practice – along with the practice of starvation and the practice of binge eating – independently positive and ceases to be only 'repairing the damage' caused by the moment of weakness during a binge, as in Orsini (2017) or Burns (2004).

---

[1]In her study, Orsini (2017) established that obese women feel dissatisfaction and frustration with their large bodies and admire and envy thin people. Therefore, she rejects the feminist position (Orbach & Mikulincer, 1998, p. 25) that a woman's life in a fat body is a protest against social pressure that every woman should look and behave in a certain way. According to the feminist critique of Orbach, obesity represents a woman's conscious refusal to conform to a preconceived image of 'normative beauty'. A much more complex relationship to one's own obesity is also confirmed in an autobiographical scientific essay on weight loss (Longhurst, 2012).

Well, sometimes I really get a feeling in these... when I feel that I might develop symptoms. Before that, there's this feeling, like... of being overwhelmed and so on... I just need to calm down a little and let it all, like, stop (...) Sometimes I can do this, but when there's a new kind of situation, like I don't know how to deal with it, especially when it has to do with my parents. In fact, I can deal with anything, but what is linked here... Here I never know where I stand, I never know how to act, be myself, something. And that's where these symptoms most often come to me because I don't know what to do with myself. Not like... And I know that they will come home. Like, in two hours and I will have to see them. And I don't know what to say to them. And that destroys me and I don't know what to do and I surrender myself to the symptom. (R 11)

Chapter 13

Spontaneous Eating and Using Food Against Internal Chaos

The interviewees imagined spontaneous feeding as a promised land – an idealised but somewhat unattainable state of normalcy, happiness and freedom from the disorder (according to Malson et al., 2011). Ambivalence is present in the descriptions of the fear of gaining weight (in accordance with the findings of Nordbø et al., 2012) and the fact that the body of the interviewees is 'actually a fat body' and that this would show if they would eat normally (e.g. R 18). Also, there is the fear, supported by earlier experiences, that the person has lost the ability to eat 'normally' guided by their own signals of hunger and satiety, i.e. that after the rules of dieting are relaxed in patients with eating disorders, binging is bound to occur (frequent transitions between diagnoses, according to Eddy et al., 2008).

> So, it's fascinating to me that I see someone eat something and they're okay with it, it's like they're not even thinking about whether they ate it or not. Like, there, I only ate that much because I was (*hungry*)... to me it's wow, how can you do that because I think three days in advance about the food I have to put in myself. So that, for me, it has become so tiring, just, like, after six years, I would really like to be free from all that, but I can't. (R 4)

Spontaneous eating would mean taking care of oneself and trusting one's inner needs, and allowing oneself spontaneous pleasures (Bachner-Melman & Oakley, 2016), which is highly problematic for most of the interviewees.

The relationship to food lives in extremes (*Food: all or nothing*), where one bite of 'forbidden food' initiates binges since the body is already 'contaminated' (the same as in Lavis, 2014). In this way, controlling food represents controlling an otherwise chaotic life (established already in Burns, 2004) and a path towards the construction of a new identity (Nordbø et al., 2006). The binary relationship in which the way of eating or abstaining from food also means personal success or failure in life is in accordance with the findings of Burns (2004). For the interviewees, food control represented a struggle against internal and external chaos (similar to Aarnio & Lindeman, 2004).

Eating Disorders in a Capitalist World, 119–122
Copyright © 2024 Jelena Balabanić Mavrović
Published under exclusive licence by Emerald Publishing Limited
doi:10.1108/978-1-80455-786-020231014

> I: In addition to what I expected (*from losing weight*) is that... Better... better control over myself, which would then automatically mean that I am better and more satisfied and happier... and then I would achieve much more...
>
> R: In terms of some kinds of successes in life?
>
> I: In the sense that it won't be difficult for me to achieve anything anymore, I mean, I'm terribly chaotic here... I can't stand my reflection in the mirror, I can't get out of bed... but when I'm where I want to be, then I will be able to get up, go outside and do what needs to be done. (R 25)

Some interviewees exhibited confusion and indecision in their statements about food and other topics, verbalising their inner chaos and loss of control over thoughts and feelings (*code: I'm lost*). This was confirmed in earlier research as a tendency for more frequent dissociation in people with eating disorders and a weak sense of one's personality (La Mela et al., 2009; Oldershaw et al., 2015).

The interviewees described their sense of being lost and their highly ambivalent attitude towards almost all important issues of life – the imperative of self-discipline, strictness towards oneself and rigidity coexist with indecision and a fragile sense of one's identity.

> Separated, lost, misguided by myself. I can't see myself at all. I rarely see myself in reality. When I see myself in reality, I get terribly scared, and then I go into some kind of illusion. But it's just, like, so hard for me... It's really hard for me to face it. (R 28)

Therefore, we can confirm that the ritualised daily schedule, behaviour rules and the moral labelling of food provide an efficient strategy of avoiding one's true needs and that they appear self-sufficient (already mentioned in Bachner-Melman & Oakley, 2016).

The interviewees conclude that they *preoccupy themselves with food so that they don't have to think about anything else*. While they are constantly preoccupied with their body, weight and food, they avoid facing the difficulties that hide behind the symptoms (in accordance with the findings of Koskina & Giovazolias, 2010).

> You can't live that long by the rules, you can't influence... You don't know when you're going to die. I'm trying not to die all the time. But realistically, I can't control it. Okay, even if you sometimes light up a cigarette and eat something that's not good. And with me it's all the time, it's like I'm fighting with it. I smoke a little, so I'm afraid of cigarettes. I eat a little of this, so I'm afraid of it. Constantly some opposing... two opposing things.

> When you release that brake, you are actually closer to death. You
> are more vulnerable, like... (R 28)

The interviewees sometimes openly connected their relationship to food and their emotional states, and they talked about focusing on food so as not to think about other things in their lives. They also indicated that sometimes they communicated with their environment through food. In addition to the self-control they exercised through starvation, some interviewees had gone through periods of seclusion and devoted themselves to work (including studying, exercising).

> Well... I don't know, in anorexia. And unfortunately, at that
> stage, after a while, you no longer have any feelings. You
> become such a... slave, and a walking skeleton who experiences
> nothing, and doesn't... and doesn't want to experience anything
> and can't... doesn't even think about anything but food... I don't
> know if there were any emotions around food at all... well, yes,
> basically crying and some great sadness started coming on only
> when I started eating, when I could feel something... (R 25)

Making decisions in other areas of life may have seemed difficult to the interviewees, due to their fear of making mistakes and the strong pressure to succeed (Nordbø et al., 2006). Some interviewees would communicate with the environment through food (which confirms the results of the study by Nordbø et al., 2006), by cooking for others, eating less than the person they were with, eating so as not to disappoint those close to them, or asking those close to them to determine what they were going to have for their meals (similar to Dalle Grave, 2015). The interviewees verbalised the closeness between different forms of eating disorders in the sense that both starvation and binge eating serve the same goal in different ways, which is the regulation of emotions. This differs from the dichotomous positioning of anorexia and bulimia in Burns (2004), where anorexia is presented as extreme self-control of emotions and bulimia as an occasional indulgence in urges. Emotions are perceived as problematic and the interviewees would numb or hide them (Fox, 2009; Petersson et al., 2021).

> I think it's punishment and possibly an escape because I don't
> want to face reality and emotions, and I'd rather eat them. It's
> easier for me to be physically sick and have a stomachache than to
> deal with it mentally. (R 27)

The multiple meanings of food and refraining from food identified in this study have already been recognised in other qualitative research. A meta study by Bryant et al. (2022) extracted similar themes from 53 studies which looked at the subjective experience of people with anorexia. It has been shown that people with anorexia perceive emotions as threatening and by restricting food they want to establish greater control over their inner world. Also, anorexia is profoundly related to the sense of one's identity since physicality is a key aspect of existence (Bryant et al., 2022). Anorexia is often perceived as a means of avoiding internal and external conflicts, like some sort of guardian or protector (Bryant et al., 2022). One of the functions of anorexia is to suppress all needs, which is combined with the desire for people to punish themselves if they are not successful in this. The meta study (Bryant et al., 2022) found that fear and the need to avoid a chaotic and threatening world is one of the key features of anorexia, which is carried out through starvation practices. Sadness and difficulties in identifying and verbalising emotions are present, and patients perceive themselves as ineffective. They have low self-esteem and often feel lonely and isolated (Bryant et al., 2022). People with anorexia hide their sadness in front of others in order not to burden them, but also so that the environment does not perceive them as 'weak' (Bryant et al., 2022). Sadness turns out to be a more acceptable emotion than anger, which was repeatedly suppressed (Beyant et al., 2022), and this is another confirmation of the thesis about patients' self-silencing through eating disorders.

Chapter 14

A Healthy Diet and Exercising – Disorder or Health?

The theme *the slippery road of a healthy lifestyle* indicates the meanings that the interviewees attached to the so-called healthy foods and exercising. For people at risk of developing an eating disorder, engaging in a healthy diet and working out can be a trigger for entering anorexia or bulimia. For many of the interviewees, orthorexic behaviour (unhealthy obsession with healthy food) was the first step towards developing an eating disorder. They listed different types of healthy diet regimes (LCHF diet, keto diet, paleo diet, clean eating, hospital diet, vegetarianism, intermittent fasting...) with which they experimented in the beginning but also during the disorder.

> In that last phase of my life, I had already learned a lot about food, so I ate little, but extremely healthy. So, I was taking various supplements, I was taking omega-threes, beta-glucans. I was taking everything there was... So my blood tests were perfect. So I was very careful about what I ingested. It was just a little bit. But I watched the calories. But I was more careful... It didn't even matter so much to me in that last (*anorexia phase*) how much I ate in terms of calories, but that it was of good quality and that there were no carbohydrates. And then, so that was, like, I looked a lot healthier, although I might have weighed less than in my previous phase (R 20)

What is particularly interesting, the interviewees in this study interpreted 'healthy eating' simultaneously as *a way to enter or exit* their eating disorders. Since orthorexic eating provides a similar sense of control and purity as an eating disorder, the obsession with healthy eating helped some of the interviewees accept more regular food consumption and facilitated recovery from anorexia and bulimia. Since orthorexic behaviour is directed towards controlling the quality of food and not controlling the quantity of food, like anorexia (Costa et al., 2017), orthorexia can be a temporary crutch for patients in overcoming the steps in recovery which include weight gain and 'normal eating' (noted already in LaMarre et al., 2015).

Eating Disorders in a Capitalist World, 123–133
Copyright © 2024 Jelena Balabanić Mavrović
Published under exclusive licence by Emerald Publishing Limited
doi:10.1108/978-1-80455-786-020231015

> I replaced that non-eating with eating only selected and healthy
> foods because very few people eat like that. (R 27)

The interviewees nevertheless pointed out that clean eating, or the so-called healthy eating, was unsustainable and that it was not the end point of healing. For them, healing would represent spontaneous eating, with which they associate concepts such as freedom, peace and normality. They have their most common experiences of spontaneous eating when hanging out with friends. However, for most of them, spontaneous eating is only a faraway 'promised land' which seems unattainable due to the insurmountable obstacle of fear of gaining weight.

> ... I have a feeling that I will never, unfortunately, never be able to
> be completely unburdened by it. But then I would at least wish,
> you know, that I could eat healthy. Okay, maybe I have that need
> for control, but then I can channel that need for control into some
> form of eating. Like veganism, so that I can be obsessed with that.
> But it doesn't matter, at least it wouldn't be this destructive in me.
> (R 21)

The interviewees, therefore, described obsessive healthy eating (orthorexia) as a risky practice for the development of anorexia or bulimia, thus confirming previous findings that eating disorders are not an anomaly or an exception from the dominant cultural practice, but rather a kind of 'crystallization of culture' (Bordo, 1993), an extreme application of normative discursive practices of contemporary Western or global culture (Malson, 2008).

When viewed through the prism of orthorexia, eating disorders only intensify some aspects of existing and generally accepted norms such as rules about recommended healthy eating, counting calories and losing weight for health purposes or as part of the war against obesity (Malson, 2008; Warin, 2003). Let us not forget that public health recommendations also divide food into permitted and prohibited, just like people with eating disorders do, whereby permitted food, such as vegetables, is clean and light, and prohibited food contains fats, oils or sugars (Warin, 2010). It can be concluded that the promotion of health contributes to the construction of social meanings of food and nutrition for women with eating disorders, together with the gender determination of thinness and media-mediated images of ideal female bodies (Malson, 2008).

> R: ...how do people feel when they eat so unhealthy?
>
> I: Well, dirty and heavy (laughs) ... and incompetent. (R 1)

Therefore, testimonies of women with eating disorders show that the current obsession with a healthy diet, widespread in Western society, 'transforms from a solution to becoming part of the problem' (Staudacher, 2018, p. 668). Other research also suggests that special 'healthy diets' (vegetarian, pescatarian, vegan, raw food, paleo or gluten free diet) can trigger eating disorders (Barnett et al.,

2016). What is particularly disturbing, even following a medically justified diet due to illness (diabetes, celiac disease) increases the risk for the development of an eating disorder (Toni et al., 2017). Part of the difficulty stems from the interpretation of the term 'diet', which is used for a wide range of occasional or permanent behaviours: from moderate and healthy behavioural changes, such as increased intake of nutritionally rich food, to extreme dietary restrictions, such as fasting (Freedman et al., 2001). There are also a number of dietary variations between these extremes – reducing carbohydrate intake and avoiding sugar are especially popular (Freedman et al., 2001).

> Cereals, well... I threw out white sugar, sugar from sugarcane and sugar beet. No refined sugar. No white flour. Palm oil, sunflower oil, God forbid. But coconut oil, with no additives, gluten free, low-fat milk, less than 1.5%, then almond milk, nuts, fruit for breakfast, green tea two or three glasses a day. Although I would drink a litre or two of it. Um... Of course bread, nothing. Pasta. If I eat pasta, I don't need bread to go with it. Um... Pizza, God forbid. Sauces are not necessary. Only vinegar, it, like, stimulates digestion, so I guess it will do. (laughs) Chewing gum no, it slows digestion down. God forbid. (R 12)

Clean eating advocates the consumption of healthy, 'clean' food, which can lead to a pathological fixation on healthy eating (Ambwani et al., 2019). Clean eating is a concept popularised through social media such as Instagram, culinary blogs and books written by celebrity non-experts describing their personal eating regimes and lifestyles. Adolescents and young people are especially likely to follow such advice (Ambwani et al., 2019), as they look for role models in their formative years and they attach great importance to their physical appearance.

> The theory is that I must be clean inside and out. I wash my hair every day, change the sheets every day, everything must be clean every day, I must vacuum the house every day and then after the third day I don't have the strength to do it anymore, and that cleanliness means there can be no food or water and that was a healthy lifestyle for me. And then I would feed on sunshine on the balcony. That was like eating to me, vitamin D. And I might take some water through a dropper just so that my mouth would not be very dry. (R 5)

There are many definitions of 'clean eating', and they typically include elements such as eating local, non-processed, organically grown food prepared in one's home (Dennett, 2016). Clean eating often includes additional strategies such as eliminating gluten, grains or dairy products (Ambwani et al., 2019). Ambwani et al. (2019) conclude that this is a heterogeneous concept based on organically grown food of plant origin, with no genetically modified ingredients, processed as little as possible, grown locally, which promotes sustainability and ecology, and contains natural sweeteners, whole grains and clean proteins. Also, clean eating reduces or completely excludes fast food, food preservatives, fats, sugar, gluten, calories and meat (Ambwani et al., 2019). People follow the clean eating diet regime mainly for health reasons, to lose weight and as a way to achieve control over eating (Ambwani et al., 2019). The desire to lose weight and the need to control one's eating are associated with the risk of disordered eating (Ambwani et al., 2019).[1]

In the words of an interviewee:

> Everything was healthy. Everything was healthy. And what was healthy for me was no carbohydrates. I consumed carbohydrates exclusively through fruits and vegetables. And I only ate granny smith apples. (*laughs*) They're, like, sour. And that was safe food. So all the proteins. Meat was safe for me. And everything was with no oil. I would also use oil because I thought it was... Fats were healthy for me. But I would add a spoonful of home-made virgin olive oil later so that I could control how much oil I used. So then, I don't know, let's say I would roast the meat, just like that, on a pan. And then I would eat it with a spoonful of olive oil. Then I ate more... And really... I ate smoked salmon quite often because it was, like, so fatty. If I treated myself to that salmon, I would have to watch my fat intake for the next two days. And so on. So nuts were most often my breakfast. (R 20)

The complex relationship between anorexia and bulimia accompanied with orthorexia and clean eating can be viewed through the fact that the symptoms of orthorexia among patients diagnosed with these types of eating disorders increased from 28% to 58% in the period three years after the treatment, while the symptoms of anorexia and bulimia decreased (Barthels et al., 2017). A possible explanation is that orthorexic behaviour serves as a strategy for patients with eating disorders to be able to eat larger amounts of food while maintaining a sense of control and autonomy (Barthels et al., 2017). Namely, for patients with bulimia

---

[1]The American Eating Disorders Association (NEDA) has warned of possible health damage caused by an extreme fixation on 'healthy eating' which resembles the consequences of anorexia (NEDA, 2019). Promoting radical attitudes such as 'sugar is the enemy' (Prevention, 2016 according to Ambwani et al., 2019) and omitting entire classes of food without medical justification (e.g. allergies) can contribute to the development of disturbed attitudes and behaviours related to food (Pemberton, 2017 according to Ambwani et al., 2019). Furthermore, Pemberton (2017, according to Ambwani et al., 2019) indicates that clean eating can mask an already existing eating disorder and prevent the individual from seeking professional help. He also states that clean eating represents nonsense presented as health advice at best. At worst, this type of diet is accepted by individuals who already have psychological difficulties and who thereby cover up a restrictive diet, which potentially has detrimental health consequences (Pemberton, 2017, according to Ambwani et al., 2019).

and minors with anorexia, the first line of treatment is family based treatment programmes (FBT) (Lock & Le Grange, 2015) or cognitive behavioural therapy for eating disorders (CBT-E) adapted according to the guidelines of the National Institute for Health and Care Excellence (NICE, 2017). These approaches sometimes involve consuming high-calorie foods within a standard diet, which is especially stressful for people recovering from eating disorders. Such an approach is in contrast to the promotion of healthy food, in which certain groups of foods (sugars, carbohydrates, fats) are frequently demonised, and people recovering from eating disorders – in addition to struggling with the primary disorder – must also deal with the pressure of their environment and the media, which often promote an orthorexic lifestyle (LaMarre et al., 2015).

> We feel dirty if I eat something unhealthy or the so-called junk food, even though we said today that we wouldn't call it that. But everyone calls it that, you can't change that. Yes, like, really, if I take just one bite of that food – it's over. If I ate I don't know how much oatmeal with almond milk that day, it all goes to hell because of one bite of one cookie. (R 12)

We can conclude that ideas and behaviours we find in patients with eating disorders have spread in the wider socio-cultural environment through the healthism movement. Daily 'self-care' is promoted in the media through a kind of methodical supervision of one's nutrition and exercising, and in this way, healthism has updated the existing dichotomies of body and spirit, emotions and thoughts, male and female principles, adding new meanings to them. The cultural shaping of hunger, desire or craving is gendered (Musolino et al., 2018), and women are still expected to control and silence the needs of their bodies.

> Well, on the paleo diet I felt like I was doing something good for myself. When I was in pure restriction, I consciously did it to take control. And then paleo is okay. Now we have taken control. Now I'm doing something good for myself. So I convinced myself that, like, this was the best way. (R 20)

In an era where obesity is publicly shamed, anorexia becomes an example of productive power, almost a cultural norm which operates through disciplinary practices (Warin, 2010). In maintaining low weight, the daily lives of people with eating disorders consist of achieving goals through self-monitoring and self-disciplining practices, which makes them feel successful and in control, a principle that is normalised through healthism, clean eating and the orthorexic lifestyle. The body becomes a project that is consciously worked on (Hanganu-Bresch, 2020).

> Um, control, no white sugar, gluten. Um... Not after six or eight o'clock or four hours before going to bed. Mandatory daily walking for at least an hour. Lots of greens, as few carbohydrates as possible,

as much protein as possible. Maybe those supplements too. Um...
You can't do this, you can't do that. (R 12)

Since for the interviewees *healthy equals thin*, and they attach almost the same
terms to a healthy life as to dieting (*purity, control, power*), we can confirm that
health and beauty overlap (Burns & Gavey, 2004) and that there is a presence of
awareness of individualised responsibility for one's health in the context of the
'war against obesity' (Malson, 2008).

When I ate like that... everything clean... I really thought that I
was worthy, good, that it gave me motivation, that it pushed me
forward, that it gave me strength, I drew strength from that. (R 1)

The interviewees perceived the benefits of a 'healthy lifestyle' similarly,
sometimes exactly, like the benefits of anorexic behaviour: *a healthy lifestyle*
brought them a feeling of power, control and purity. For most interviewees, only
a thin body is a healthy body, so many of them equate health and thinness (with a
minority affirming the importance of a fit and firm body).

... again like some sort of power because I ate an apple instead of
something else, and, like, an apple is healthy and automatically I
have power, while others don't. (R 3)

Development of eating disorders because of the desire to eat healthier has been
observed in other research (Kinzl et al., 2006; McGovern et al., 2020), and this
indicates that orthorexia is an obsessive or pathological preoccupation with
healthy eating, with emotional consequences in the form of anxiety or discomfort
if a person breaks self-imposed rules (Cena et al., 2019). The overlapping of the
meanings of 'healthy food' and 'dieting' is supported by recent research on
orthorexia (Barthels et al., 2017), which opens up the possibility of understanding
orthorexia as a 'milder variant' of anorexia, where, in addition to the focus on
healthy food, there is also a focus on physical appearance. However, instead of a
thin body as in classic anorexia, in orthorexia the goal is the appearance of a
healthy body (Bartherls et al., 2017).

What is particularly interesting here is the fact that orthorexia can be *a step
towards healing*. Our interviewees perceived eating the so-called healthy food as
an acceptable step towards food consumption since it provided them with a sense
of structure, control and predictability, which they normally had when they fasted
and did their diet regimes (Barthels et al., 2017). In the research by Segura-Garcia
et al. (2015), more than half of the people had symptoms of orthorexia nervosa
after their treatment for anorexia, which is in line with the results of our study.
Barthels et al. (2017) also confirmed the positive influence of orthorexic behaviour
on recovery from anorexia, in terms of strengthening the sense of competence and
autonomy of the patient. They also recommend a planned implementation of
orthorexic eating as the first step in recovery from anorexia (Barthels et al., 2017).

... I had to make a pact with myself (*laughs*). I had to do it in order to move in the direction of healing and self-love... That pact was, okay, if you've decided that you're going to live and that you're going to... um... gain weight because you have to, they told you that you had to, so you have to... then do it properly and then eat healthy food, so that you can be healthy and beautiful... instead of, like... gaining weight randomly... (R 25)

Some interviewees highlighted *the unsustainability of clean eating*, since they saw clean or healthy eating as just another form of dieting (Burns & Gavey, 2004). They stated that the so-called unhealthy or forbidden food caused them to have bad feelings, such as guilt, shame and a fear of gaining weight (Burns, 2004). Enjoying eating junk food and revolting against the control of dietary rules through eating junk food reiterates the meanings attached to the construction of bulimic binge eating (Eli, 2018). Therefore, for some interviewees, eating unhealthy food represents a revolt against the tyranny of control and the rigid rules of the so-called healthy life (and/or disorders).

... I associate that food, junk food, which means sweets, snacks, with some sort of happiness. Because I'd have them at birthday parties, I'd have them when we were having a good time and all that, and I, like, don't deserve that food because I don't deserve to enjoy myself and be happy, and then when I allow myself to enjoy that food, then I'm not good enough because I can't enjoy it all the time. It can't always be my birthday, like, hello. (R 28)

The healthy-unhealthy food dichotomy within the so-called healthy lifestyle framework reflects the relationship between self-control in anorexia/restriction and enjoyment/guilt/rebellion in binge eating, only in this case instead of thinness, health is highlighted as the supreme principle (Barthels et al., 2017).

Among the interviewees in this study, working out was defined as a companion to a 'healthy diet' for the purpose of getting a lean and slender body (Håman et al., 2015). Obsessive exercise is one of the frequent compensatory behaviours in anorexia and bulimia (APA, 2013), and it is carried out excessively, compulsively and to the detriment of one's health (Achamrah et al., 2016; Fietz et al., 2014). This compulsive working out is often accompanied by eating the so-called clean food, and it also creates a sense of duty and control of one's life through intense physical activity. The interviewees distinguished between healthy and obsessive exercising and they wondered if they would ever be able to engage in regular, recreational sports which would not be associated with the prevention of obesity and calorie consumption through sports. Some interviewees entered their eating disorder through the use of mobile phone apps for weight loss and exercising, and others because of their desire to get better at sports or dancing classes they were already taking.

> I wanted to start competing in fitness and I reached a certain body weight with which I was satisfied, but even at that time I lost that instinctive relationship with food. I was on a restrictive diet. And quite spontaneously one day, I had dinner my mum made for me, I was already, like... I was happy with my weight, but I was hungry, always hungry. I only ate certain foods, and it just occurred to me like a flash: well, you could eat all of this and then throw it up. And you will be able to do it. Try it now. Without even thinking about what would happen later. (R 10)

Some interviewees stated that the very *beginning of their eating disorder* was related to *playing sports or dancing*, which is in line with research that speaks of the high prevalence of disturbed attitudes towards the body and food in athletes and dancers (Currie, 2010; Sundgot-Borgen & Torstveit, 2004). A metastudy (Smolak et al., 2000) has shown that female athletes are at a higher risk of developing eating disorders than non-athletes, especially in sports which emphasise a slim appearance (disciplines with an important aesthetic component) or sports with weight categories. In sports with weight categories, aesthetic sports or in dancing, compensatory behaviours such as dehydration, self-induced vomiting, abuse of laxatives and diuretics are widely used to reduce body weight, so that they can be considered part of the subculture of these sports (Sundgot-Borgen & Torstveit, 2010). Reduced eating with intense training in female athletes can lead to the loss of menstruation and later osteoporosis. These related conditions are called the female sports triad (Sundgot-Borgen & Torstveit, 2010). The interviewees who associated the onset of eating disorders with playing sports or dancing pointed out that they had experienced weight loss, comparison with the bodies of other athletes or dancers, a distorted view of their body as fat and mood changes (which is in accordance with the study by Mencias et al., 2012).

> In the sixth form I started taking dance classes. It was competitive dancing. Like, strict, rigid, perfectionist, as I am myself, so it went really well, a nice package. And I think it's there that I first started... "Well, do you really have to eat after training?" (R 15)

The harmful influence of obsessive training on the mental and physical health of patients with eating disorders is in accordance with the research of the fitness subculture by Ferguson et al. (2020). This group of researchers pointed out that beneath the superficial idea of empowering women through fitspiration lurks a dynamic similar to that of eating disorders. The never-ending project of the body encourages the individuals to maintain a continuous critical attitude towards themselves, whereby they continuously conduct self-monitoring for the purpose of perpetual self-improvement. Given that the goal of an athletic body is to reduce the amount of subcutaneous fat and to increase muscle mass to a certain extent, people are exposed to cycles of starvation and training in order to get an ideal body, which can never be fully achieved (Ferguson et al., 2020). Internal contradictions and tensions between the empowering potential of playing sports and the self-objectifying attitude and self-monitoring practices of members of the fitspiration movement indicate a high risk of impaired self-esteem and disordered eating (Robinson et al., 2017). Ferguson et al. (2020) concluded that in their research on the fitspiration movement, there was no trace of empowerment and emancipation of women who strove for the ideal athletic body. Exercising can also be part of self-monitoring and self-control techniques in building *a strong, healthy-looking body.*

> ... well, the first thing for me was excessive training and restriction, that is to say everything, every day I threw out more and more food and reduced my portions more and more, but that was totally, like, totally in line with that goal, that, like, "me now, that's my goal" because, like, "I've been able to do it so far, I can do it even more." And I was like constantly, "I can do more and more." In the end, I trained every day, literally, like, ate what would fit on a small plate, all of it together. I ate very little, but I was always full of energy (R 11)

The presence of bulimic behaviour patterns in the fitspiration community has been confirmed in the form of a 'cheat day'. One day a week – usually Friday or Saturday – is planned in advance as a day of binge eating, followed by 6 days of restriction, training and living 'properly' (Murray et al., 2018).

Just like following public health instructions on the so-called healthy diet is in accordance with the dominant discourse on maintaining a healthy body through regular exercise, so is the attitude towards exercising in patients with anorexia and bulimia (Malson, 2008). Therefore, it is not easy to determine the difference between *obsessive* and *healthy exercise* (Currie, 2010), and the interviewees themselves tended to minimise the weight, length or harmfulness of the physical activity they performed (Kolnes, 2016).

> When sports cease to be pleasurable for me, when this physical activity itself turns into challenging myself, "you can do better, you can do it harder, this is not good enough", that's a sign to me that it's a disorder. It's exercising because of the disorder. And when I exercise and I don't get these voices, then I exercise healthily. And I haven't been able to get to the point for a very long time where I can work out without having that critic behind me, that thing that keeps challenging me. I go for a bike ride and that bike ride turns into chaos. Something in my head... I get into an argument in my head. And that's a big problem for me because I need sports to feel good. In a way, I'm addicted, I guess because of that serotonin or something. It's something that makes me who I am. And then there's also... I don't know (R 28)

The interviewees emphasised the need to exercise at all costs, regardless of whether they were tired, what their physical condition was, what the weather was like or what time of day it was (*obsessive exercise; sports as duty and control*), which is in line with previous research (Kolnes, 2016; Moola et al., 2015; Young et al., 2015). Patients are caught in a vicious cycle of eating and exercising, and they have a hard time resisting their internal compulsion to exercise, which is 'stronger than reason' (Kolnes, 2016, p. 1).

> I had to walk. I had to run. I couldn't not do it. So I suffered terribly when it started. That walking. It wasn't like part of a healthy life, it was really a compulsion. So that was terrible for me. If I didn't wake up at six in the morning and go for a run first thing, I had a terrible day. And, like, it was as if I had eaten more. It was the same. It was the same compulsion. And, like, no matter what the temperature was outside. Regardless... So I'd be out in the rain, in the snow, in the blizzard. I would get dressed and I had to run, walk. I had to. (R 20)

The feeling of losing control over oneself and yielding to the need for obsessive exercise is in contrast to *the fuelling of the self* (Axelsen, 2009; Kolnes, 2012) that patients feel after the exercise. The interviewees described how, for them, exercising was a way to prevent weight gain and that it served to burn calories after a meal, thus continuing the previously mentioned idea of 'calorie burning' while exercising (Churruca et al., 2017). For some interviewees, food had to be earned by exercising and fasting, which was perceived as 'good behaviour' (Churruca et al., 2017).

> ... sometimes I eat that (*bread*) which is, like, not good, and it can really cause me to be anxious. But, you know, training saves me. (R 6)

Some of the interviewees continuously monitored their calorie intake and calories burned through exercise on their mobile phone apps for weight loss and exercise. It was precisely those apps that promoted a 'healthy lifestyle' that triggered the onset of the disorder. This is in accordance with research which has found a link between the use of these mobile apps and the presence of disordered eating in the sense that people who use them have more dietary restrictions and an unhealthy preoccupation with food (Embacher et al., 2018; Hefner et al., 2016; Plateau et al., 2018; Simpson & Mazzeo, 2017). However, for the time being, there are no available longitudinal studies on the possible causality of this influence. Apps like MyFitnessPal greatly contribute to the development of eating disorders by further disrupting the vulnerable individual's fragile relationship with their body and hunger and satiety signals (Pennesi & Wade, 2016). Research confirms that similar mobile apps are widely used by people with eating disorders, and 73% of users estimate that the use of these applications for counting calories and recording exercise contributes to the maintenance of eating disorders (Levinson et al., 2017).

I think that's what happened in the summer when I went with my high school friend to (*name of café*) for pancakes. She also had a problem with her weight and so on. She told me about the MyFitnessPal app because, like, I was already getting into that a little bit, so, like, I should check it out. And yadda yadda. And I started typing it in, and after two or three months there was no need to type anymore. I already knew all sorts of things. And instead of studying, I actually studied what I was allowed to eat, what combinations I wasn't allowed to eat, how many calories there were in which food... It was, like, really... And exercising. (R 12)

The practice of counting calories has become widely accepted or even encouraged by public health officials, so the Department of Health and Social Care in the United Kingdom (2022) requires that the caloric value of food be displayed in eating establishments and on groceries in stores. Such legislation has once again put people with eating disorders in a specific position – for them public health recommendation becomes a toxic symptom of their relationship to food.

Daily monitoring of food and physical activity becomes a way of monitoring oneself (Levinson et al., 2017). These practices are constructed as activities that undoubtedly lead to health, and in society, health is perceived as the responsibility of the individual (Churruca et al., 2017) and a necessary prerequisite for *a good life* or even *a good life* per se (Crawford, 2006, p. 404).

R: So, how do you feel then (*when you exercise*)?

I: Well, like, I keep everything under control because I'm taking care of my body, I work out, I don't let myself go, it's that word again - yes. Um, taking care of myself, like. I'm not lying in bed, I'm moving about. (R 9)

Our interviewees identified health and beauty as a single notion (Murray et al., 2010), whereby achieving a lean and firm body becomes an essential aspect of acceptable modern Westernised femininity (Dworkin & Wachs, 2009, p. 37). In some of the interviewees, the awareness of the harmfulness of obsessive sports raised the question of possible further sport activities without risking the aggravation of eating disorder symptoms (in line with the considerations of sports addiction by Lichtenstein et al., 2014).

I mean, that orthorexia is definitely a new trend as well as ... the self-delusion that... that you're in the gym to get fit, and you're actually there to be thin. (R 25)

Other interviewees offered an ideal image of desirable personal health through balanced food, regular exercise, socialising and preservation of mental health (*exercise-food-socialising-mental health*), which is something that has not been recorded in previous research.

Chapter 15

The Context of Growing Up: Confirmation of the Biopsychosocial Model of the Emergence of the Disorder

The theme *Different ways of growing up* addresses the second research question about the social meanings which women with eating disorders attach to certain shapes of the female body (thin/fat) and food, eating and abstaining from food in a particularly interesting way. This theme provides a retrospective look at the childhood years of women with eating disorders by analysing their early relationship with their own bodies and food.

The interviewees described various experiences from their childhoods and early youth, and there doesn't seem to be a single path that would lead to the development of an eating disorder, which is in line with earlier research (Culbert et al., 2015). The interviewees gave testimonials of quite diverse attitudes towards food in their early childhood. Some of them were considered *picky, thin children* (which is in accordance with the findings of Yilmaz et al., 2018a), some had *the usual attitude towards food* and some were *chubby children who liked to eat a lot* (in accordance with the study of Sahoo et al., 2015). Such findings confirm the current scientific consensus that no one is predestined for the development of anorexia or bulimia, and risk factors in the form of genetic predisposition or personality traits only become expressed under the influence of the environment (Fairweather-Schmidt & Wade, 2015).

In the same way, we can interpret the interviewees' *experience of themselves as a child*: a chubby child is at increased risk of developing an eating disorder due to the introduction of emotional eating as a way of emotional self-regulation (Sutin et al., 2017; Vollrath et al., 2011), but also social stigmatisation of obesity, and family (Dahill et al., 2021) and peer pressure towards the normative appearance (Copeland et al., 2015). A child with increased body weight is at greater risk of turning to unhealthy ways of regulating body weight (Evans et al., 2016; Veses et al., 2014). The perception of oneself as *a happy and satisfied child* is in accordance with the findings where in girls the concern about the appearance of one's body appears mostly in pre-puberty and puberty (Stice et al., 2002; Volpe et al., 2016). The body changes that take place at that time are accompanied by a number of psycho-social changes that can further stimulate the emergence of eating disorders (van Eeden et al., 2020). Some of the interviewees saw themselves

Eating Disorders in a Capitalist World, 135–140
Copyright © 2024 Jelena Balabanić Mavrović
Published under exclusive licence by Emerald Publishing Limited
doi:10.1108/978-1-80455-786-020231016

as ambitious and versatile students, matching the profile of the 'perfect child' or 'golden girl' described in the vast literature on eating disorders (Hurst & Zimmer-Gembeck, 2015; Lloyd et al., 2014). The literature mentions insecurity as a risk factor for the development of eating disorders (Hughes, 2012; Schaumberg et al., 2019; Tasca et al., 2013), while rebelliousness in girls has not been directly linked to the study of the childhood influences which precede the development of anorexia or bulimia.

> That is, my parents, I have to explain this, they were never parents who would make any demands on me. I also had excellent marks in school. I didn't have to be encouraged. I am the one who... (*encouraged*) myself. I guess that's just my character, I am a perfectionist and that I am very hard on myself. That's how I was. (R 20)

What is common to the vast majority of the interviewees is the focus on food and physical appearance present in their birth families. Their parents or extended family members emphasised the importance of eating healthy food and having a slim body appearance. The interviewees regularly received messages from the environment that appearance was important. In addition to the influence of their parents, they were also teased by their peers while they were growing up, or there were some incidents involving experts. Experts recommended diets, prescribed weight loss programmes or actively encouraged girls to lose weight in other ways, which they perceived as contributing to their later disordered eating (consistent with the findings on the dangers of 'medical dieting' in Cena et al., 2017; Patton et al., 1999).

> I started gaining weight. I wasn't really that much overweight, but I was fatter and since my dad is quite fat, my mom would constantly watch me and him... she would constantly make these suggestions that we go on some sort of Montignac diet because my grandfather was also on that diet, but he really needed it because of his diabetes, and so in the seventh grade I went on that diet, healthy eating, whatever you call it, I don't know. And that lasted about three or four months. I lost 10 kilos, dad lost 40 kilos and yes. That's where it started. (R 9)

If the parents or extended family members are focused on the so-called a healthy diet, this can contribute to the development of eating disorders in people who possess biological or psychological vulnerabilities (Kluck, 2008; O'Connor & Van Esterik, 2008). The imposition of parental will and difficulties in the relationship with the mother and/or father as risk factors for the development of anorexia and bulimia for our interviewees are in accordance with previous findings (Haworth-Hoeppner, 2000).

A study by Haworth-Hoeppner (2000) singled out three types of family influences for the development of anorexia: a focus on food and appearance, strict supervision/control over children and a critical, cold family atmosphere.

> And I remember what I wanted to mention about the synchronized swimming coach, like, she made this comment... a girl asked her why some people can't compete, and she said that in today's world, the most important thing is to be thin in order to be successful. I might have been 11 or 12 years old at the time, but it got so etched in my memory. You have to be thin in order to be successful. (R 5)

Other studies have also confirmed that the parents' disturbed attitude towards food and their criticism of their children's appearance affects the development of body dissatisfaction in young people (Davison & Birch, 2004; Haines et al., 2008; Wertheim et al., 2002). In some studies, excessive control over the child by the parents is associated with the development of anorexia in later years, especially the mother's highly protective behaviour (Le Grange et al., 2010). Some studies have found that the parents of girls who developed bulimia expressed high expectations from their daughters, were emotionally distant and criticised their body shape and weight in the period before the onset of the disorder (Le Grange et al., 2010).

Smolak, Levine and Schermer (1999) showed that the more often mothers talked about their children's weight, the more worried the children were about their physical appearance, the more body dissatisfaction they expressed and the more often they tried to lose weight through various restrictive diets.

> There was always this terrible control at home, especially in my father's family. On my mother's side, there wasn't that much control, there was more freedom on my mother's side. Terrible control from dad's side. And constant fear – when will he go ballistic, when will he go ballistic because I've just put... because he can see me eating something. So, there's some kind of lunch, and he'll suddenly go ballistic because I'm eating potatoes or something. (R 28)

Describing how the eating disorder began in their lives, the interviewees confirmed the idea of a 'perfect storm' (Frank, 2016) – a series of cumulative influences and predispositions that are directly or indirectly related to the beginning of difficulties in relation to the body and food. For most of the interviewees, this happened at a turning point in their lives: the transition from elementary to high school, transition from high school to college, their parents' divorce or an illness in the family. Berge et al. (2012) singled out six types of life transitions that constitute a risk for the development of an eating disorder if the young individual does not have sufficient support: school transition, death of a family member, changes in the parental relationship/divorce, relocation/significant job change, illness/hospitalisation, abuse, sexual assault or incest. Berge et al. (2012) conclude that it is important to observe the family context or wider life circumstances of the so-called transitions which can be a risk factor for the development of an eating disorder.

The interviewees also reported difficulties in their parents' marriage, which is not a specific factor in the emergence of eating disorders, but can contribute to the creation of emotional insecurity in the child. Namely, along with other mediating influences, marital conflict between the parents in early childhood can increase the risk of developing a disturbed relationship with food in adolescents (Bi et al., 2017; George et al., 2014). Several of the interviewees pointed out that they wanted to get their parents' attention through their thinness, which is in line with the insights of Nordbø et al. (2006) about the physical communication of psychological stress in anorexia patients.[1]

Most interviewees pointed out that, while growing up, they had received *messages about the importance of physical appearance* in different ways through peer teasing (which has already been investigated by Fairweather-Schmidt & Wade, 2017; Quiles et al., 2013), but also through pressure from doctors, nutritionists and trainers to become thin. Research shows that it is important to approach weight correction in children responsibly and professionally (Jebeile et al., 2019), otherwise dietary regimes in overweight children could increase the risk of the development of eating disorders (Memon et al., 2020). Other studies (Arthur-Cameselle & Quatromoni, 2014; Hines et al., 2019; Vaughan et al., 2004) also indicate how powerful the focus on physical appearance in sports and the role of coaches are.

> Not probably, but it is certainly connected with elementary school, with weighing in gym class where you literally felt like, God forgive me, like cattle going to the cattle scales because they told you in front of everyone: "You are too fat. You have to stop eating. Don't drink sodas." So many things. I mean, it was a totally wrong approach towards a child. (R 22)

The period of insecurity and psychological suffering at the time when girls start getting their curves and when they go through physical changes can be quite turbulent (Gailledrat et al., 2016), since their position in society also changes and they learn behaviours related to their gender role (Holmes et al., 2017). Some of the basic values related to the female gender role are the idealisation of thinness as a beauty ideal and the importance of dieting (Nagata et al., 2020). The vast majority of the interviewees started their first diet with the goal of *losing just a little bit of weight* (which confirms the findings of an earlier study by Stice & Presnell, 2010).

---

[1] It is also important to highlight the devastating impact which eating disorders have on the parents and other family members, who go through the intense experience of caring for a sick family member, and who themselves feel anxiety, anger, frustration and guilt (Hillege et al., 2006).

'Dieting' represents the normative behaviour of girls in modern Western society (Nagata et al., 2020), and adolescence is the period when people become 'morbidly preoccupied with what others think of them' (Harter, 2006, p. 541). The interviewees in our study singled out the influence of close female individuals from their own generation – friends, sisters, roommates, cousins – who taught them how to diet, who were their role models and who 'introduced them into the world' of normative femininity (in line with the results of Eisenberg & Neumark-Sztainer, 2010; Sawka et al., 2015). The influence of peer groups and a close circle of female friends shows that imitating close role models and the need to belong can encourage young girls to develop body dissatisfaction and engage in unhealthy ways of maintaining their weight (Keel & Forney, 2013). It has been shown that attitudes about the desirability of losing weight in girls' peer groups influence their desire to be thin, lower the satisfaction with their appearance and worsen their self-esteem, which was measured one year later (Dohnt & Tiggemann, 2006). To put it succinctly, if the best friend or sister of a girl with other risk factors is on a diet or is vomiting, this increases the probability that she will start engaging in these unhealthy behaviours herself, which was confirmed in the statements of some of the interviewees.

> ... In January I met a girl who was my beauty ideal and... I knew what was wrong with her, but I didn't know that I had the same problem as she did. And she was my hero. I watched her and compared myself to her on a daily basis and she must have felt it because she was into it very deeply, very much, she wasn't getting treatment or anything. And then she would always come to my class (*the person's name*) and ask me how I was, what I ate that day, if I ate at all, how much water I drank, she'd tell me I had to flush everything from my body and things like that. I didn't get what was happening and then it all went like that for months... (R 5)

The interviewees also emphasised the influence of the media, the internet and social media (which was already found in the studies of Saul & Rodgers, 2018; Spettigue & Henderson, 2004), from which they also collected information about restrictive and so-called healthy eating, but also about purging methods. For some interviewees, the promotion of diets, idealisation of thinness and having a perfect appearance as well as content related to thinspiration or fitspiration movements in the media represented an incentive for restrictive practices and exercise (the same as in studies Branley & Covey, 2017; Juarascio et al., 2010; Robinson et al., 2017). Paradoxically, even media content which fights against anorexia and bulimia can unintentionally promote harmful behaviours (Logrieco et al., 2021). Thus, it has been shown that anti-Pro-Ana content on popular social media such as TikTok encourages viewers to imitate the symptoms (Logrieco et al., 2021).

> And I was just telling the girls where I got the idea from. I asked them how they got the idea. I got the idea from Pink's video

> "Stupid girl"... who's fighting it, but someone who has been in this situation obviously got the idea of what to do. And so it started. Yes. (R 30)

In addition to all of the above, as part of the initial jigsaw puzzle of creating conditions for the development of an eating disorder, the interviewees also pointed out school stress, which for many is combined with perfectionistic efforts to be the best. Research shows that untreated eating disorders are associated with poorer school performance, while patients with eating disorders who receive therapy do better in school than the control group (Claydon & Zullig, 2020). High perfectionism in patients with eating disorders (Bardone-Cone et al., 2006) leads to seeking confirmation of self-worth in external achievements (school marks) (Krafchek, 2017).

> I started going out only when I was 18. Before then it was, like, you had to get straight A's, you had to have excellent marks, you had to get into a great college. Like, I told my parents when I was ten that I would go to university, that I would finish university at the age of 23 and that I would have a successful career. And that was the only thing that was important in my life, for me to be successful. To have a career, like, a big one. That was it. (R 4)

Perceived scholastic failure or the fear of failure represented a burden for low self-esteem in most of the interviewees (Mora et al., 2017; Stoeber et al., 2017). In this study, withdrawal from society, the weakening of established social bonds, as well as the feeling of not belonging (in accordance with the findings of Levine, 2012) were also found, which in some of the interviewees took on a depressive image of avoiding social situations, lying in bed and listlessness (in accordance with the research of Godart et al., 2006; Mattar et al., 2012).

In conclusion, the interviewees today place the beginning of their eating disorder in a certain stressful period of life, which varies from case to case, spanning from the lower grades of elementary school to the first years of college. In a period of major life changes which often (but not always) coincided with entering puberty and gaining curves, there was an overlap of various influences that led to harmful practices in relation to food and the body. In most of the interviewees' birth families, there was an increased focus on appearance and food. Almost all of the interviewees started dieting in order to 'lose a little weight', and dieting was confirmed as the strongest risk factor in the development of anorexia and bulimia. The interviewees modelled their dieting on close female figures (friends, elder sisters, cousins) or on information about weight loss collected from the media or via the internet and social media. Frequently, the onset of the eating disorder was accompanied by increased stress at school or university and family changes (divorce, relocation, illness or death). The onset of the disorder was often associated with withdrawal from society and isolation.

Chapter 16

Final Discussion

The findings of the study reveal a rich, complex and often contradictory inner world of women with eating disorders. The analysis of the in-depth interviews sheds light on the issues of social meanings related to female and male gender roles, as well as the meanings attributed to the shapes of the female body and various eating practices.

In summarising the attitudes of these women towards gender stereotypes, we come across two key female gender role stereotypes: the traditional woman as a victim and the superwoman. The traditional woman as a victim is a negative stereotype perceived as undesirable and threatening to the identity of the interviewees, and they actively and consciously reject it through various strategies. The dominant ways of rejecting this traditional female gender role stereotype are: refusing to grow up and take on the adult female role as such (regressive strategy), identifying with another, modern stereotype of the superwoman (perfectionist, neoliberal strategy) or taking over certain elements of the male gender role (masculinisation).

It is important to note that patients with eating disorders usually combine all three strategies, which results in a tendency towards an undifferentiated gender identity, i.e. a low intensity of female or male gender role traits. The title of the theme 'insecure femininity' summarises the prevailing attitude towards the female gender role among the interviewees.

Considering what has been said, we expect that in the near future transgender issues will present themselves as an answer to the problem of undifferentiated gender for patients with eating disorders.[1] Also, in the context of the proliferation of definitions of sexual orientation in contemporary Western society outside the framework of LGBT categories, it is possible that girls and women with anorexia and bulimia will more frequently identify as asexual compared to the general population.

As we have stated, one of the ways of forming a female gender role different from the traditional stereotype of the woman as a victim is to try to follow the stereotype of the superwoman, who is seen as a woman who has to be successful

---

[1]According to the research by Grammer et al. (2021), certain categories of transgender and non-binary people have a higher risk of developing eating disorders, which was also confirmed by Simone et al. (2022).

Eating Disorders in a Capitalist World, 141–150
Copyright © 2024 Jelena Balabanić Mavrović
Published under exclusive licence by Emerald Publishing Limited
doi:10.1108/978-1-80455-786-020231017

in all aspects of her life (career, motherhood, marriage) and is at the same time beautiful and attractive. In this stereotype, the liberal capitalist myth of the individual who reaps all social benefits through hard work is combined with the legacy of the woman liberation movement about a woman who can (and must) achieve all her professional and private goals. The superwoman is also strongly based on the media-mediated image of a 'perfect' woman living a 'perfect' life.

It seems reasonable to put forward the thesis that the interviewees are torn between the negatively viewed traditional stereotype of the female role and the (too) perfect stereotype of the new emancipated neoliberal woman, who represents the 'winner who takes it all' – success at work and in the family, physical beauty and 'self-care'. This internal conflict contributes to the development of eating disorders. Most interviewees were highly ambivalent towards the superwoman stereotype. They did not accept their own femininity and that they did not really know how to be an adult woman. The interviewees still felt threatened by the negative stereotype of the traditional definition of a woman as someone who is destined to have a subordinate role in society, someone who is expected to be obedient and willing to make sacrifices.

However, like the traditional female role, this new stereotype imposes a vision of normative femininity in an equally harmful way – the role of the superwoman who is seemingly powerful and equal to the man, but is similarly hegemonic and suppresses authentic human experience, weaknesses or the right to be different.

It should be borne in mind that it was in the capitalist society at the height of the women's liberation movement that eating disorders exploded. We could debate on the pressure of numerous life choices and opportunities that (apparently or really) girls and young women face in a neoliberal society and on the individual failure in a society of 'equal opportunities' for men and women. As healthcare is reduced to personal responsibility in Western society (Crawford, 1980), ignoring any structural, economic and socio-cultural influences, the search for personal identity and social status in women with anorexia and bulimia is also viewed as a completely intimate, private project. That project is seemingly devoid of social and structural constraints and is blessed with imagined infinite potentials, while every mistake is viewed as a result of one's own shortcomings and incompetence. Many women with eating disorders are paralysed by the feeling that they face a world in which they have yet to prove their worth alone, especially since the developed society of late capitalism falsely promises them that they can and must 'get anything they want'. In this research, this is symbolised by the modern myth of the superwoman.

Apart from the female gender role, the interviewees in this study question or openly reject motherhood and their sexuality, which they are afraid of and repulsed by. They feel that eating disorders protect them from growing up (into women). Thus, they apply the strategy of delaying and staying in the 'waiting room of the female gender role' while they hold onto the role of a little or an adolescent girl. The fact that they find the male gender role attractive is visible in their idealisation of some segments of traditional masculinity, which they view as a path towards social power, but also personal strength, self-discipline and self-confidence.

As we have already mentioned, the normative construction of the female gender is associated with body dissatisfaction and a higher incidence of eating disorders in the female population (Ata et al., 2015). It is quite possible that the interviewees 'boycott' the cultural construction of a woman as someone who fulfils certain social expectations related to the reproductive role and the sexualisation of her body and who occupies a subordinate and limited place in the family and society in accordance with the traditional female role. Staying in the 'waiting room of the female gender role' represents a peaceful and temporary solution to the cultural conflict related to gender identity, whereby the activist potential or possible social rebellion of people with anorexia or bulimia is transferred to their intimate space, where it remains unconscious and directed against them. An extremely diverse group of statements gathered around the most represented code 'I want to remain a little girl' indicates poorly profiled and sometimes contradictory expectations of the female role, which are nevertheless postponed since the key strategy is regression or infantilisation, i.e. prolonging one's childhood. This set of meanings could be further interpreted through a psychological perspective and object relations theory (Gander et al., 2015; Lawrence, 2008), which links eating disorders and fears of separation, family entanglement and difficulties in individualising of adolescent girls.

Some of the interviewees are deeply determined by their experiences of sexual trauma; therefore, they reject the female gender role already at the level of their bodies, whose curves remind them of past events but also carry the potential for retraumatisation. They reject the components which are socially related to the female gender role – the curvy female body, sexuality and reproduction or marriage.

It should be noted that the sample also holds a group of statements gathered around the relative acceptance of the gender role to which the positive qualities of motherhood, a happy relationship and female sexuality associated with pleasure and love are attributed. The interviewees perhaps best present the interpretations of the objectification theory that, through the fear of gaining weight, patients with eating disorders want to achieve social ideals of beauty and get closer to the image of a desirable female body (code: *so we can be perfect for the man*).

Therefore, we can conclude that patients with eating disorders mostly reject the female gender role because of the negative characteristics attributed to the traditional female role, but also due to unrealistically high expectations attributed to the role of the superwoman. For some, a kind of 'adulthood waiting room', i.e. delaying the acceptance of the female gender role, was reinforced by traumatic sexual experiences that further distanced them from accepting the gender role of a woman, which is perceived as threatening and dangerous.

Earlier research on the relationship between gender roles and eating disorders is not unambiguous. The results of this qualitative research indirectly confirm an earlier study by Hepp et al. (2005), according to which patients with eating disorders belong to the group of non-binary individuals, in the sense that they score low on the scales of femininity and masculinity. This contrasts with the study by Sarner-Levin et al. (2018), in which anorexia patients scored lower for masculine traits (e.g. assertiveness, independence, dominance) but higher for feminine (such as tenderness, sensitivity, shyness, sensitivity to the needs of others). The same authors note that gender-specific characteristics could vary over time.[2]

How can these deviations be explained? It seems to me that the answer lies in the separation of different aspects of femininity and masculinity, which would dissolve the monolithic understanding of gender concepts and open the door to a subtler analysis. A possible interpretation of the findings is that the interviewees retain some aspects of their femininity, such as self-silencing of emotions and putting other people's needs before their own, while rejecting others (lenience, physical femininity and love for children). Furthermore, distinguishing between current self-evaluation and desired psycho-emotional functioning ('what I am vs. what I would like to be') might also help in understanding the relationship of patients with eating disorders towards gender roles. In the research quoted above, which links femininity and anorexia (Sarner-Levin et al., 2018), affected girls also rejected the idea of the traditional female role as being subservient to the man, which indicates the need to distinguish femininity from the normative female role.

Something similar was done in an older study by Paxton and Sculthorpe (1991), in which they separated the 'positive' from the 'negative' traits of femininity and masculinity and linked them to disordered eating. This way, the authors tested two opposing models for the aetiology of eating disorders. One is the socio-cultural model by Boskind-White and White (1986), according to which modern girls are still raised with traditional values to be 'passive, gentle and afraid of competition' (Boskind-White & White, 1986, p. 363, according to Paxton & Sculthorpe, 1991) and are excessively subject to the ideal of femininity. Therefore, they use harmful weight control practices to feel more secure in a thinner body (Paxton & Sculthorpe, 1991). Another socio-cultural model, that of Steiner-Adair (1986), emphasises that girls growing up in the Western society value masculine characteristics such as independence and personal autonomy more, and this comes into conflict with their developmental needs for finding fulfilment through relationships. Therefore, Steiner-Adair (1986) expects that girls with eating disorders will strive more towards the ideal of masculinity and will be dissatisfied with the difference between their actual masculinity (e.g. self-efficacy, self-esteem) and the ideal. A study by Paxton and Sculthorpe (1991) showed that both models work if a distinction is made between positive and negative characteristics of masculinity and femininity. People with eating disorders were found to believe that they possess negative characteristics of femininity (e.g. lack of independence, need for approval, timidity, weakness, self-criticism, anxiety, worrying), and they exhibited a greater discrepancy between their perception of themselves and the ideal male characteristics (e.g. strength of character, confidence, high performance at work). Also, a difference was found between people with anorexia and people with bulimia – people with bulimia scored lower in their self-perception of positive masculine traits, which can be explained by a certain type of autonomy and self-control which sufferers of anorexia exhibit in their daily relationship with

---

[2]The results of increased femininity may also have been influenced by the condition of anorexia (malnutrition, physical weakness, dependence on others).

food. It is possible that the inconsistency of the findings of various studies on gender roles and eating disorders is partly due to the different psychological profiles of patients with anorexia and bulimia. I assume that the sample would change further if we also included patients with binge-eating disorders. It is possible that patients with different types of eating disorders (restrictive, purgative, binge eating) differ in relation to gender roles.

The positive masculinity of today can be understood as a protective factor against eating disorders since it promotes individualism, listening to one's needs and representing one's beliefs (Bem, 1974). However, if a person strives for these characteristics but fails to realise them, then this internal discrepancy becomes a source of personal suffering and it encourages them to realise a new, ideal self through behaviours towards the body and food.

Accordingly, intertwining social and individual factors that become manifest in eating disorders should be considered. The positive correlation between self-lessness and femininity speaks of the expectations of the gender role of the woman as one who takes care of others and neglects her own needs (Sarner-Levin et al., 2018). The neoliberal stereotype of the superwoman as an ideal integration of male and female characteristics offers an apparent solution, but it also creates new problems of excessive, contradictory expectations that our interviewees found very burdensome.

Hilde Bruch, who repeatedly emphasised the low self-esteem of anorexia patients, while describing the disorder itself as a 'desperate struggle for a self-respecting identity' (Bruch, 1973, p. 250), offered an explanation which can greatly help in understanding the complex relationship people with eating disorder have with gender roles. If in a capitalist society masculine characteristics are highly valued and femininity is defined through a negative, traditional pattern or as a fantastic integration of masculine traits, helpful in the professional world, while retaining positive feminine traits in the private sphere, for vulnerable girls and young women such a choice can be too taxing, and identifying with gender roles in a conflicting way can contribute to the development of an eating disorder.

As for the male gender stereotypes, the traditional stereotype of a strong man who does not show emotions is dominant, but there are hints for possible conceptualisations of other stereotypical male gender roles: the modern emotional man (egalitarian parenting and financial equality), the narcissist (a man who strives to achieve the muscular ideal), the sexual predator and the sissy (an incompetent man who is with a capable woman).

For some of the interviewees, the values attributed to the male gender role were positive and desirable, and they had repeatedly wished to be a man. This was especially the case if they wanted to achieve a sense of confidence, control and power through the eating disorder, as these are qualities attributed to men. In a way, the interviewees felt more successful and superior with extreme weight loss, which brought them closer to the male gender role. They believed that it was more difficult to be a woman in society and that as men they would be privileged.

The interviewees who saw the male gender role as something undesirable and repulsive were the ones who had experienced sexual trauma. They were not attracted to either the female or male gender role, but rather to that of a child. For them, traits attributed to any gender role were undesirable; therefore, they were actively focused on erasing all signs of adulthood from their bodies, as well as on maintaining the social status of a child or an adolescent. Unresolved family relationships and painful separation processes further strengthened the conscious refusal to grow up and made them take on an eating disorder as a strategy to prolong their childhood or adolescence.

Furthermore, the interviewees who had experienced a conflicted upbringing (conflict with their parents) and had had problematic sexual relationships (self-punishment through promiscuity), valued the male gender role more and wanted to be men since men are protected from sexual aggression.

We can conclude that the attitude towards gender roles is crucial for understanding eating disorders. This attitude is not unambiguous and is characterised by internal conflicting expectations and meanings, and probably influenced by a segmentation of the sample, which should be further verified in future research.

In this research, we followed a combined approach to the aetiology of eating disorders (Keel & Klump, 2003), accepting anorexia as universally present in most societies throughout history, while looking at bulimia through the prism of a culture-bound syndrome (Keel & Klump, 2003). The presented data analysis supports the thesis that anorexia and bulimia are closely related to the attitude towards gender roles, although this relationship is very complex and probably undergoes transformations as cultural changes happen. For young girls and women, the body and the attitude towards food are a place of struggle for their own identity in different societies and historical periods. If there is enough food, the manipulation of food and body becomes a strong message, the inner conflicts of young individuals become materialised, simultaneously painful intimate acts but also public testimonies of disagreement with and resistance to the circumstances in which they live.

I would agree with Beck et al. (2017), who show that the time before a girl gets her first period (ages 13–17) is crucial for the effective prevention of eating disorders. Expressing fear, sadness and disgust related to menstruation (and sexual maturation into a woman) is risky for the later development of eating disorders, which once again shows how the study of gender roles in patients is relevant for understanding the social context of the emergence of eating disorders.

The extent to which culture and eating disorders are intertwined is further described in the themes that speak about social meanings related to food, eating and abstaining from food. In patients with eating disorders, we encounter current prevailing trends in Western society in relation to 'healthy food': following the rules of clean eating, orthorexia and the healthism movement and fit inspo/fitness attitude towards food. In forming their relationship with food, patients with eating disorders rely on a mixture of scientific data and nutritional advice presented through social and mainstream media, and these are interpreted through the intimate prism of an individual's search for self-realisation through proper eating, a perfect physical appearance and 'self-care'.

In order to fully understand one's relationship with food, it should be brought into connection with one's relationship to one's body, which is crucial for the formation of identity of people with eating disorders. The body and food determine and complement each other – the body 'testifies' to one's eating habits, and the meanings given to food reflect the values related to living in the body and have to do with issues of desire, hunger and relationships with other people (already mentioned in Coveney, 2006).

Within the framework of neoliberal ideology, health has become a personal concern, and finding a solution for one's health-related problems is understood as a matter of personal choice (Crawford, 1980). Therefore, so body size and shape are indicators of personal choices which have nothing to do with any social, cultural, physical or economic constraints (Rich et al., 2004). Within this narrative, a thin and slim body signifies health and beauty, and being overweight is constructed as unhealthy and as a consequence of an irresponsible lifestyle of an individual (Malson, 2009). Given that the experience of one's body is extremely important for the creation of a personal identity, the socio-cultural context plays an integral role in how these experiences are (re)produced (Malson, 2009). We can conclude that stigmatising obesity as a global health crisis further reinforces existing moralising meanings related to fat and thin bodies (Malson, 2009).

The findings have confirmed that for patients with anorexia and bulimia, the public health narrative of the war against obesity in which body weight has become a sign of health is harmful. The interviewees interpret a thin body as proof of the 'propriety' of a person who 'behaves correctly' (Malson, 2009). Individuals who think their body deviates from the expected norm perceive themselves as people who are in some way inadequate, unacceptable or wrong (Malson, 2009).[3]

Ever since the World Health Organization (WHO) declared war on the global obesity epidemic in 2000, numerous calculations of increased health care costs due to complications in overweight or obese individuals (Kouris-Blazos & Wahlquist, 2007) have been carried out, further justifying public pressure towards weight loss. In such an environment, where the public narrative is directed towards the stigmatisation of obesity and encouraging individuals to reduce their daily calorie and fat intake by 20–25% (WHO, 2000), individuals with risk factors for the development of eating disorders encounter increased challenges in forming a healthy self-image (Malson et al., 2009). Binge-eating disorder, which has been included in the *Diagnostic and Statistical Manual of Mental Disorders* by the American Psychiatric Association since 2013, is often accompanied by increased body weight and obesity, so focusing on reducing body weight can worsen the actual symptoms of the disorder (Dalle Grave, 2015) or prompt the affected person to develop another form of eating disorders (anorexia or bulimia; Stice et al., 2002).

---

[3]Although the rate of obesity among children has doubled in the last 50 years (Forth, 2014) and one in three children in the United States is overweight or obese, the stigmatisation of obese children has also significantly increased in this period (Andreyeva et al., 2008). Children play less often with their overweight peers, and they judge them more often as lonely, lazy, stupid, ugly and dirty (Puhl & Latner, 2007). These stereotypes are present in children as early as at the age of 3, and they increase with age (Puhl & Latner, 2007).

These arguments are supported by the findings which discuss the focus on food and appearance in the birth families of the interviewees, and the question arises of how the prevention of obesity should be implemented and healthy eating habits promoted, thus reducing the harmful potential that such an endeavour might include. In addition to the parents and the extended family, important adults from the child's surroundings whose job is to educate and guide young people were singled out as risk influences: coaches, teachers, doctors and nutritionists. They were perceived as people who can also convey the message that body shape and weight are extremely important for the child's future.

Most of the conclusions on the attitudes of patients towards food and the body in this book represent a continuation of already established scientific interpretations. *The body as the basis of identity* of patients, *Magical food* and *Different ways of growing up* additionally confirm the already familiar phenomena of denying and rejecting one's own body in patients with eating disorders, a repulsive attitude towards fatness, as opposed to the thin ideal, and the focus on the appearance and shape of one's body as the 'centre of the world'.

What I see as a contribution to understanding the complex micro-world of anorexia and bulimia is the understanding of binge eating and vomiting as possible initial behaviours in some forms of the disorder and the emphasis on the dual character of orthorexia.

Through their powerful statements, the interviewees emphasised that for some of them the intense experience of binge eating or the feeling of emptiness after the expulsion of food and emotions through vomiting was the main driving force of the disorder, while starvation or restriction represented a rest between purgative practices. This is a visible departure from the previous conceptualisation of bulimia as failed anorexia and the perception of binge eating and vomiting only as unwanted consequences of dietary practices. In this way, binge eating and vomiting acquire an independent meaning, and for some of the interviewees they were the first form and the driving force of the disorder.

Very often the interviewees perceived their urges to consume food as threatening, destructive and difficult to tame (Burns, 2004). Countless times, people with eating disorders have emphasised how crucial it is to have control over themselves because if they were free and did what they wanted, this would lead to a complete 'disintegration of the system' or, as the interviewees put it, living in external and internal chaos. The idea that the needs and, in fact, the authentic personalities of the interviewed women are something dangerous and infinitely threatening and bad, like 'a tiger in a cage' (Tangram wellness, 2022) is interesting. At the same time, patients with eating disorders apply various approaches to solving the problem of the destructive potential of their own personality. They use different procedures of emotional self-regulation or self-silencing (Geller et al., 2000) – in anorexia, patients decide to 'kill' or 'tame' the tiger by not eating, but they are aware that the tiger can only die if they themselves die. Every eating carries the possibility that the person will lose control, and therefore for some patients it is seemingly easier to keep fasting than to eat moderately. Binge eating and vomiting also offer a temporary way out to 'contain' the caged tiger. This way, self-destructiveness is supposedly controlled by planning periods of eating/ binge eating in advance and indulging in the 'lower urges' without control, and then, through purging (vomiting, laxative abuse) or compensating behaviours (obsessive exercise, starvation), the tiger is once again metaphorically locked in the cage and the patient can reassume the role of a self-controlled and socially well-adapted woman.

Understanding orthorexia as a risky practice for the development of an eating disorder highlights the importance of having a responsible prevention of obesity programme and implies that there should be a change in the way the need for a healthy diet is communicated through social media, the internet and the institutions: schools, sports clubs, doctor's offices. The fact that many of the interviewees cite conversations with experts (nutritionists, school doctors, gynaecologists, etc.) as triggers for their entering eating disorders is simply devastating. But, notably, for some interviewees, orthorexia was at the same time a way out of the disorder. Because it provides a similar sense of control and purity to an eating disorder, the obsession with healthy eating helped some interviewees accept more regular food consumption. It may be useful for therapeutic purposes to consider orthorexic eating as an initial part of the recovery path from anorexia and bulimia.

By reading social meanings attached to food, eating and abstaining from food, we can conclude that disordered eating has little to do with food itself or indeed with body weight, but that it rather reflects wider social relations which include power and control, within which individuals fail to achieve recognition and the feeling of authenticity (Evans et al., 2011). Therefore, while studying the social imprint in the world of the meaning of people with eating disorders, it is necessary to go beyond the obsession with thinness and the fear of gaining weight (Katzman & Lee, 1997) in order to encompass their whole living experience.

If we interpret eating disorders exclusively as personal pathology, without understanding the cultural context in which the disorders originate, anorexia and bulimia will continue to destroy the lives of thousands of women (Tully, 2015). Therefore, the critical feminist perspective (Malson, 2008) points to a multitude of modern Western cultural narratives and practices which constitute and regulate normative femininity and to their inextricable connection with the construction of 'eating disorders'. Here, eating disorders are not understood as clinical entities separate from a 'normal, healthy' society, but as complex, heterogeneous and changing common denominators for a set of individuals, bodies and bodily practices which are socially and historically situated within (rather than outside) contemporary Western cultures (Malson, 2008). Eating disorders are an expression of many sometimes contradictory societal values, concerns and dilemmas related to 'being a woman' (Malson, 2008, p. 113). I believe that in the future the issue of gender roles will prove to be even more important in understanding eating disorders, since young people are increasingly questioning their gender identity and social expectations related to gender.

I would like to stress that in this book I have presented a study based on the analysis of in-depth interviews of 30 girls and women. The findings and conclusions are based on the collected data. In the interpretation of these findings, I emphasised dominant trends, which necessarily requires simplification. I am aware that the results presented here are not completely exhaustive and that the individual stories of patients contain experiences that go well beyond the conclusions of this study. This is important for me to say if you, as a reader suffering from an eating disorder, have not found yourself in these analyses. In generalisations, individual differences are inevitably ignored. I would like to point out that I did not want to hurt anyone with my analysis, and in my writing I tried to be respectful and protect the dignity of people with eating disorders, as well as their relatives.

Bibliography

Aarnio, K., & Lindeman, M. (2004). Magical food and health beliefs: A portrait of believers and functions of the beliefs. *Appetite*, *43*(1), 65–74. https://doi.org/10.1016/j.appet.2004.03.002

Achamrah, N., Coeffier, M., & Dechelotte, P. (2016). Physical activity in patients with anorexia nervosa. *Nutrition Reviews*, *74*, 301–311.

Ainsworth, M. D., & Bell, S. M. (1970). Attachment, exploration, and separation: Illustrated by the behavior of one-year-olds in a strange situation. *Child Development*, *41*(1), 49–67. https://doi.org/10.2307/1127388

Aldao, A., Nolen-Hoeksema, S., & Schweizer, S. (2010). Emotion-regulation strategies across psychopathology: A meta-analytic review. *Clinical Psychology Review*, *30*(2), 217–237. https://doi.org/10.1016/j.cpr.2009.11.004

Allmark, P., Boote, J., & Chambers, E. (2009). Ethical issues in the use of in-depth interviews. *Literature Review and Discussion Research Ethics*, *5*(2), 48. https://doi.org/10.1177/174701610900500203

Almeida, B., Machado, S., Fonseca, C., Fragoeiro, C., & Monteiro, L. (2019). "The Golden Cage" revisiting Hilde Bruch revolutionary concepts on anorexia nervosa. EPA 2019, 27th European Congrea of Psychiatry, Warsaw. https://doi.org/10.26226/morressier.5c642bdf9ae8fb00131ce734

Alvesson, M. (2003). Beyond neopositivists, romantics, and localists: A reflexive approach to interviews in organizational research. *The Academy of Management Review*, *28*(1), 13–33. https://doi.org/10.2307/30040687

Ambwani, S., Shippe, M., Gao, Z., & Austin, S. B. (2019). Is #cleaneating a healthy or harmful dietary strategy? Perceptions of clean eating and associations with disordered eating among young adults. *Journal of Eating Disorders*, *3*, 7–17. https://doi.org/10.1186/s40337-019-0246-2

American Psychiatric Association. (1994). *Diagnostic and statistical manual of mental disorders: DSM-IV* (4th ed.). American Psychiatric Association. http://www.psychiatryonline.com/DSMPDF/dsm-iv.pdf

American Psychiatric Association, DSM-5 Task Force. (2013). *Diagnostic and statistical manual of mental disorders: DSM-5™* (5th ed.). American Psychiatric Publishing, Inc. https://doi.org/10.1176/appi.books.9780890425596

Anderson-Fye, E. P. (2004). A "coca-cola" shape: Cultural change, body image, and eating disorders in San Andrés, Belize. *Culture Medicine and Psychiatry*, *28*(4), 561–595. https://doi.org/10.1007/s11013-004-1068-4

Andreyeva, T., Puhl, R. M., & Brownell, K. D. (2008). Changes in perceived weight discrimination among Americans, 1995–1996 through 2004–2006. *Obesity*, *16*(5), 1129–1134.

Antaki, C., Billig, M., Edwards, D., & Potter, J. (2003). Discourse analysis means doing analysis: A critique of six analytic shortcomings. https://doi.org/10.5565/rev/athenea.64Corpus. https://repository.lboro.ac.uk/articles/journal_contribution/

Discourse_analysis_means_doing_analysis_a_critique_of_six_analytic_shortcom
ings/9473747

Aradas, J., Sales, D., Rhodes, P., & Conti, J. (2019). "As long as they eat"? Therapist experiences, dilemmas and identity negotiations of Maudsley and family-based therapy for anorexia nervosa. *Journal of Eating Disorders, 7*(26). https://doi.org/ 10.1186/s40337-019-0255-1

Arcelus, J., Mitchell, A. J., Wales, J., & Nielsen, S. (2011). Mortality rates in patients with anorexia nervosa and other eating disorders. A meta-analysis of 36 studies. *Archives of General Psychiatry, 68*(7), 724–731. https://doi.org/10.1001/ archgenpsychiatry.2011.74

Arcelus, J., Yates, A., & Whiteley, R. (2012). Romantic relationships, clinical and sub-clinical eating disorders: A review of the literature. *Sexual and Relationship Therapy, 27*(2), 147–161. https://doi.org/10.1080/14681994.2012.696095

Armstrong, J. G., & Roth, D. M. (1989). Attachment and separation difficulties in eating disorders: A preliminary investigation. *International Journal of Eating Disorders, 8*(2), 141–155. https://doi.org/10.1002/1098-108X(198903)8:2<141:: AID-EAT2260080203>3.0.CO;2-E

Arthur-Cameselle, J. N., & Quatromoni, P. (2014). A qualitative analysis of female collegiate athletes' eating disorder recovery experiences. *Sport Psychologist, 28,* 334–346.

Ata, R., Schaefer, L. M., & Thompson, J. K. (2015). Sociocultural theories of eating disorders. In M. Levine & L. Smolak (Eds.), *The Wiley-Blackwell handbook of eating disorders* (pp. 269–282). John Wiley and Sons, Ltd.

Atkinson, P., & Coffey, A. (2002). Revisiting the relationship between participant observation and interviewing. In J. F. Gubrium & J. A. Holstein (Eds.), *Handbook of interview research* (pp. 801–814). Sage.

Axelsen, M. (2009). The power of leisure: "I was an anorexic; I'm now a healthy triathlete". *Leisure Sciences, 31*(4), 330–346.

Bacanu, S. A., Bulik, C. M., Klump, K. L., Fichter, M. M., Halmi, K. A., Keel, P., Kaplan, A. S., Mitchell, J. E., Rotondo, A., Strober, M., Treasure, J., Woodside, D. B., Sonpar, V. A., Xie, W., Bergen, A. W., Berrettini, W. H., Kaye, W. H., & Devlin, B. (2005). Linkage analysis of anorexia and bulimia nervosa cohorts using selected behavioral phenotypes as quantitative traits or covariates. *American Journal of Medical Genetics Neuropsychiatric Genetics, 139B*(1), 61–68.

Bachner-Melman, R., & Oakley, B. (2016). Giving 'til it hurts': Eating disorders and pathological altruism. In Y. Latzer & D. Stein (Eds.), *Bio-psycho-social contributions to understanding eating disorders.* https://doi.org/10.1007/978-3-319-32742-6_7

Banchefsky, S., & Park, B. (2016). The "new father": Dynamic stereotypes of fathers. *Psychology of Men & Masculinity, 17*(1), 103–107. https://doi.org/10.1037/ a0038945

Bang, L., Treasure, J., Rø, Ø., & Joos, A. (2017). Advancing our understanding of the neurobiology of anorexia nervosa: Translation into treatment. *Journal of Eating Disorders, 1,* 5–38. https://doi.org/10.1186/s40337-017-0169-8

Bardone-Cone, A. M., Hunt, R. A., & Watson, H. J. (2018). An overview of conceptualizations of eating disorder recovery, recent findings, and future directions. *Current Psychiatry Reports, 20*(9), 79. https://doi.org/10.1007/s11920-018-0932-9

Bardone-Cone, A. M., Sturm, K., Lawson, M. A., Robinson, D. P., & Smith, R. (2010, March). Perfectionism across stages of recovery from eating disorders. *International Journal of Eating Disorders*, *43*(2), 139–148. https://doi.org/10.1002/eat.20674

Bardone-Cone, A. M., Wonderlich, S. A., Frost, R. O., Bulik, C. M., Mitchell, J. E., Uppala, S., & Simonich, H. (2006). Perfectionism and eating disorders: Current status and future directions. *Clinical Psychology Review*, *27*(3), 384–405. https://doi.org/10.1016/j.cpr.2006.12.005

Barnett, M. J., Dripps, W. R., & Blomquist, K. K. (2016). Organivore or organorexic? Examining the relationship between alternative food network engagement, disordered eating, and special diets. *Appetite*, *1*(105), 713–720. https://doi.org/10.1016/j.appet.2016.07.008

Barthels, F., Meyer, F., Huber, T., & Pietrowsky, R. (2017). Orthorexic eating behaviour as a coping strategy in patients with anorexia nervosa. *Eating and Weight Disorders*, *22*(2), 269–276. https://doi.org/10.1007/s40519-016-0329-x

Bartky, S. L. (1988). Foucault, femininity, and the modernization of patriarchal power. In I. Diamond & L. Quinby (Eds.), *Feminism and foucault: Reflections of resistance*. Northeastern University Press.

Batista, M. (2019). *Psihološka prilagodba i sociokulturni stavovi u adolescentica s anoreksijom nervozom*. Doktorski rad. Sveučilište u Zagrebu.

Becker, A. E. (2004). Television, disordered eating, and young women in Fiji: Negotiating body image and identity during rapid social change. *Culture Medicine and Psychiatry*, *28*(4), 533–559. https://doi.org/10.1007/s11013-004-1067-5

Becker, A. E., Burwell, R. A., Gilman, S. E., Herzog, D. B., & Hamburg, P. (2002). Eating behaviours and attitudes following prolonged exposure to television among ethnic Fijian adolescent girls. *The British Journal of Psychiatry: The Journal of Mental Science*, *180*, 509–514. https://doi.org/10.1192/bjp.180.6.509

Becker, A. E., Fay, K. E., Agnew-Blais, J., Khan, A. N., Striegel-Moore, R. H., & Gilman, S. E. (2011). Social network media exposure and adolescent eating pathology in Fiji. *The British Journal of Psychiatry: The Journal of Mental Science*, *198*(1), 43–50. https://doi.org/10.1192/bjp.bp.110.078675

Beck, T., Mancuso, A., & Petrides, J. (2017). Eating disorders and menarche: Can emotions toward the first period provide insight into future eating disorder development? *Psychology*, *08*(11), 1718–1727. https://doi.org/10.4236/psych.2017.811113

Behar, A. R., De la Barrera, C. M., & Michelotti, C. J. (2002). Gender differences in attitudes towards eating behaviors. *Revista médica de Chile*, *130*(9), 964–975. http://doi.org/10.4067/S0034-98872002000900002

Bekker, M. H. J., & Boselie, K. A. H. M. (2002). Gender and stress: Is gender role stress? A re-examination of the relationship between feminine gender role stress and eating disorders. *Stress and Health*, *18*(3), 141–149.

Bell, R. M. (1985). *Holy anorexia*. University of Chicago Press.

Bell, K., Coulthard, H., & Wildbur, D. (2017). Self-disgust within eating disordered groups: Associations with anxiety, disgust sensitivity and sensory processing. *European Eating Disorders Review*, *25*(5), 373–380. https://doi.org/10.1002/erv.2529

Bem, S. L. (1974). The measurement of psychological androgyny. *Journal of Consulting and Clinical Psychology, 42*(2), 155–162. https://doi.org/10.1037/h0036215

Bemporad, J. R. (1997). Cultural and historical aspects of eating disorders. *Theoretical Medicine, 18*(4), 401–420.

Berge, J. M., Loth, K., Hanson, C., Croll-Lampert, J., & Neumark-Sztainer, D. (2012). Family life cycle transitions and the onset of eating disorders: A retrospective grounded theory approach. *Journal of Clinical Nursing, 21*(9–10), 1355–1363. https://doi.org/10.1111/j.1365-2702.2011.03762.x

Berrettini, W. (2004). The genetics of eating disorders. *Psychiatry, 1*(3), 18–25.

Bi, S., Haak, E. A., Gilbert, L. R., & Keller, P. S. (2017). Children exposed to marital conflict exhibit more disordered eating behaviors: Child emotional insecurity and anxiety as mechanisms of risk. *Journal of Child and Family Studies, 26*, 3112–3122. https://doi.org/10.1007/s10826-017-0811-8

Birksted-Breen, D. (1986). Phallus, penis and mental space. *International Journal of Psycho-Analysis, 77*, 649–657.

Björk, T., & Ahlström, G. (2008). The patient's perception of having recovered from an eating disorder. *Health Care for Women International, 29*(8), 926–944. https://doi.org/10.1080/07399330802269543

Boisvert, J. A., & Harrell, W. A. (2013). The role of sexual orientation as risk and protective factors for eating disorder symptomatology in women. In J. Marich (Ed.), *The psychology of women: Diverse perspectives from the modern world* (pp. 93–107). Nova Science Publishers.

Bordo, S. (1993). *Unbearable weight: Feminism, Western culture and the body.* University of California Press.

Bordo, S. (2012). *Beyond the anorexic paradigm: Re-thinking 'eating' disorders.* Routledge Handbook of Body Studies.

Boroughs, M., & Thompson, J. K. (2002). Exercise status and sexual orientation as moderators of body image disturbance and eating disorders in males. *International Journal of Eating Disorders, 31*(3), 307–311. https://doi.org/10.1002/eat.10031

Borzekowski, D. L. G., Schenk, S., Wilson, J. L., & Peebles, R. (2010). e-Ana and e-Mia: A content analysis of pro–eating disorder web sites. *American Journal of Public Health, 100*(2010), 1526–1534. https://doi.org/10.2105/AJPH.2009.172700

Boskind-Lodahl, M. (1976). Cinderella's stepsisters: A feminist perspective on anorexia nervosa and bulimia. *Signs: Journal of Women in Culture and Society, 2*, 342–356.

Boskind-White, M., & White, W. C. (1986). Bulimarexia: A historical-sociocultural perspective. In K. D. Brownell & J. P. Foreyt (Eds.), *Handbook of eating disorders: Physiology, psychology, and treatment of obesity, anorexia, and bulimia.* Basic Books.

Bourdieu, P. (1986). The forms of capital. In J. Richardson (Ed.), *Handbook of theory and research for the sociology of education.* Greenwood.

Bowlby, J. (1962/1982). *Attachment and loss.* Basic Books.

Boyd, C., Abraham, S., Maala, L., Luscombe, G., & Taylor, A. (2009). Time since menarche, weight gain and body image awareness among adolescent girls: Onset of eating disorders? *Journal of Psychosomatic Obstetrics & Gynecology, 30*, 89–94.

Branca, F., Nikogosian, H., & Lobstein, T. (2007). *The challenge of obesity in the WHO European region and the strategies for response.* World Health Organization.

Branley, D. B., & Covey, J. (2017). Pro-ana versus pro-recovery: A content analytic comparison of social media users' communication about eating disorders on Twitter and Tumblr. *Frontiers in Psychology*, *8*, 1356. https://doi.org/10.3389/fpsyg.2017.01356

Bratman, S., & Knight, D. (2000). *Health food junkies: Overcoming the obsession with healthful eating*. Broadway Book.

Braun, V., & Clarke, V. (2013). *Successful qualitative research: A practical guide for beginners*. SAGE Publication.

Braun, V., & Clarke, V. (2019). Reflecting on reflexive thematic analysis. *Qualitative Research in Sport, Exercise and Health*, *11*(4), 589–597. https://doi.org/10.1080/2159676X.2019.1628806

Bretherton, I. (1992). The origins of attachment theory: John Bowlby and Mary Ainsworth. *Developmental Psychology*, *28*(5), 759–775. https://doi.org/10.1037/0012-1649.28.5.759

Brewster, D. H., Nowell, S. L., & Clark, D. N. (2015). Risk of oesophageal cancer among patients previously hospitalised with eating disorder. *Cancer Epidemiology*, *39*(3), 313–320. https://doi.org/10.1016/j.canep.2015.02.009

Brown, B. (2010). *The gifts of imperfection: Let go of who you think you're supposed to be and embrace who you are*. Hazelden Publishing.

Bruch, H. (1973). *Eating disorders: Obesity, anorexia nervosa, and the person within*. Basic Books.

Bruch, H. (1978). *The golden cage: The enigma of anorexia nervosa*. Harvard University Press.

Brumberg, J. J. (1982). Chlorotic girls, 1870–1920: A historical perspective on female adolescence. *Child Development*, *53*(6), 1468–1477.

Brumberg, J. J. (1989). *Fasting girls*. Vintage Books.

Bryant, E., Aouad, P., Hambleton, A., Touyz, S., & Maguire, S. (2022, August 1). 'In an otherwise limitless world, I was sure of my limit.'† Experiencing Anorexia Nervosa: A phenomenological metasynthesis. *Front Psychiatry*, *13*, 894178. https://doi.org/10.3389/fpsyt.2022.894178

Brytek-Matera, A. (2021). Vegetarian diet and orthorexia nervosa: A review of the literature. *Eating and Weight Disorders*, *26*(1), 1–11. https://doi.org/10.1007/s40519-019-00816-3

Buchholz, A., Henderson, K. A., Hounsell, A., Wagner, A., Norris, M., & Spettigue, W. (2007). Self-silencing in a clinical sample of female adolescents with eating disorders. *Journal of the Canadian Academy of Child and Adolescent Psychiatry* [*Journal de l'Académie canadienne de psychiatrie de l'enfant et de l'adolescent*], *16*(4), 158–163.

Bulatao, R. A., & Anderson, N. B. (Eds.). (2004). *Understanding racial and ethnic differences in health in late life: A research agenda*. National Research Council (US) Panel on Race, Ethnicity, and Health in Later Life. National Academies Press. https://www.ncbi.nlm.nih.gov/books/NBK24685/

Bulik, C. M. (2014). The challenges of treating anorexia nervosa. *Lancet*, *383*, 105–106. https://doi.org/10.1016/S0140-6736(13)61940-6

Bulik, C. M., Devlin, B., Bacanu, S., Thornton, L., Klump, K. L., Fichter, M. M., Halmi, K. A., Kaplan, A. S., Strober, M., Woodside, D. B., Bergen, A. W., Ganjei, J. K., Crow, S., Mitchell, J., Rotondo, A., Mauri, M., Cassano, G., Keel, P., Berrettini, W. H., & Kaye, W. H. (2003). Significant linkage on chromosome 10p in families with bulimia nervosa. *The American Journal of Human Genetics, 72,* 200–207.

Bulik, C. M., Flatt, R., Abbaspour, A., & Carroll, I. (2019). Reconceptualizing anorexia nervosa. *Psychiatry and Clinical Neurosciences, 73*(9), 518–525. https://doi.org/10.1111/pcn.12857

Burgard, D. (2010). What's weight got to do with it? In M. Maine, B. Hartman, D. McGilley, & W. Bunnell (Eds.), *Treatment of eating disorders. Bridging the research – Practice gap.* Elsevier Inc.

Burns, M. (2004). Eating like an ox: Femininity and dualistic constructions of bulimia and anorexia. *Feminism & Psychology, 14*(2), 269–295. https://doi.org/10.1177/0959-353504042182

Burns, M., & Gavey, N. (2004). 'Healthy weight' at what cost? 'Bulimia' and a discourse of weight control. *Journal of Health Psychology, 9*(4), 549–565. https://doi.org/10.1177/1359105304044039

Bynum, C. W. (1987). *Holy feast and holy fast: The religious significance of food to medieval women.* University of California Press.

Calogero, R. M., Tantleff-Dunn, S., & Thompson, J. K. (Eds.). (2011). *Self-objectification in women: Causes, consequences, and counteractions.* American Psychological Association. https://doi.org/10.1037/12304-000

Campos, P. F. (2004). *The obesity myth.* Githam Books.

Carey, M., & Preston, C. (2019). Investigating the components of body image disturbance within eating disorders. *Frontiers in Psychiatry, 10,* 635. https://doi.org/10.3389/fpsyt.2019.00635

Carney, T., Tait, D., & Touyz, S. (2007). Coercion is coercion? Reflections on trends in the use of compulsion in treating anorexia nervosa. *Australasian Psychiatry, 15*(5), 390–395. https://doi.org/10.1080/10398560701458202

Carney, T., Wakefield, A., Tait, D., & Touyz, S. (2006). Reflections on coercion in the treatment of severe anorexia nervosa. *Israel Journal of Psychiatry and Related Sciences, 43*(3), 159–165.

Carr, J., Kleiman, S. C., Bulik, C. M., Bulik-Sullivan, E. C., & Carroll, I. M. (2016). Can attention to the intestinal microbiota improve understanding and treatment of anorexia nervosa? *Expert Review of Gastroenterology & Hepatology, 10,* 565–569.

Cascino, G., Castellini, G., Stanghellini, G., Ricca, V., Cassioli, E., Ruzzi, V., Monteleone, P., & Monteleone, A. M. (2019). The role of the embodiment disturbance in the anorexia nervosa psychopathology: A network analysis study. *Brain Sciences, 9*(10), 276. https://doi.org/10.3390/brainsci9100276

Castellini, G., Lelli, L., Lo Sauro, C., Fioravanti, G., Vignozzi, L., Maggi, M., Faravelli, C., & Ricca, V. (2019). Anorectic and bulimic patients suffer from relevant sexual dysfunctions. *The Journal of Sexual Medicine, 9,* 2590–2599.

Cena, H., Barthels, F., Cuzzolaro, M., Bratman, S., Brytek-Matera, A., Dunn, T., Varga, M., Missbach, B., & Donini, L. M. (2019). Definition and diagnostic criteria for orthorexia nervosa: A narrative review of the literature. *Eating and Weight Disorders, 24*(2), 209–246. https://doi.org/10.1007/s40519-018-0606-y

Cena, H., Stanford, F. C., Ochner, L., Fonte, M. L., Biino, G., De Giuseppe, R., Taveras, E., & Misra, M. (2017). Association of a history of childhood-onset obesity and dieting with eating disorders. *Eating Disorders, 25*(3), 216–229. https://doi.org/10.1080/10640266.2017.1279905

Chua, N. Y. L. (2020). *How do individuals with anorexia nervosa (AN) experience the voice dialogue method in the context of experiencing an internal eating disorder voice? A Thematic Analysis.* Doctoral thesis, UCL.

Churruca, K., Perz, J., & Ussher, J. M. (2014). Uncontrollable behavior or mental illness? Exploring constructions of bulimia using Q methodology. *Journal of Eating Disorders*, 2–22. http://www.jeatdisord.com/content/2/1/22

Churruca, K., Ussher, J. M., & Perz, J. (2016). Just desserts? Exploring constructions of food in women's experiences of bulimia. *Qualitative Health Research, 27*(10), 1491–1506. https://doi.org/10.1177/1049732316672644

Cinquegrani, C., & Brown, D. H. K. (2018). 'Wellness' lifts us above the Food Chaos': A narrative exploration of the experiences and conceptualisations of Orthorexia Nervosa through online social media forums. *Qualitative Research in Sport, Exercise and Health, 10*(5), 585–603. https://doi.org/10.1080/2159676X.2018.1464501

Clay, D. L. (2015). The phenomenology of anorexia nervosa: The intertwining meaning of gender and embodiment. In Z. Bekirogullari & M. Y. Minas (Eds.), *Health and Health Psychology – icH&Hpsy 2015. European proceedings of social and behavioural sciences* (Vol. 5, pp. 22–41). Future Academy. https://doi.org/10.15405/epsbs.2015.07.4

Claydon, E., & Zullig, K. J. (2020). Eating disorders and academic performance among college students. *Journal of American College Health, 68*(3), 320–325. https://doi.org/10.1080/07448481.2018.1549556

Clough, B. (2016). Anorexia, capacity, and best interests: Developments in the court of protection since the Mental Capacity Act 2005. *Medical Law Review, 24*(3), 434–445. https://doi.org/10.1093/medlaw/fww037

Cocca, C. (2016). *Superwomen: Gender, power, and representation.* Bloomsbury Academic.

Coelho, J. S., Ouellet-Courtois, C., Purdon, C., & Steiger, H. (2015). Susceptibility to cognitive distortions: The role of eating pathology. *Journal of Eating Disorders, 3*, 31. https://doi.org/10.1186/s40337-015-0068-9

Colls, R. (2007). Materialising bodily matter: Intra-action and the embodiment of 'fat'. *Geoforum, 38*(2), 353–365.

Connell, R. W. (2005). Change among the gatekeepers: Men, masculinities, and gender equality in the global arena. *Research Library Core, 30*(3).

Connell, R. W., & Messerschmidt, J. W. (2005). Hegemonic masculinity: Rethinking the concept. *Gender & Society, 19*, 829.

Conti, J., Rhodes, P., & Adams, H. (2016). Listening in the dark: Why we need stories of people living with severe and enduring anorexia nervosa. *Journal of Eating Disorders, 4*(33). https://doi.org/10.1186/s40337-016-0117-z

Cooper, C. (2010). Fat studies: Mapping the field. *Sociology Compass, 4*, 1020–1034. https://doi.org/10.1111/j.1751-9020.2010.00336.x

Copeland, W. E., Bulik, C. M., Zucker, N., Wolke, D., Lereya, S. T., & Costello, E. J. (2015). Does childhood bullying predict eating disorder symptoms? A prospective, longitudinal analysis. *International Journal of Eating Disorders, 48*(8), 1141–1149. https://doi.org/10.1002/eat.22459

Corstorphine, E., Mountford, V., Tomlinson, S., Waller, G., & Meyer, C. (2007). Distress tolerance in the eating disorders. *Eating Behaviors, 8*, 91–97. https://doi.org/10.1016/j.eatbeh.2006.02.003

Costa, C. B., Hardan-Khalil, K., & Gibbs, K. (2017). Orthorexia nervosa: A review of the literature. *Issues in Mental Health Nursing, 38*(12), 980–988. https://doi.org/10.1080/01612840.2017.1371816

Coveney, J. (2006). *Food, morals and meaning the pleasure and anxiety of eating.* Routledge.

Crawford, R. (1980). Healthism and the medicalization of everyday life. *International Journal of Health Services, 10*(3), 365–388. https://doi.org/10.2190/3H2H-3XJN-3KAY-G9NY

Crawford, R. (2006). Health as a meaningful social practice. *Health, 10*(4), 401–420. https://doi.org/10.1177/1363459306067310

Crichton, P. (1996). Were the Roman emperors Claudius and Vitellius bulimic? *International Journal of Eating Disorders, 19*, 203–207.

Crow, S. J., & Eckert, E. D. (2016). Anorexia nervosa and bulimia nervosa. In *The medical basis of psychiatry* (4th ed., pp. 211–228). Springer. https://doi.org/10.1007/978-1-4939-2528-5_12

Crow, S. J., Peterson, C. B., Swanson, S. A., Raymond, N. C., Specker, S., Eckert, E. D., & Mitchell, J. E. (2009). Increased mortality in bulimia nervosa and other eating disorders. *American Journal of Psychiatry, 166*(12), 1342–1346. https://doi.org/10.1176/appi.ajp.2009.09020247

Culbert, K. M., Racine, S. E., & Klump, K. L. (2011). The influence of gender and puberty on the heritability of disordered eating symptoms. In *Behavioral neurobiology of eating disorders* (pp. 177–185). Springer.

Culbert, K. M., Racine, S. E., & Klump, K. L. (2015). Research Review: What we have learned about the causes of eating disorders – A synthesis of sociocultural, psychological, and biological research. *Journal of Child Psychology and Psychiatry, 56*(11), 1141–1164. https://doi.org/10.1111/jcpp.12441

Currie, A. (2010). Sport and eating disorders – Understanding and managing the risks. *Asian Journal of Sports Medicine, 1*(2), 63–68. https://doi.org/10.5812/asjsm.34864

D'Abundo, M., & Chally, P. (2004). Struggling with recovery: Participant perspectives on battling an eating disorder. *Qualitative Health Research, 14*(8), 1094–1106. https://doi.org/10.1177/1049732304267753

Dahill, L. M., Touyz, S., Morrison, N. M. V., & Hay, P. (2021). Parental appearance teasing in adolescence and associations with eating problems: A systematic review. *BMC Public Health, 21*, 450. https://doi.org/10.1186/s12889-021-10416-5

Dalle, G. R. (2015). *Kako pobijediti poremećaje hranjenja?* Veble.

Dallos, R. (2001). ANT—Attachment Narrative Therapy: Narrative and attachment theory approaches in systemic family therapy with eating disorders. *Journal of Family Psychotherapy, 12*(2), 43–72. https://doi.org/10.1300/J085v12n02_04

Dallos, R., & Denford, S. A. (2008). A qualitative exploration of relationship and attachment themes in families with an eating disorder. *Clinical Child Psychology and Psychiatry, 13*(2), 305–322. https://doi.org/10.1177/1359104507088349

Danner, U. N., Sanders, N., Smeets, P. A., van Meer, F., Adan, R. A., Hoek, H. W., & van Elburg, A. A. (2012). Neuropsychological weaknesses in anorexia nervosa: Set-shifting, central coherence, and decision making in currently ill and recovered women. *International Journal of Eating Disorders, 45*(5), 685–694. https://doi.org/10.1002/eat.22007

Davis, C., Claridge, G., & Fox, J. (2000, January). Not just a pretty face: Physical attractiveness and perfectionism in the risk for eating disorders. *International*

Journal of Eating Disorders, *27*(1), 67–73. https://doi.org/10.1002/(sici)1098-108x(200001)27:1<67::aid-eat7>3.0.co;2-f

Davison, K. K., & Birch, L. L. (2004). Predictors of fat stereotypes among 9-year-old girls and their parents. *Obesity Research*, *12*(1), 86–94. https://doi.org/10.1038/oby.2004.12

De Beauvoir, S. (1997 [1949]). *The second sex* (H. M. Parshley, Trans., Ed.). Vintage Books.

Degrassi. (2006). The next generation: Our lips are sealed. Part One. Season 5, Episode 15.

Dell'Osso, L., Abelli, M., Carpita, B., Pini, S., Castellini, G., Carmassi, C., & Ricca, V. (2016). Historical evolution of the concept of anorexia nervosa and relationships with orthorexia nervosa, autism, and obsessive-compulsive spectrum. *Neuropsychiatric Disease and Treatment*, *12*, 1651–1660. https://doi.org/10.2147/NDT.S108912

Dennett, C. A. (2016). A no-nonsense guide to clean eating. Chicago Health. https://chicagohealthonline.com/a-no-nonsense-guide-to-clean-eating/. Accessed on November 06, 2018.

Denzin, N. K., & Lincoln, Y. S. (1998). Entering the field of qualitative research. In N. K. Denzin & Y. S. Lincoln (Eds.), *Collecting and interpreting qualitative materials* (pp. 1–34). Sage.

Department of Health and Social Care, UK. (2022). https://www.gov.uk/government/news/new-calorie-labelling-rules-come-into-force-to-improve-nations-health

Diekman, A. B., Eagly, A. H., Johnston, A. M., Dovidio, J. F., Hewstone, F., Glick, P. G., & Esses, V. M. (2010). Social structure. In *The Sage handbook of prejudice, stereotyping, and discrimination* (pp. 209–224). Sage. https://doi.org/10.4135/9781446200919.n13

DiNicola, V. (1990). Anorexia multiform: Self starvation in historical and cultural context. Part 2: Anorexia nervosa as a cultural reactive syndrome. *Transcultural Psychiatric Research Review*, *27*, 245–286.

Dodge, E. (2016). Forty years of eating disorder-focused family therapy – The legacy of 'psychosomatic families'. *Advances in Eating Disorders*, *4*(2), 219–227. https://doi.org/10.1080/21662630.2015.1099452

Dohnt, H., & Tiggemann, M. (2006). The contribution of peer and media influences to the development of body satisfaction and self esteem in young girls: A prospective study. *Developmental Psychology*, *42*, 929–936.

Dour, H. J., & Theran, S. A. (2011). The interaction between the superhero ideal and maladaptive perfectionism as predictors of unhealthy eating attitudes and body esteem. *Body Image*, *8*, 93–96.

Dunn, T. M., & Bratman, S. (2016). On orthorexia nervosa: A review of the literature and proposed diagnostic criteria. *Eating Behaviors*, *21*, 11–17. https://doi.org/10.1016/j.eatbeh.2015.12.006

Durif-Bruckert, C., & Armand, C. (2007). *La nourriture et nous: Corps imaginaire et normes sociales*.

Dworkin, S. L., & Wachs, F. L. (2009). *Body panic: Gender, health, and the selling of fitness*. New York University Press.

Eagly, A. H., Nater, C., Miller, D. I., Kaufmann, M., & Sczesny, S. (2020). Gender stereotypes have changed: A cross-temporal meta-analysis of U.S. public opinion polls from 1946 to 2018. *American Psychologist, 75*(3), 301–315. https://doi.org/10.1037/amp0000494

Eddy, K. T., Dorer, D. J., Franko, D. L., Tahilani, K., Thompson-Brenner, H., & Herzog, D. B. (2008). Diagnostic crossover in anorexia nervosa and bulimia nervosa: Implications for DSM-V. *American Journal of Psychiatry, 165*(2), 245–250. https://doi.org/10.1176/appi.ajp.2007.07060951

Eiring, K., Wiig Hage, T., & Reas, D. L. (2021). Exploring the experience of being viewed as "not sick enough": A qualitative study of women recovered from anorexia nervosa or atypical anorexia nervosa. *Journal of Eating Disorders, 9*, 142. https://doi.org/10.1186/s40337-021-00495-5

Eisenberg, M. E., & Neumark-Sztainer, D. (2010). Friends' dieting and disordered eating behaviors among adolescents five years later: Findings from Project EAT. *Journal of Adolescent Health, 47*(1), 67–73. https://doi.org/10.1016/j.jadohealth.2009.12.030

Eli, K. (2015). Binge eating as a meaningful experience in bulimia nervosa and anorexia nervosa: A qualitative analysis. *Journal of Mental Health, 24*(6), 363–368. https://doi.org/10.3109/09638237.2015.1019049

Eli, K. (2018). Striving for liminality: Eating disorders and social suffering. *Transcultural Psychiatry, 55*(4), 475–494. https://doi.org/10.1177/1363461518757799

Embacher, M. K., McGloin, R., & Atkin, D. (2018). Body dissatisfaction, neuroticism, and female sex as predictors of calorie-tracking app use amongst college students. *Journal of American College Health, 66*(7), 608–616.

Engeln-Maddox, R., Miller, S. A., & Doyle, D. M. (2011). Test of objectification theory in gay, lesbian, and heterosexual community samples: Mixed evidence for proposed pathways. *Sex Roles, 65*(7–8), 518–532. https://doi.org/10.1007/s11199-011-9958-8

Ensign, J. (2003). Ethical issues in qualitative health research with homeless youths. *Journal of Advanced Nursing, 43*(1), 43–50.

Ernhout, C., Babington, P., & Childs, M. (2015). What's the relationship? Non-suicidal self-injury and eating disorders. In *The Information Brief Series, Cornell. Research Program on Self-Injury and Recovery.* Cornell University.

Escobar-Koch, T., Banker, J. D., Crow, S., Cullis, J., Ringwood, S., Smith, G., Van Furth, E., Westin, K., & Schmidt, U. (2010). Service users' views of eating disorder services: An international comparison. *International Journal of Eating Disorders, 43*(6), 549–559. https://doi.org/10.1002/eat.20741

Espeset, E. M., Gulliksen, K. S., Nordbø, R. H., Skårderud, F., & Holte, A. (2012). The link between negative emotions and eating disorder behaviour in patients with anorexia nervosa. *European Eating Disorders Review, 20*(6), 451–460. https://doi.org/10.1002/erv.2183

Evans, E. H., Adamson, A. J., Basterfield, L., Le Couteur, A., Reilly, J. K., Reilly, J. J., & Parkinson, K. N. (2016). Risk factors for eating disorder symptoms at 12 years of age: A 6-year longitudinal cohort study. *Appetite, 108*, 12–20. https://doi.org/10.1016/j.appet.2016.09.005

Evans, E. J., Hay, P. J., Mond, J., Paxton, S. J., Quirk, F., Rodgers, B., Jhajj, A. K., & Sawoniewska, M. A. (2011). Barriers to help-seeking in young women with eating disorders: A qualitative exploration in a longitudinal community survey. *Eating Disorders, 19*(3), 270–285. https://doi.org/10.1080/10640266.2011.566152

Faija, C. L., Tierney, S., Gooding, P. A., Peters, S., & Fox, J. R. E. (2017). The role of pride in women with anorexia nervosa: A grounded theory study. *Psychology and Psychotherapy: Theory, Research and Practice*, *90*(4), 567–585. https://doi.org/10.1111/papt.12125

Fairburn, C. G. (2008). *Cognitive behavior therapy and eating disorders* (Vol. 100, p. 12). The Guilford Press.

Fairburn, C. G., Cooper, Z., & Shafran, R. (2003). Cognitive behaviour therapy for eating disorders: A "transdiagnostic" theory and treatment. *Behaviour Research and Therapy*, *41*(5), 509–528. https://doi.org/10.1016/s0005-7967(02)00088-8

Fairweather-Schmidt, A., & Wade, T. D. (2015). Do genetic and environmental influences on disordered eating change from early to late adolescence? *Journal of Eating Disorders*, *3*(Suppl. 1), O10. https://doi.org/10.1186/2050-2974-3-s1-o10

Fairweather-Schmidt, A., & Wade, T. (2017). Weight-related peer-teasing moderates genetic and environmental risk and disordered eating: Twin study. *British Journal of Psychiatry*, *210*(5), 350–355. https://doi.org/10.1192/bjp.bp.116.184648

Farrell, A. E. (2011). *Fat shame: Stigma and the fat body in American culture*. New York University Press.

Fassino, S., Amianto, F., Gramaglia, C., Facchini, F., & Abbate Daga, G. (2004). Temperament and character in eating disorders: Ten years of studies. *Eating and Weight Disorders*, *9*(2), 81–90.

Ferguson, C. J., Muñoz, M. E., Garza, A., & Galindo, M. (2014). Concurrent and prospective analyses of peer, television and social media influences on body dissatisfaction, eating disorder symptoms and life satisfaction in adolescent girls. *Journal of Youth and Adolescence*, *43*(1), 1–14. https://doi.org/10.1007/s10964-012-9898-9

Ferguson, S., Brace-Govan, J., & Welsh, B. (2020). Complex contradictions in a contemporary idealised feminine body project. *Journal of Marketing Management*. https://doi.org/10.1080/0267257X.2020.172155

Fietz, M., Touyz, S., & Hay, P. (2014). A risk profile of compulsive exercise in adolescents with an eating disorder: A systematic review. *Advances in Eating Disorders*, *2*, 241–263.

Finch, J. (1993). It's great to have someone to talk to. In M. Hammersley (Ed.), *Social Research: Philosophy, politics and practice* (pp. 166–180). Open University. Sage.

Fine, M. (2002). *Disruptive voices: The possibilities for feminist research*. University of Michigan Press.

Finlay, L. (2002). "Outing" the researcher: The provenance, process, and practice of reflexivity. *Qualitative Health Research*, *12*(4), 531–545. https://doi.org/10.1177/104973202129120052

Firestone, S. (1970). *The dialectic of sex: The case for feminist revolution*. Bantam Book.

Fishman, C. (2005). *Enduring change in eating disorders: Interventions with long-term results*. Routledge.

Fitzsimmons-Craft, E. E. (2011). Social psychological theories of disordered eating in college women: Review and integration. *Clinical Psychology Review*, *31*(7), 1224–1237. https://doi.org/10.1016/j.cpr.2011.07.011

Flak, S. R. (2021). *The infuence of maternal body-shaming comments and bodily shame on portion size*. Doctoral dissertation, University of South Florida.

Fontana, A., & Frey, J. H. (1998). Interviewing: The art of science. In N. K. Denzin, & Y. S. Lincoln (Eds.), *Collecting and interpreting qualitative materials* (pp. 47–78). Sage Publications, Inc.

Forbush, K., & Watson, D. (2006). Emotional inhibition and personality traits: A comparison of women with anorexia, bulimia, and normal controls. *Annals of Clinical Psychiatry, 18*(2), 115–121. https://doi.org/10.1080/10401230600614637

Forrest, L. N., Smith, A. R., & Swanson, S. A. (2017). Characteristics of seeking treatment among U.S. adolescents with eating disorders. *International Journal of Eating Disorders.* https://doi.org/10.1002/eat.22702

Forth, C. E. (2013). The qualities of fat: Bodies, history, and materiality. *Journal of Material Culture, 18*(2). https://doi.org/10.1177/1359183513489496

Forth, C. E. (2014). Materializing fat. In C. E. Forth & A. Leitch (Eds.), *Fat: Culture and materiality.* Bloomsbury.

Forth, C. E., & Leitch, A. (2014). *Fat: Culture and Materiality.* Bloomsbury.

Fournier, V. (2002). Fleshing out gender: Crafting gender identity on women's bodies. *Body & Society, 8*(2), 55–77. https://doi.org/10.1177/1357034X02008002004

Fox, J. R. E. (2009). A qualitative exploration of the perception of emotions in anorexia nervosa: A basic emotion and developmental perspective. *Clinical Psychology & Psychotherapy, 16*, 276–302. https://doi.org/10.1002/cpp.631

Fox, J. R. (2009). Eating disorders and emotions. *Clinical Psychology & Psychotherapy, 16*(4), 237–239. https://doi.org/10.1002/cpp.625

Fox, J. R., & Diab, P. (2013). An exploration of the perceptions and experiences of living with chronic anorexia nervosa while an inpatient on an Eating Disorders Unit: An Interpretative Phenomenological Analysis (IPA) study. *Journal of Health Psychology, 20*(1), 27–36. https://doi.org/10.1177/1359105313497526

Fox, J., & Vendemia, M. A. (2016). Selective self-presentation and social comparison through photographs on social networking sites. *Cyberpsychology, Behavior, and Social Networking, 19*(10), 593–600. https://doi.org/10.1089/cyber.2016.0248

Frank, G. K. (2016). The perfect storm – A bio-psycho-social risk model for developing and maintaining eating disorders. *Frontiers in Behavioral Neuroscience, 10*, 44. https://doi.org/10.3389/fnbeh.2016.00044

Fredrickson, B. L., & Roberts, T. A. (1997). Objectification theory: Toward understanding women's lived experiences and mental health risks. *Psychology of Women Quarterly, 21*(2), 173–206. https://doi.org/10.1111/j.1471-6402.1997.tb00108.x

Freedman, M. R., King, J., & Kennedy, E. (2001). Popular diets: A scientific review. *Obesity Research, 9*(Suppl. 1), 1S–40S. https://doi.org/10.1038/oby.2001.113

Frey, I. (2020). Anorexia's failed little sisters: Reflections on researching bulimia as a former bulimic. *Social Theory & Health, 18*, 138–151. https://doi.org/10.1057/s41285-019-00100-5

Fuchs, T. (2021). The disappearing body: Anorexia as a conflict of embodiment. *Eating and Weight Disorders.* https://doi.org/10.1007/s40519-021-01122-7

Fuchs, T. (2022). The disappearing body: Anorexia as a conflict of embodiment. *Eating and Weight Disorders, 27*, 109–117. https://doi.org/10.1007/s40519-021-01122-7

Fullagar, S. (2009). Negotiating the neurochemical self: Anti-depressant consumption in women's recovery from depression. *Health: An Interdisciplinary Journal for the Social Study of Health, Illness and Medicine, 13*(3), 389–406.

Gailledrat, L., Rousselet, M., Venisse, J. L., Lambert, S., Rocher, B., Remaud, M., Guilleux, A., Sauvaget, A., Eyzop, E., & Grall-Bronnec, M. (2016). Marked body shape concerns in female patients suffering from eating disorders: Relevance of a clinical sub-group. *PLoS One*, *11*(10), e0165232. https://doi.org/10.1371/journal.pone.0165232

Galić, B. (2002). Moć i rod. *Revija za Sociologiju*, *23*(3–4), 225–238.

Galić, B. (2008). Rodni identitet i seksizam u hrvatskom društvu. In I. Cifrić (Ed.), *Relacijski identiteti: Prilozi istraživanju identiteta hrvatskog društva* (pp. 153–183). Hrvatsko sociološko društvo, Institut za društvena istraživanja, Zavod za sociologiju Odsjeka za sociologiju Filozofskog fakulteta, Zagreb.

Galmiche, M., Déchelotte, P., Lambert, G., & Tavolacci, M. P. (2019). Prevalence of eating disorders over the 2000–2018 period: A systematic literature review. *The American Journal of Clinical Nutrition*, *109*, 1402–1413. https://doi.org/10.1093/ajcn/nqy342

Gander, M., Sevecke, K., & Buchheim, A. (2015). Eating disorders in adolescence: Attachment issues from a developmental perspective. *Frontiers in Psychology*. https://doi.org/10.3389/fpsyg.2015.01136

Gearhardt, A. N., White, M. A., & Potenza, M. N. (2011). Binge eating disorder and food addiction. *Current Drug Abuse Reviews*, *4*(3), 201–207. https://doi.org/10.2174/1874473711104030201

Geller, J., Brown, K. E., Zaitsoff, S. L., Bates, M. E., Menna, R., & Dunn, E. C. (2008). Assessing readiness for change in adolescents with eating disorders. *Psychological Assessment*, *20*, 63–69. http://doi.org/10.1037/1040-3590.20.1.63

Geller, J., Cockell, S. J., Hewitt, P. L., Goldner, E. M., & Flett, G. L. (2000). Inhibited expression of negative emotions and interpersonal orientation in anorexia nervosa. *International Journal of Eating Disorders*, *28*(1), 8–19. https://doi.org/10.1002/1098-108x(200007)28:1<8::aid-eat2>3.0.co;2-u

George, M. W., Fairchild, A. J., Cummings, E. M., & Davies, P. T. (2014). Marital conflict in early childhood and adolescent disordered eating: Emotional insecurity about the marital relationship as an explanatory mechanism. *Eating Behaviors*, *15*(4), 532–539. https://doi.org/10.1016/j.eatbeh.2014.06.006

Giles, D. (2006). Constructing identities in cyberspace: The case of eating disorders. *British Journal of Social Psychology*, *45*(3), 463–477. https://doi.org/10.1348/014466605X53596

Gill, R. (2007). *Gender and the media*. Polity Press.

Gilligan, C., Lyons, N. P., & Hanmer, T. J. (Eds.). (1990). *Making connections: The relational worlds of adolescent girls at Emma Willard School*. Harvard University Press.

Gilman, S. L. (2010). *Obesity: The biography*. Oxford University Press.

Glashouwer, K. A., & de Jong, P. J. (2021). The revolting body: Self-disgust as a key factor in anorexia nervosa. *Current Opinion in Psychology*, *41*, 78–83. https://doi.org/10.1016/j.copsyc.2021.03.008

Godart, N. T., Perdereau, F., Rein, Z., Berthoz, S., Wallier, J., Jeammet, P., & Flament, M. F. (2006). Comorbidity studies of eating disorders and mood disorders. Critical review of the literature. *Journal of Affective Disorders*, *97*(1–3), 37–49. https://doi.org/10.1016/j.jad.2006.06.023

Godier, L. R., & Park, R. J. (2015). Does compulsive behavior in anorexia nervosa resemble an addiction? A qualitative investigation. *Frontiers in Psychology*, *6*, 1608. https://doi.org/10.3389/fpsyg.2015.01608

Gordon, R. A. (2000). *Eating disorders: Anatomy of a social epidemic* (2nd ed.). Blackwell Publishing.

Gordon, R. A. (2015). The history of bulimia nervosa. In M. P. Levine & L. Smolak (Eds.), *The Wiley handbook of eating disorders* (Vol. 1, pp. 25–39). Wiley.

Gorman, K. A., & Fritzsche, B. A. (2002). The good-mother stereotype: Stay at home (or wish that you did!). *Journal of Applied Social Psychology*, *32*(10), 2190–2201. https://doi.org/10.1111/j.1559-1816.2002.tb02069.x

Gottlieb, G. (2003). On making behavioral genetics truly developmental. *Human Development*, *46*(6), 337–355. https://www.jstor.org/stable/26763768. Accessed on August 28, 2021.

Grammer, A. C., Vazquez, M., Fitzsimmons-Craft, E., Fowler, L., Rackoff, G., Schvey, N., Lipson, S., Newman, M., Eisenberg, D., Taylor, C., & Wilfley, D. (2021). Characterizing eating disorder diagnosis and related outcomes by sexual orientation and gender identity in a National Sample of college students. *Eating Behaviors*, *42*. https://doi.org/10.1016/j.eatbeh.2021.101528

Green, A. (2001). *Life narcissism death narcissism*. Free Association Books.

Green, M. A., Davids, C. M., Skaggs, A. K., Riopel, C. M., & Hallengren, J. J. (2008). Femininity and eating disorders. *Eating Disorders: The Journal of Treatment and Prevention*, *16*(4), 283–293.

Gremillion, H. (2002). In fitness and in health: Crafting bodies in the treatment of anorexia nervosa. *Signs*, *27*(2), 381–414. https://doi.org/10.1086/495691

Grenfell, J. W. (2006). Religion and eating disorders: Towards understanding a neglected perspective. *Feminist Theology*, *14*(3), 367–387. https://doi.org/10.1177/0966735006063775

Grice, D. E., Halmi, K. A., Fichter, M. M., Strober, M., Woodside, D. B., Treasure, J. T., Kaplan, A. S., Magistretti, P. J., Goldman, D., Bulik, C. M., Kaye, W. H., & Berrettini, W. H. (2002). Evidence for a susceptibility gene for anorexia nervosa on chromosome 1. *The American Journal of Human Genetics*, *70*, 787–792.

Griffin, J., & Berry, E. M. (2003). A modern day holy anorexia? Religious language in advertising and anorexia nervosa in the west. *European Journal of Clinical Nutrition*, *57*, 43–51.

Grosz, E. (1994). *Volatile bodies: Towards a corporeal feminism*. Routledge.

Guest, G. (2006). How many interviews are enough? An experiment with data saturation and variability. *Field Methods*, *18*, 59–82. https://doi.org/10.1177/1525822X05279903

Gustafsson, S. A., Edlund, B., Davén, J., Kjellin, L., & Norring, C. (2011). How to deal with sociocultural pressures in daily life: Reflections of adolescent girls suffering from eating disorders. *Journal of Multidisciplinary Healthcare*, *4*, 103–110. https://doi.org/10.2147/JMDH.S17319

Habermas, T. (2005). On the uses of history in psychiatry: Diagnostic implications for anorexia nervosa. *International Journal of Eating Disorders*, *38*(2), 167–182.

Habermas, T. (2015). History of anorexia nervosa. In M. P. Levine & L. Smolak (Eds.), *The Wiley handbook of eating disorders* (Vol. 1, pp. 11–24). Wiley.

Haferkamp, N., Eimler, S. C., Papadakis, A., & Kruck, J. V. (2012). Men are from Mars, women are from Venus? Examining gender differences in self-presentation on social networking sites. *Cyberpsychology, Behavior, and Social Networking*, *15*(2). https://doi.org/10.1089/cyber.2011.0151

Haines, E. L., Deaux, K., & Lofaro, N. (2016). The times they are a-changing ... or are they not? A comparison of gender stereotypes, 1983–2014. *Psychology of Women Quarterly*, *40*(3), 353–363. https://doi.org/10.1177/0361684316634081

Haines, J., Neumark-Sztainer, D., Hannan, P. J., & Robinson-O'Brien, R. (2008). Child versus parent report of parental influences on children's weight-related attitudes and behaviors. *Journal of Pediatric Psychology*, *33*, 783–788.

Hall, A., & Hay, P. J. (1991). Eating disorder patient referrals from a population region 1977–1986. *Psychological Medicine*, *21*(3), 697–701. https://doi.org/10.1017/S0033291700022339

Halmi, K. A. (2005a). Multimodal treatment of eating disorders. *World Psychiatry*, *4*(2), 69–73.

Halmi, K. A. (2005b). Obsessive-compulsive personality disorder and eating disorders. *Eating Disorders*, *13*(1), 85–92. https://doi.org/10.1080/10640260590893683

Håman, L., Barker-Ruchti, N., Patriksson, G., & Lindgren, E. C. (2015). Orthorexia nervosa: An integrative literature review of a lifestyle syndrome. *International Journal of Qualitative Studies on Health and Well-Being*, *10*, 26799. https://doi.org/10.3402/qhw.v10.26799

Hambrook, D., Oldershaw, A., Rimes, K., Schmidt, U., Tchanturia, K., Treasure, J., Richards, S., & Chalder, T. (2011). Emotional expression, self-silencing, and distress tolerance in anorexia nervosa and chronic fatigue syndrome. *British Journal of Clinical Psychology*, *50*(3), 310–325. https://doi.org/10.1348/014466510X519215

Hanganu-Bresch, C. (2020). Orthorexia: Eating right in the context of healthism. *Medical Humanities*, *46*, 311–322.

Harman, A. (2016). Exercising moral authority: The power of guilt in health and fitness discourses. *IJFAB: International Journal of Feminist Approaches to Bioethics*, *9*(2), 12–45. https://doi.org/10.3138/ijfab.9.2.12

Harrison, K. (2003). Television viewers' ideal body proportions: The case of the curvaceously thin woman. *Sex Roles*, *48*, 255–264. https://doi.org/10.1023/A:1022825421647

Harter, S. (2006). The self. In W. Damon & R. M. Lerner (Eds.), *Handbook of child psychology* (6th ed., Vol. 3, pp. 505–570). John Wiley.

Hart, K., & Kenny, M. E. (1997). Adherence to the super woman ideal and eating disorder symptoms among college women. *Sex Roles*, *36*, 461–478.

Haworth-Hoeppner, S. (2000). The critical shapes of body image: The role of culture and family in the production of eating disorders. *Journal of Marriage and Family*, *62*(1), 212–227. https://doi.org/10.1111/j.1741-3737.2000.00212.x

Hay, P. J. (2012). Avoid being 'tyrannised' by the evidence: Reflections on family-based treatment in adolescent anorexia nervosa. *Australian and New Zealand Journal of Psychiatry*, *46*(11), 1102–1103.

Hayes, J. F., Fitzsimmons-Craft, E. E., Karam, A. M., Jakubiak, J., Brown, M. L., & Wilfley, D. E. (2018). Disordered eating attitudes and behaviors in youth with overweight and obesity: Implications for treatment. *Current Obesity Reports*, *7*(3), 235–246. https://doi.org/10.1007/s13679-018-0316-9

Haynos, A. F., & Fruzzetti, A. E. (2011). Anorexia nervosa as a disorder of emotion dysregulation: Evidence and treatment implications. *Clinical Psychology: Science and Practice, 18*(3), 183–202. https://doi.org/10.1111/j.1468-2850.2011.01250.x

Hefner, V., Dorros, S. M., Jourdain, N., Liu, C., Tortomasi, A., Greene, M. P., & Alverez, C. (2016). Mobile exercising and tweeting the pounds away: The use of digital applications and microblogging and their association with disordered eating and compulsive exercise. *Cogent Social Sciences, 2*(1), 1–11.

Heinberg, L. J., Coughlin, J. W., Pinto, A. P., Haug, N., Brode, C., & Guarda, A. S. (2008). Validation and predictive utility of the Sociocultural Attitudes Toward Appearance Questionnaire for Eating Disorders (SATAQ-ED): Internalization of sociocultural ideals predicts weight gain. *Body Image, 5*(3), 279–290. https://doi.org/10.1016/j.bodyim.2008.02.001

Henderson, Z. B., Fox, J. R. E., Trayner, P., & Wittkowski, A. (2019). Emotional development in eating disorders: A qualitative metasynthesis. *Clinical Psychology & Psychotherapy, 26*(4), 440–457. https://doi.org/10.1002/cpp.2365

Hentschel, T., Heilman, M. E., & Peus, C. V. (2019). The multiple dimensions of gender stereotypes: A current look at men's and women's characterizations of others and themselves. *Frontiers in Psychology.* https://doi.org/10.3389/fpsyg.2019.00011

Hepp, U., Spindler, A., & Milos, G. (2005). Eating disorder symptomatology and gender role orientation. *International Journal of Eating Disorders, 37*, 227–233.

Hesse-Biber, S. (1991). Women, weight and eating disorders. *Women's Studies International Forum, 14*(3), 173–191. https://doi.org/10.1016/0277-5395(91)90109-U

Hesse-Biber, S., Leavy, P., Quinn, C. E., & Zoino, J. (2006). The mass marketing of disordered eating and eating disorders: The social psychology of women, thinness and culture. *Women's Studies International Forum, 29*(2), 208–224. https://doi.org/10.1016/j.wsif.2006.03.007

Hillege, S., Beale, B., & McMaster, R. (2006). Impact of eating disorders on family life: Individual parents' stories. *Journal of Clinical Nursing, 15*(8), 1016–1022. https://doi.org/10.1111/j.1365-2702.2006.01367.x

Hines, J. C., Wendorf, W., Hennen, A. N., Hauser, K. L., Mitchell, M. M., & Homa, J. M. (2019). How do lean and non-lean female collegiate athletes view the eating disorder education they receive from their coaches? *International Journal of Sports Science & Coaching, 14*, 169–178.

Hinney, A., Scherag, S., & Hebebrand, J. (2010). Chapter 9 – Genetic findings in anorexia and bulimia nervosa. In C. Bouchard (Ed.), *Progress in molecular biology and translational science* (Vol. 94, pp. 241–270). Academic Press. https://doi.org/10.1016/B978-0-12-375003-7.00009-1

Hipple Walters, B., Adams, S., Broer, T., & Bal, R. (2016). Proud2Bme: Exploratory research on care and control in young women's online eating disorder narratives. *Health, 20*(3), 220–241. https://doi.org/10.1177/1363459315574118

Hoek, H. W., van Harten, P. N., Hermans, K. M., Katzman, M. A., Matroos, G. E., & Susser, E. S. (2005). The incidence of anorexia nervosa on Curaçao. *American Journal of Psychiatry, 162*(4), 748–752. https://doi.org/10.1176/appi.ajp.162.4.748

Hoek, H. W., & van Hoeken, D. (2003). Review of the prevalence and incidence of eating disorders. *International Journal of Eating Disorders, 34*(4), 383–396.

Hoffman, R. M., & Borders, L. D. (2001). Twenty-five years after the Bem Sex-Role Inventory: A reassessment and new issues regarding classification variability. *Measurement and Evaluation in Counseling and Development, 34*, 39–55.

Holland, G., & Tiggemann, M. (2017). "Strong beats skinny every time": Disordered eating and compulsive exercise in women who post fitspiration on Instagram. *International Journal of Eating Disorders, 50*(1), 76–79. https://doi.org/10.1002/eat.22559

Holmes, S. (2014). Between feminism and anorexia: An autoethnography. *International Journal of Cultural Studies.* https://doi.org/10.1177/136787791 4561831

Holmes, S. (2018). Responses to warnings about the impact of eating disorders on fertility: A qualitative study. *Sociology of Health & Illness*, 1–17. https://doi.org/10.1111/1467-9566.12676

Holmes, J. (2019). Anorexia and the Trojan Horse: A reflexive review of written psychoanalytic encounters with anorexic patients. *Journal of Child Psychotherapy, 45*(1), 71–86. https://doi.org/10.1080/0075417X.2019.1617766

Holmes, S., Drake, S., & Odgers, K. (2017). Feminist approaches to anorexia nervosa: A qualitative study of a treatment group. *Journal of Eating Disorders, 5*, 36. https://doi.org/10.1186/s40337-017-0166-y

Hudson, J. I., Hiripi, E., Pope, H. G., Jr., & Kessler, R. C. (2007). The prevalence and correlates of eating disorders in the National Comorbidity Survey Replication. *Biological Psychiatry, 61*(3), 348–358. https://doi.org/10.1016/j.biopsych.2006.03.040

Hughes, E. K. (2012). Comorbid depression and anxiety in childhood and adolescent anorexia nervosa: Prevalence and implications for outcome. *Clinical Psychologist, 16*(1), 15–24. https://doi.org/10.1111/j.1742-9552.2011.00034.x

Hurst, K., & Zimmer-Gembeck, M. (2015). Focus on perfectionism in female adolescent anorexia nervosa. *International Journal of Eating Disorders, 48*(7), 936–941. https://doi.org/10.1002/eat.22417

Jack, D. C., & Dill, D. (1992). The Silencing the Self Scale: Schemas of intimacy associated with depression in women. *Psychology of Women Quarterly, 16*(1), 97–106. https://doi.org/10.1111/j.1471-6402.1992.tb00242.x

Jackson, S. C., Keel, P. K., & Lee, Y. H. (2006). Trans-cultural comparison of disordered eating in Korean women. *International Journal of Eating Disorders, 39*(6), 498–502. https://doi.org/10.1002/eat.20270

Jacquemot, A. M. M. C., & Park, R. (2020). The role of interoception in the pathogenesis and treatment of anorexia nervosa. *A Narrative Review Frontiers in Psychiatry, 11.* https://doi.org/10.3389/fpsyt.2020.00281. https://www.frontiersin.org/articles/10.3389/fpsyt.2020.00281

Jebeile, H., Gow, M. L., Baur, L. A., Garnett, S. P., Paxton, S. J., & Lister, N. B. (2019). Treatment of obesity, with a dietary component, and eating disorder risk in children and adolescents: A systematic review with meta-analysis. *Obesity Reviews: An Official Journal of the International Association for the Study of Obesity, 20*(9), 1287–1298. https://doi.org/10.1111/obr.12866

Jenkins, J., & Ogden, J. (2011). Becoming 'whole' again: A qualitative study of women's views of recovering from anorexia nervosa. *European Eating Disorders Review, 20*(1), e23–e31. https://doi.org/10.1002/erv.1085

Joffe, H. (2011). Thematic analysis. In D. Harper & A. R. Thompson (Eds.), *Qualitative research methods in mental health and psychotherapy: A guide for students and practitioners.* John Wiley & Sons, Ltd. http://doi.org/10.1002/9781119973249.ch15

Jones, A. M., & Buckingham, J. T. (2005). Self-esteem as a moderator of the effect of social comparison on women's body image. *Journal of Social and Clinical Psychology, 24,* 1164–1187.

Jones, D. J., Fox, M. M., Babigian, H. M., & Hutton, H. E. (1980). Epidemiology of anorexia nervosa in Monroe County, New York: 1960–1976. *Psychosomatic Medicine, 42,* 551–558.

Jones, L., Harmer, C., Cowen, P., & Cooper, M. (2008). Emotional face processing in women with high and low levels of eating disorder related symptoms. *Eating Behaviors, 9*(4), 389–397. https://doi.org/10.1016/j.eatbeh.2008.03.001

Jönsson, S., & Lukka, K. (2006). There and back again. Doing interventionist research in management accounting. In C. S. Chapman & A. G. Hopwood (Eds.), *Handbook of management accounting research* (pp. 375–397). Elsevier.

Joshi, R., Herman, C., & Polivy, J. (2004). Self-enhancing effects of exposure to thin-body images. *The International Journal of Eating Disorders, 35,* 333–441. https://doi.org/10.1002/eat.10253

Juarascio, A. S., Shoaib, A., & Timko, C. A. (2010). Pro-eating disorder communities on social networking sites: A content analysis. *Eating Disorders, 18*(5), 393–407. https://doi.org/10.1080/10640266.2010.511918

Jureković, I. (2021). Internetsko ponašanje osoba oboljelih od poremećaja hranjenja: kvalitativna studija (Diplomski rad). https://urn.nsk.hr/urn:nbn:hr:131:616708

Kakhi, S., & McCann, J. (2016, November/December). Psych Anorexia nervosa: Diagnosis, risk factors and evidence-based treatments. *Progress in Neurology and Psychiatry, 20*(6), 24–29c.

Kalm, L. M., & Semba, R. D. (2005). They starved so that others be better fed: Remembering Ancel Keys and the Minnesota experiment. *The Journal of Nutrition, 135,* 1347–1352.

Karsay, K., & Schmuck, D. (2019). "Weak, sad, and lazy fatties": Adolescents' explicit and implicit weight bias following exposure to weight loss reality TV shows. *Media Psychology, 22,* 60. https://doi.org/10.1080/15213269.2017.1396903

Katzman, M. A., Hermans, K. M., Van Hoeken, D., & Hoek, H. W. (2004). Not your "typical island woman": Anorexia nervosa is reported only in subcultures in Curaçao. *Culture Medicine and Psychiatry, 28*(4), 463–492. https://doi.org/10.1007/s11013-004-1065-7

Katzman, M. A., & Lee, S. (1997). Beyond body image: The integration of feminist and transcultural theories in the understanding of self starvation. *International Journal of Eating Disorders, 22*(4), 385–394. https://doi.org/10.1002/(sici)1098-108x(199712)22:4<385::aid-eat3>3.0.co;2-i

Katzmarzyk, P. T., & Davis, C. (2001). Thinness and body shape of Playboy centerfolds from 1978 to 1998. *International Journal of Obesity, 25,* 590–592.

Keel, P. K., & Forney, K. J. (2013). Psychosocial risk factors for eating disorders. *International Journal of Eating Disorders, 46*(5), 433–439.

Keel, P. K., & Klump, K. L. (2003). Are eating disorders culture-bound syndromes? Implications for conceptualizing their etiology. *Psychological Bulletin, 129,* 747–769.

Kelly, M. (2016). The nutrition transition in developing Asia: Dietary change, drivers and health impacts. In *Eating, Drinking: Surviving* (pp. 83–90). https://doi.org/10.1007/978-3-319-42468-2_9

Kent, L. (2001). Fighting abjection: Representing fat women. In J. E. Braziel & K. Le Besco (Ed.), *Bodies out of bounds, fatness and transgressions*. University of California Press.

Kerr-Gaffney, J., Mason, L., Jones, E., Hayward, H., Ahmad, J., Harrison, A., Loth, E., Murphy, D., & Tchanturia, K. (2020). Emotion recognition abilities in adults with anorexia nervosa are associated with autistic traits. *Journal of Clinical Medicine, 9*(4), 1057. https://doi.org/10.3390/jcm9041057

Keski-Rahkonen, A. (2007). Epidemiology and course of anorexia nervosa in the community. *American Journal of Psychiatry, 164*(8), 1259–1265. https://doi.org/10.1176/appi.ajp.2007.06081388

Keski-Rahkonen, A., Hoek, H. W., Linna, M. S., Raevuori, A., Sihvola, E., Bulik, C. M., Rissanen, A., & Kaprio, J. (2008). Incidence and outcomes of bulimia nervosa: A nationwide population-based study. *Psychological Medicine, 39*(5), 823–831. https://doi.org/10.1017/S0033291708003942

Keys, A., Brozek, J., Henshel, A., Mickelson, O., & Taylor, H. L. (1950). *The biology of human starvation* (pp. 1–2). University of Minnesota Press.

Khalsa, S. S., Craske, M. G., Li, W., Vangala, S., Strober, M., & Feusner, J. D. (2015, November). Altered interoceptive awareness in anorexia nervosa: Effects of meal anticipation, consumption and bodily arousal. *International Journal of Eating Disorders, 48*(7), 889–897. https://doi.org/10.1002/eat.22387

Khalsa, S. S., Craske, M. G., Li, W., Vangala, S., Strober, M., & Feusner, J. D. (2015). Altered interoceptive awareness in anorexia nervosa: Effects of meal anticipation, consumption and bodily. *International Journal of Eating Disorders.*

Kim, Y., Landgraf, A., & Colabianchi, N. (2020). Living in high-SES neighborhoods is protective against obesity among higher-income children but not low-income children: Results from the healthy communities study. *Journal of Urban Health, 97*(2), 175. https://doi-org.ezproxy.nsk.hr/10.1007/s11524-020-00427-9

Kinzl, J. F., Hauer, K., Traweger, C., & Kiefer, I. (2006). Orthorexia nervosa in dieticians. *Psychotherapy and Psychosomatics, 75*, 395–396. https://doi.org/10.1159/000095447

Kleiman, S. C., Carroll, I. M., Tarantino, L. M., & Bulik, C. M. (2015). Gut feelings: A role for the intestinal microbiota in anorexia nervosa? *International Journal of Eating Disorders, 48*, 449–451.

Kluck, A. (2008). Family factors in the development of disordered eating: Integrating dynamic and behavioral explanations. *Eating Behaviors, 9*, 471–483.

Kolnes, L. J. (2012). Embodying the body in anorexia nervosa–a physiotherapeutic approach. *Journal of Bodywork and Movement Therapies, 16*(3), 281–288. http://www.ncbi.nlm.nih.gov/pubmed/22703737

Kolnes, L. J. (2016). 'Feelings stronger than reason': Conflicting experiences of exercise in women with anorexia nervosa. *Journal of Eating Disorders, 4*, 6. https://doi.org/10.1186/s40337-016-0100-8

Korn, J., Vocks, S., Rollins, L. H., Thomas, J. J., & Hartmann, A. S. (2020). Fat-phobic and non-fat-phobic anorexia nervosa: A conjoint analysis on the importance of shape and weight. *Frontiers in Psychology.* https://doi.org/10.3389/fpsyg.2020.00090

Koubaa, S., Hallstrom, T., & Hirschberg, A. L. (2008). Early maternal adjustment in women with eating disorders. *International Journal of Eating Disorders, 41*, 405–410.

Kouris-Blazos, A., & Wahlqvist, M. L. (2007). Health economics of weight management: Evidence and cost. *Asia Pacific Journal of Clinical Nutrition, 16*(Suppl. 1), 329–338.

Koutek, J., Kocourkova, J., & Dudova, I. (2016). Suicidal behavior and self-harm in girls with eating disorders. *Neuropsychiatric Disease and Treatment, 12*, 787–793. https://doi.org/10.2147/NDT.S103015

Kozak, M., Frankenhauser, H., & Roberts, T. A. (2009). Objects of desire: Objectification as a function of male sexual orientation. *Psychology of Men & Masculinity, 10*(3), 225–230. https://doi.org/10.1037/a0016257

Krafchek, J. (2017). *Stress and coping in academically high-achieving females before the onset of disordered eating: The role of academic achievement.* Thesis, Monash University. https://doi.org/10.4225/03/594b51e0f38b2

Kravvariti, V., & Gonidakis, F. (2016). Eating disorders and sexual function. *Psychiatriki, 27*(2), 136–143. https://doi.org/10.22365/jpsych.2016.272.136

Kristeva, J. (1982). *Powers of horror. An essay on abjection.* Columbia University Press.

Kvale, S., & Brinkmann, S. (2009). *Interviews: Learning the craft of qualitative research interviewing* (2nd ed.). Sage Publications, Inc.

La Mela, C., Maglietta, M., Castellini, G., Amoroso, L., & Lucarelli, S. (2009). Dissociation in eating disorders: Relationship between dissociative experiences and binge-eating episodes. *Comprehensive Psychiatry, 51*(4), 393–400. https://doi.org/10.1016/j.comppsych.2009.09.008

LaMarre, A., Rice, C., & Bear, M. (2015). Unrecoverable? Prescriptions and possibilities for eating disorder recovery. In N. Khanlou & F. B. Pilkington (Eds.), *Women's mental health: Resistance and resilience in community and society* (pp. 145–160). Springer International Publishing. https://doi.org/10.1007/978-3-319-17326-9_10

Lamoureux, M. M. H., & Bottorff, J. L. (2005). "Becoming the real me": Recovering from anorexia nervosa. *Health Care for Women International, 26*(2), 170–188. https://doi.org/10.1080/07399330590905602

Lavis, A. (2014). Materialities and metaphors of fat in the lived experiences of individuals with anorexia. In C. E. Forth & A. Leitch (Eds.), *Fat: Culture and materiality.* Bloomsbury.

Lavis, A. (2018). Not eating or tasting other ways to live: A qualitative analysis of 'living through' and desiring to maintain anorexia. *Transcultural Psychiatry, 55*(4), 454–474. https://doi.org/10.1177/1363461518785796

Lawrence, M. (2008). *The anorexic mind.* Karnac Books.

Le Gallais, T. (2008). Wherever I go there I am: Reflections on reflexivity and the research stance. *Reflective Practice, 9*(2), 145–155. https://doi.org/10.1080/14623940802005475

Le Grange, D., Lock, J., Loeb, K., & Nicholls, D. (2010). Academy for eating disorders position paper: The role of the family in eating disorders. *International Journal of Eating Disorders, 43*(1), 1.

LeBesco, K. (2004). *Revolting bodies? The struggle to redefine fat identity.* University of Massachusetts Press.

LeBesco, K., & Braziel, J. E. (2001). Editor's introduction. In J. E. Braziel & K. LeBesco (Eds.), *Bodies out of bounds. Fatness and transgression* (pp. 1–13). University of California Press.

Lee, S., Ho, T. P., & Hsu, L. K. (1993). Fat phobic and non-fat phobic anorexia nervosa: A comparative study of 70 Chinese patients in Hong Kong. *Psychological Medicine, 23*(4), 999–1017.

Lee, S., & Lee, A. M. (2000). Disordered eating in three communities of China: A comparative study of female high school students in Hong Kong, Shenzhen, and rural Hunan. *International Journal of Eating Disorders, 27*(3), 317–327. https://doi.org/10.1002/(sici)1098-108x(200004)27:3<317::aid-eat9>3.0.co;2-2

Leslie, M., Lambert, E., & Treasure, J. (2019). Towards a translational approach to food addiction: Implications for bulimia nervosa. *Current Addiction Reports, 6,* 258–265. https://doi.org/10.1007/s40429-019-00264-0

Levine, M. P. (2012). Loneliness and eating disorders. *Journal of Psychology, 146*(1–2), 243–257. https://doi.org/10.1080/00223980.2011.606435

Levine, M. P., & McVey, G. L. (2015). Prevention, prevention science, and an ecological perspective: A framework for programs, research, and policy. In D. Beck-Ellsworth (Ed.), *Understanding eating disorders: Risk factors, diagnosis, treatment and recovery (Part VI: Introduction Staying off the path: A world without eating disorders)* (pp. 269–291). Cognella Academic Publishing.

Levine, M. P., & Murnen, S. K. (2009). "Everybody knows that mass media are/are not [pick one] a cause of eating disorders": A critical review of evidence for a causal link between media, negative body image, and disordered eating in females. *Journal of Social and Clinical Psychology, 28*(1), 9–42. https://doi.org/10.1521/jscp.2009.28.1.9

Levine, M. P., & Smolak, L. (1992). Toward a model of the developmental psychopathology of eating disorders: The example of early adolescence. In J. H. Crowther, D. L. Tennenbaum, S. E. Hobfoll, & M. A. P. Stephens (Eds.), *The etiology of bulimia nervosa: The individual and familial context* (pp. 59–80). Hemisphere Publishing Corp.

Levine, M. P., & Smolak, L. (1996). Media as a context for the development of disordered eating. In L. Smolak, M. P. Levine, & R. Striegel-Moore (Eds.), *The developmental psychopathology of eating disorders: Implications for research, prevention, and treatment* (pp. 235–257). Lawrence Erlbaum Associates.

Levinson, C. A., Fewell, L., & Brosof, L. C. (2017). My Fitness Pal calorie tracker usage in the eating disorders. *Eating Behaviors, 27,* 14–16.

Levinson, C. A., Fewell, L., & Brosof, L. C. (2017, December). My Fitness Pal calorie tracker usage in the eating disorders. *Eating Behaviors, 27,* 14–16. https://doi.org/10.1016/j.eatbeh.2017.08.003

Levitt, J. L. (2007). Treating eating disorder patients who have had traumatic experiences: A self-regulatory approach. *Eating Disorders, 15,* 359–372.

Lichtenstein, M. B., Christiansen, E., Elklit, A., Bilenberg, N., & Støving, R. K. (2014). Exercise addiction: A study of eating disorder symptoms, quality of life, personality traits and attachment styles. *Psychiatry Research, 215*(2), 410–416. https://doi.org/10.1016/j.psychres.2013.11.010

Lilienfeld, S. O., Ritschel, L. A., Lynn, S. J., Cautin, R. L., & Latzman, R. D. (2013). Why many clinical psychologists are resistant to evidence-based practice: Root causes and constructive remedies. *Clinical Psychology Review, 33*(7), 883–900. https://doi.org/10.1016/j.cpr.2012.09.008

Li, N. P., Smith, A. R., Yong, J. C., & Brown, T. A. (2014). Intrasexual competition and other theories of eating restriction. In V. A. Weekes-Shackelford & T. K. Shackelford (Eds.), *Evolutionary perspectives on human sexual psychology and behavior, evolutionary psychology* (Vol. 2014, pp. 323–346). Springer Science Business Media. https://doi.org/10.1007/978-1-4939-0314-6_17

Lloyd, S., Yiend, J., Schmidt, U., & Tchanturia, K. (2014). Perfectionism in anorexia nervosa: Novel performance based evidence. *PLoS One, 9*(10), e111697. https://doi.org/10.1371/journal.pone.0111697

Lock, J., & Le Grange, D. (2015). *Treatment manual for anorexia nervosa: A family-based approach* (2nd ed.). Guilford Publications.

Lock, J., & Le Grange, D. (2018). Family-based treatment: Where are we and where should we be going to improve recovery in child and adolescent eating disorders. *International Journal of Eating Disorders, 52*(4), 481–487.

Logrieco, G., Marchili, M. R., Roversi, M., & Villani, A. (2021, January 25). The paradox of Tik Tok anti-pro-anorexia videos: How social media can promote non-suicidal self-injury and anorexia. *International Journal of Environmental Research and Public Health, 18*(3), 1041. https://doi.org/10.3390/ijerph18031041

Lois, J. (2010). The emporal emotion work of motherhood: Homeschoolers' strategies for managing time shortage. *Gender & Society, 24*(4), 421–446. http://doi.org/10.1177/0891243210377762

Longhurst, R. (2012). Becoming smaller: Autobiographical spaces of weight loss. *Antipode, 44*(3), 871–888.

Long, S., Wallis, D., Leung, N., & Meyer, C. (2011). 'All eyes are on you': Anorexia nervosa patientperspectives of in-patient mealtimes. *Journal of Health Psychology, 17*(3), 419–428. https://doi.org/10.1177/1359105311419270

Lupton, D. (1996). *Food, the body and the self.* Sage.

da Luz, F. Q., Hay, P., Touyz, S., & Sainsbury, A. (2018). Obesity with comorbid eating disorders: Associated health risks and treatment approaches. *Nutrients, 10*(7), 829. https://doi.org/10.3390/nu10070829

MacArthur, H. J. (2019). Beliefs about emotion are tied to beliefs about gender: The case of men's crying in competitive sports. *Frontiers in Psychology, 10*, 2765. https://doi.org/10.3389/fpsyg.2019.02765

MacKay, K. (2020). The 'tyranny of reproduction': Could ectogenesis further women's liberation? *Bioethics, 34*(4), 346–353. https://doi.org/10.1111/bioe.12706

Maclaran, P., & Kravets, O. (2018). *Feminist perspectives in marketing: Past, present, and future.* Routledge.

Madden, S. (2015). Biopsychiatric theories of eating disorders. In M. P. Levine & L. Smolak (Eds.), *The Wiley handbook of eating disorders* (Vol. 1, pp. 25–39). Wiley.

Madden, S., Miskovic-Wheatley, J., Wallis, A., Kohn, M., Lock, J., Le Grange, D., Jo, B., Clarke, S., Rhodes, P., Hay, P., & Touyz, S. (2015). A randomized controlled trial of in-patient treatment for anorexia nervosa in medically unstable adolescents. *Psychological Medicine, 45*(2), 415–427. https://doi.org/10.1017/S0033291714001573

Madowitz, J., Matheson, B. E., & Liang, J. (2015, September). The relationship between eating disorders and sexual trauma. *Eating and Weight Disorders, 20*(3), 281–293. https://doi.org/10.1007/s40519-015-0195-y

Mahalik, J. R., Morray, E. B., Coonerty-Femiano, A., Ludlow, L. H., Slattery, S. M., & Smiler, A. (2005). Development of the conformity to feminine norms inventory. *Sex Roles, 52*(7–8), 417–435.

Maine, M., & Bunnell, D. W. (2010). A perfect biopsychosocial storm: Gender, culture, and eating disorders. In M. Maine, B. H. McGilley, & D. W. Bunnell (Eds.), *Treatment of eating disorders: Bridging the research–practice gap* (pp. 3–16). Elsevier Academic Press. https://doi.org/10.1016/B978-0-12-375668-8.10001-4. ISBN 9780123756688.

Malson, H. (1998). *The thin woman: Feminism, post-structuralism and the social psychology of anorexia nervosa.* Routledge.

Malson, H. (2008). Deconstructing un/healthy body-weight and weight management. In *Critical Bodies* (pp. 27–42). Palgrave Macmillan. https://doi.org/10.1057/9780230591141_2

Malson, H. (2009). Appearing to disappear: Postmodern feminities and self-starved subjectivities. In H. Malson & M. Burns (Eds.), *Critical feminist perspectives on eating dis/orders* (pp. 135–145). Routledge.

Malson, H., Bailey, L., Clarke, S., Treasure, J., Anderson, G., & Kohn, M. (2011). Un/imaginable future selves: A discourse analysis of in-patients' talk about recovery from an 'eating disorder. *European Eating Disorders Review, 19*(1), 25–36. https://doi.org/10.1002/erv.1011

Malson, H., & Burns, M. (2009). Re-theorising the slash of dis-order: An introduction to critical feminist approaches to eating dis/orders. In H. Malson & M. Burns (Eds.), *Critical feminist approaches to eating dis/orders* (pp. 1–6). Routledge.

Malson, H., Riley, S., & Markula, P. (2009). Beyond psychopathology: Interrogating (Dis)orders of body weight and body management. *Journal of Community and Applied Social Psychology, 19*(5), 331–335. https://doi.org/10.1002/casp.1019

Malson, H., & Ussher, J. M. (1996). Body poly-texts: Discourses of the anorexic body. *Journal of Community and Applied Social Psychology, 6,* 267–280.

Marques, C., Simão, M., Guiomar, R., & Castilho, P. (2021). Self-disgust and urge to be thin in eating disorders: How can self-compassion help? *Eating and Weight Disorders.* https://doi.org/10.1007/s40519-020-01099-9

Martino, S., & Lauriano, S. (2013). Feminist identity and the superwoman ideal. *Journal of Behavioral Health, 2*(2), 167–172.

Martín, J., Padierna, A., van Wijngaarden, B., Aguirre, U., Anton, A., Muñoz, P., & Quintana, J. M. (2015). Caregivers consequences of care among patients with eating disorders, depression or schizophrenia. *BMC Psychiatry, 15,* 124. https://doi.org/10.1186/s12888-015-0507-9

Mattar, L., Thiébaud, M.-R., Huas, C., Cebula, C., & Godart, N. (2012). Depression, anxiety and obsessive–compulsive symptoms in relation to nutritional status and outcome in severe anorexia nervosa. *Psychiatry Research, 200,* 513–517.

Mc Arthur, H. J. (2019). Beliefs about emotion are tied to beliefs about gender: The case of men's crying in competitive sports. *Frontiers in Psychology.* https://doi.org/10.3389/fpsyg.2019.02765

McGee, B. J., Hewitt, P. L., Sherry, S. B., Parkin, M., & Flett, G. L. (2005). Perfectionistic self-presentation, body image, and eating disorder symptoms. *Body Image, 2*(1), 29–40. https://doi.org/10.1016/j.bodyim.2005.01.002

McGovern, L., Gaffney, M., & Trimble, T. (2020) The experience of orthorexia from the perspective of recovered orthorexics. *Eating and Weight Disorders – Studies on Anorexia, Bulimia and Obesity*. https://doi.org/10.1007/s40519-020-00928-1

McRobbie, A. (2009). *The aftermath of feminism: Gender, culture and social change*. Sage Publications Ltd.

McRobbie, A. (2015). Notes on the Perfect. *Australian Feminist Studies, 30*(83), 3–20. https://doi.org/10.1080/08164649.2015.1011485

Mehler, P. S., & Brown, C. (2015). Anorexia nervosa – Medical complications. *Journal of Eating Disorders, 3*(11). https://doi.org/10.1186/s40337-015-0040-8

Mehler, P. S., & Rylander, M. (2015). Bulimia nervosa – Medical complications. *Journal of Eating Disorders, 3*(12). https://doi.org/10.1186/s40337-015-0044-4

Mellon, C. (1990). *Naturalistic inquiry for library science: Methods and applications for research, evaluation, and teaching*: Greenwood.

Memon, A. N., Gowda, A. S., Rallabhandi, B., Bidika, E., Fayyaz, H., Salib, M., & Cancarevic, I. (2020). Have our attempts to curb obesity done more harm than good? *Cureus, 12*(9), e10275. https://doi.org/10.7759/cureus.10275

Mencias, T., Noon, M., & Hoch, A. Z. (2012). Female athlete triad screening in National Collegiate Athletic Association Division I athletes: Is the preparticipation evaluation form effective? *Clinical Journal of Sport Medicine, 22*, 122–125.

Mensinger, J. L., Bonifazi, D. Z., & LaRosa, J. (2007). Perceived gender role prescriptions in schools, the superwoman ideal, and disordered eating among adolescent girls. *Seks Roles, 57*, 557–568.

Mento, C., Silvestri, M. C., Muscatello, M. R. A., Rizzo, A., Celebre, L., Praticò, M., Zoccali, R. A., & Bruno, A. (2021, February 23). Psychological impact of pro-anorexia and pro-eating disorder websites on adolescent females: A systematic review. *International Journal of Environmental Research and Public Health, 18*(4), 2186. https://doi.org/10.3390/ijerph18042186

Micali, N., Hagberg, K. W., Petersen, I., & Treasure, J. L. (2013). The incidence of eating disorders in the UK in 2000–2009: Findings from the General Practice Research Database. *BMJ Open, 3*(5), e002646. https://doi.org/10.1136/bmjopen-2013-002646

Miles, M. B., Huberman, A. M., & Saldana, J. (2019). *Qualitative data analysis a methods sourcebook* (4th ed.). Arizona State University.

Miller, K. (2016). *The shocking results of Yahoo health's body-positivity survey*. https://www.yahoo.com/lifestyle/the-shockingresults-of-yahoo-1332510105509942.html?guccounter=1. Accessed on January 15, 2019.

Miller, M. N., & Pumariega, A. J. (2001). Culture and eating disorders: A historical and cross-cultural review. *Psychiatry: Interpersonal and Biological Processes, 64*(2), 93–110. https://doi.org/10.1521/psyc.64.2.93.18621

Minichiello, V., Aroni, R., & Hays, T. (2008). *In-depth interviewing* (3rd ed.). Pearson Education Australia.

Minuchin, S., & Fishman, C. (1981). *Family therapy techniques* (pp. 28–49). Harvard University Press.

Minuchin, S., Rosman, B. L., & Baker, L. (1978). *Psychosomatic families: Anorexia nervosa in context*. Harvard University Press.

Moola, F. J., Gairdner, S., & Amara, C. (2015). Speaking on behalf of the body and activity: Investigating the activity experiences of Canadian women living with

anorexia nervosa. *Mental Health and Physical Activity*, *8*, 44–55. https://doi.org/
10.1016/j.mhpa.2015.02.002

Mora, F., Rojo, S. F., Banzo, C., & Quintero, J. (2017). The impact of self-esteem on eating disorders. *European Psychiatry*, *41*, S558. https://doi.org/10.1016/j.eurpsy.2017.01.802

Moroze, R. M., Dunn, T. M., Holland, J. C., Yager, J., & Weintraub, P. (2014). Microthinking about micronutrients: A case of transition from obsessions about healthy eating to near-fatal "orthorexia nervosa" and proposed diagnostic criteria. *Psychosomatics*, *56*(4), 397–403. https://doi.org/10.1016/j.psym.2014.03.003

Morse, J. M. (2000). Determining sample size. *Qualitative Health Research*, *10*, 3–5. https://doi.org/10.1177/104973200129118183

Mortimer, R. (2019). Pride before a fall: Shame, diagnostic crossover, and eating disorders. *Bioethical Inquiry*, *16*, 365–374. https://doi.org/10.1007/s11673-019-09923-3

Moulding, N. T. (2016). Gendered intersubjectivities in narratives of recovery from an eating disorder. *Journal of Women and Social Work*, *31*(1), 70–83. https://doi.org/10.1177/0886109915576519

Mulders-Jones, B., Mitchison, D., Girosi, F., & Hay, P. (2017). Socioeconomic correlates of eating disorder symptoms in an Australian population-based sample. *PLoS One*, *12*(1), e0170603. https://doi.org/10.1371/journal.pone.0170603

Mumford, L. (1961). Forum, vomitorium, bath. In *The city in history*. Harcourt Brace Jovanovich Inc.

Munro, C., Randell, L., & Lawrie, S. M. (2017). An integrative bio-psycho-social theory of anorexia nervosa. *Clinical Psychology & Psychotherapy*, *24*(1), 1–21. https://doi.org/10.1002/cpp.2047

Murray, T. R. (2001). *Recent theories of human development*. Sage Publications.

Murray, S. B., Pila, E., Mond, J. M., Mitchison, D., Blashill, A. J., Sabiston, C. M., & Griffiths, S. (2018). Cheat meals: A benign or ominous variant of binge eating behavior? *Appetite*, *130*, 274–278. https://doi.org/10.1016/j.appet.2018.08.026

Murray, S. B., Rieger, E., & Touyz, S. W. (2010). Muscle dysmorphia and the DSM-V conundrum: Where does it belong? A review paper. *International Journal of Eating Disorders*, *43*, 483–491.

Musolino, C., Warin, M., & Gilchrist, P. (2018). Positioning relapse and recovery through a cultural lens of desire: A South Australian case study of disordered eating. *Transcultural Psychiatry*, *55*(4), 534–550. https://doi.org/10.1177/1363461518778669

Musolino, C., Warin, M., Wade, T., & Gilchrist, P. (2015). 'Healthy anorexia': The complexity of care in disordered eating. *Social Science & Medicine*, *139*, 18–25. https://doi.org/10.1016/j.socscimed.2015.06.030

Nagata, J. M., Ganson, K. T., & Murray, S. B. (2020). Eating disorders in adolescent boys and young men: An update. *Current Opinion in Pediatrics*, *32*(4), 476–481. https://doi.org/10.1097/MOP.0000000000000911

Nandy, A. (1988). *Science, hegemony and violence: A requiem for modernity*. Oxford University Press.

Nasser, M. A. (1993). A prescription of vomiting: Historical footnotes. *International Journal of Eating Disorders*, *13*, 129–131.

Nasser, M., Katzman, M., & Gordon, R. (2001). *Eating disorders and cultures in transition*. Taylor & Francis.

National Institute for Health and Excellence UK. (2017). *Eating disorders: Recognition and treatment.* NICE guideline [NG69]. https://www.nice.org.uk/ guidance/ng69

NEDA. Orthorexia. (2018). https://www.nationaleatingdisorders.org/learn/byeating-disorder/other/orthorexia. Accessed on August 3, 2019.

Nefeli, K., & Giovazolias, T. (2010). The effect of attachment insecurity in the development of eating disturbances across gender: The role of body dissatisfaction. *The Journal of Psychology: Interdisciplinary and Applied, 144*(5), 449–471.

Neumark-Sztainer, D. (2005). Can we simultaneously work toward the prevention of obesity and eating disorders in children and adolescents? *International Journal of Eating Disorders, 38*(3), 220–227. https://doi.org/10.1002/eat.20181

Nevin, S. M., & Vartanian, L. R. (2017). The stigma of clean dieting and orthorexia nervosa. *Journal of Eating Disorders, 5,* 37. https://doi.org/10.1186/s40337-017-0168-9

Nicholls, D., Statham, R., Costa, S., Micali, N., & Viner, R. M. (2016). Childhood risk factors for lifetime bulimic or compulsive eating by age 30 years in a British national birth cohort. *Appetite, 105,* 266–273. https://doi-org.ezproxy.nsk.hr/ 10.1016/j.appet.2016.05.036

Nicolosi, G. (2006). Biotechnologies, alimentary fears and the orthorexic society. *Tailoring Biotechnologies, 2*(3), 37–56.

NIMH National Institute for Mental Health, NCS-R: 2001–2003. https:// www.nimh.nih.gov/health/statistics/eating-disorders

Nordbø, R. H., Espeset, E. M., Gulliksen, K. S., Skårderud, F., & Holte, A. (2006). The meaning of selfstarvation: Qualitative study of patients' perception of anorexia nervosa. *International Journal of Eating Disorders, 39,* 556–564.

Nordbø, R. H. S., Espeset, E. M. S., Gulliksen, K. S., Skårderud, F., Geller, J., & Holte, A. (2012). Reluctance to recover in anorexia nervosa. *European Eating Disorders Review, 20*(1), 60–67. https://doi.org/10.1002/erv.1097

Norwood, S. J., Bowker, A., Buchholz, A., Henderson, K. A., Goldfield, G., & Flament, M. F. (2011). Self-silencing and anger regulation as predictors of disordered eating among adolescent females. *Eating Behaviors, 12*(2), 112–118. https://doi.org/10.1016/j.eatbeh.2011.01.009

Nunn, K., Frampton, I., Fuglset, T. S., Törzsök-Sonnevend, M., & Lask, B. (2011). Anorexia nervosa and the insula. *Medical Hypotheses, 76*(3), 353–357. https:// doi.org/10.1016/j.mehy.2010.10.038

Nunn, K., Frampton, I., Gordon, I., & Lask, B. (2008). The fault is not in her parents but in her insula—A neurobiological hypothesis of anorexia nervosa. *European Eating Disorders Review, 16*(5), 355–360. https://doi.org/10.1002/erv.890

O'Shaughnessy, R., & Dallos, R. (2009). Attachment research and eating disorders: A review of the literature. *Clinical Child Psychology and Psychiatry, 14*(4), 559–574. https://doi.org/10.1177/1359104509339082

O'Connor, R. A., & Van Esterik, P. (2008). De-medicalizing anorexia: A new cultural brokering. *Anthropology Today, 24*(5), 6–9. https://doi.org/10.1111/j.1467-8322.2008.00611.x

Odgers, C. L., & Jensen, M. R. (2020, June). Adolescent development and growing divides in the digital age. *Dialogues in Clinical Neuroscience, 22*(2), 143–149. https://doi.org/10.31887/DCNS.2020.22.2/codgers

O'Hara, L., & Taylor, J. (2018). What's wrong with the 'war on obesity?' A narrative review of the weight-centered health paradigm and development of the 3C framework to build critical competency for a paradigm shift. *SAGE Open*, 1–28. https://doi.org/10.1177/2158244018772888

Oldershaw, A., Lavender, T., Sallis, H., Stahl, D., & Schmidt, U. (2015). Emotion generation and regulation in anorexia nervosa: A systematic review and meta-analysis of self-report data. *Clinical Psychology Review*, *39*, 83–95. https://doi.org/10.1016/j.cpr.2015.04.005

Oldershaw, A., Startup, H., & Lavender, T. (2019). Anorexia nervosa and a lost emotional self: A psychological formulation of the development, maintenance, and treatment of anorexia nervosa. *Frontiers in Psychology*, *10*, 219. https://doi.org/10.3389/fpsyg.2019.00219

Orbach, S. (1986). *Hunger strike: The Anorectic's struggle as a metaphor for our age*. Faber & Faber.

Orbach, S. (2009). *Bodies*. Picador.

Orbach, I., & Mikulincer, M. (1998). The Body Investment Scale: Construction and validation of a body experience scale. *Psychological Assessment*, *10*(4), 415–425. https://doi.org/10.1037/1040-3590.10.4.415

Orsini, G. (2017) "Hunger hurts, but starving works". The moral conversion to eating disorders. *Culture Medicine and Psychiatry*, *41*(1), 111–141. https://doi.org/10.1007/s11013-016-9507-6

Overstreet, N. M., Quinn, D. M., & Agovha, V. B. (2010). Beyond thinness: The influence of a curvaceous body ideal on body dissatisfaction in Black and White women. *Sex Roles*, *63*, 91–103. https://doi.org/10.1007/s11199-010-9792-4

Pacanowski, C. R., Pisetsky, E. M., Berg, K. C., Crosby, R. D., Crow, S. J., Linde, J. A., Mitchell, J. E., Engel, S. G., Klein, M. H., Smith, T. L., Le Grange, D., Wonderlich, S. A., & Peterson, C. B. (2016, August). Self-weighing behavior in individuals with eating disorders. *International Journal of Eating Disorders*, *49*(8), 817–821. https://doi.org/10.1002/eat.22537

Palazzoli, M. S. (1985). Anorexia nervosa: A syndrome of the affluent society. *Journal of Strategic & Systemic Therapies*, *4*(3), 12–16. https://doi.org/10.1521/jsst.1985.4.3.12

Palmeira, L., Pinto-Gouveia, J., & Cunha, M. (2016). The role of weight self-stigma on the quality of life of women with overweight and obesity: A multi-group comparison between binge eaters and non-binge eaters. *Appetite*. https://doi-org.ezproxy.nsk.hr/10.1016/j.appet.2016.07.015

Palmer, L. C. (2008). Crossing the Color Line. *Journal of Feminist Family Therapy*, *19*(4), 21–41. https://doi.org/10.1300/J086v19n04_02

Park, J., Lee, D. S., Shablack, H., Verduyn, P., Deldin, P., Ybarra, O., Jonides, J., & Kross, E. (2016). When perceptions defy reality: The relationships between depression and actual and perceived Facebook social support. *Journal of Affective Disorders*, *200*, 37–44. http://doi.org/10.1016/j.jad.2016.01.048

Parkes, C. M. (1995). Guidelines for conducting ethical bereavement research. *Death Studies*, *19*(2), 171–181.

Parry-Jones, B., & Parry-Jones, W. L. (1991). Bulimia: An archival review of its history in psychosomatic medicine. *International Journal of Eating Disorders*, *10*(2), 129–143. https://doi.org/10.1002/1098-108X(199103)10:2<129::AID-EAT2260100202>3.0.CO;2-I

Parsons, T. (1959). The social structure of the family. In R. N. Anshen (Ed.), *The family: Its functions and destiny*. Harper and Row.

Patching, J., & Lawler, J. (2009). Understanding women's experiences of developing an eating disorder and recovering: A life-history approach. *Nursing Inquiry, 16*(1), 10–21. https://doi.org/10.1111/j.1440-1800.2009.00436.x

Patton, G. C., Selzer, R., Coffey, C., Carlin, J. B., & Wolfe, R. (1999). Onset of adolescent eating disorders: Population based cohort study over 3 years. *BMJ (Clinical Research Ed.), 318*(7186), 765–768. https://doi.org/10.1136/bmj.318.7186.765

Paxton, S. J., & Sculthorpe, A. (1991). Disordered eating and sex role characteristics in young women: Implications for sociocultural theories of disturbed eating. *Sex Roles, 24*, 587–598. https://doi.org/10.1007/BF00288415

Peebles, R., Wilson, J. L., & Lock, J. D. (2011, March). Self-injury in adolescents with eating disorders: Correlates and provider bias. *Journal of Adolescent Health, 48*(3), 310–313. https://doi.org/10.1016/j.jadohealth.2010.06.017

Pemberton, M. (2017). Horrifying toll the clean eating fad is taking on young women. Daily Mail. http://www.dailymail.co.uk/health/article-4709100/Horrifying-toll-clean-eating-fad-taking-young-women.html

Pennesi, J. L., & Wade, T. D. (2016). A systematic review of the existing models of disordered eating: Do they inform the development of effective interventions? *Clinical Psychology Review, 43*, 175–192. https://doi.org/10.1016/j.cpr.2015.12.004

Perloff, R. M. (2014). Social media effects on young women's body image concerns: Theoretical perspectives and an agenda for research. *Sex Roles, 71*(11–12), 363–377. https://doi.org/10.1007/s11199-014-0384-6

Petersson, S., Gullbing, L., & Perseius, K. I. (2021). Just like fireworks in my brain – A Swedish interview study on experiences of emotions in female patients with eating disorders. *Journal of Eating Disorders, 9*(1), 24. https://doi.org/10.1186/s40337-021-00371-2

Phillipou, A., Rossell, S. L., Castle, D. J., & Gurvich, C. (2022). Interoceptive awareness in anorexia nervosa. *Journal of Psychiatric Research, 148*, 84–87. https://doi.org/10.1016/j.jpsychires.2022.01.051

Pike, K. M., & Borovoy, A. (2004). The rise of eating disorders in Japan: Issues of culture and limitations of the model of "westernization". *Culture Medicine and Psychiatry, 28*(4), 493–531.

Pike, K. M., & Dunne, P. E. (2015). The rise of eating disorders in Asia: A review. *Journal of Eating Disorders, 3*, 33. https://doi.org/10.1186/s40337-015-0070-2

Piran, N. (2010). A feminist perspective on risk factor research and on the prevention of eating disorders. *The Journal of Treatment & Prevention, 18*(3), 183–198. https://doi.org/10.1080/10640261003719435

Piran, N., & Cormier, H. C. (2005). The social construction of women and disordered eating patterns. *Journal of Counseling Psychology, 52*(4), 549–558. https://doi.org/10.1037/0022-0167.52.4.549

Piran, N., & Teall, T. (2012). The developmental theory of embodiment. In G. McVey, M. P. Levine, N. Piran, & H. B. Ferguson (Eds.), *Preventing eating-related and weight-related disorders: Collaborative research, advocacy, and policy change* (pp. 169–198). Wilfred Laurier University Press.

Pittock, A. (2014). *How are anorexia nervosa and spirituality connected, and what implications does this have for treatment?* Royal College of Psychiatry. https://

www.rcpsych.ac.uk/docs/default-source/members/sigs/spirituality-spsig/alexandra-pittock-anorerxia-nervosa-and-spirituality.pdf?sfvrsn=e9002559_2

Plateau, C. R., Bone, S., Lanning, E., & Meyer, C. (2018). Monitoring eating and activity: Links with disordered eating, compulsive exercise, and general wellbeing among young adults. *International Journal of Eating Disorders, 51*(11), 1270–1276.

Polit, D. F., & Beck, C. T. (2010). Generalization in quantitative and qualitative research: Myths and strategies. *International Journal of Nursing Studies, 47*(11), 1451–1458. https://doi.org/10.1016/j.ijnurstu.2010.06.004

Poorani, A. (2012). *Who determines the ideal body? A Summary of Research Findings on Body Image.* New Media and Mass Communication.

Powers, B. A., & Knapp, T. (2010). *"Halo effect". Dictionary of nursing and research* (4th ed.). Springer Publishing Company.

Preti, A., de Girolamo, G., Vilagut, G., Alonso, J., Graaf, R. D., Bruffaerts, R., Demyttenaere, K., Pinto-Meza, A., Haro, J. M., & Morosini, P. (2009). ESEMeD-WMH Investigators. The epidemiology of eating disorders in six European countries: Results of the ESEMeD-WMH project. *Journal of Psychiatric Research, 43*(14), 1125–1132. https://doi.org/10.1016/j.jpsychires.2009.04.003

Price, T., Zebitz, M., Giraldi, A., Lokind, T. S., Treasure, J., & Sjögren, J. M. (2020). Sexual function and dysfunction among women with anorexia nervosa: A systematic scoping review. *International Journal of Eating Disorders, 53*(9), 1377–1399.

Prinstein, M. J., Nesi, J., & Telzer, E. H. (2020). Commentary: An updated agenda for the study of digital media use and adolescent development – Future directions following Odgers & Jensen (2020). *Journal of Child Psychology and Psychiatry, 61,* 349–352. https://doi.org/10.1111/jcpp.13219

Puhl, R. M., & Latner, J. D. (2007). Stigma, obesity, and the health of the nation's children. *Psychological Bulletin, 133*(4), 557–580.

Puhl, R. M., Moss-Racusin, C. A., & Schwartz, M. B. (2007). Internalization of weight bias: Implications for binge eating and emotional well-being. *Obesity, 15*(1), 19–23. https://doi.org/10.1038/oby.2007.521

Qu, S. Q., & Dumay, J. (2011). The qualitative research interview. *Qualitative Research in Accounting and Management, 8*(3), 238–264. https://ssrn.com/abstract=2058515

Quiles, M. Y., Quiles, S. M. J., Pamies Aubalat, L., Botella Ausina, J., & Treasure, J. (2013). Peer and family influence in eating disorders: A meta-analysis. *European Psychiatry, 28*(4), 199–206. https://doi.org/10.1016/j.eurpsy.2012.03.005

Radin, A. P. (2003). *"Fictitious facts: The case of the vomitorium". APAClassics.org. American Philological Association. Archived from the original on 2003-03-20.* https://www.history.com/news/vomitoriums-fact-or-fiction

Rancourt, D., Schaefer, L. M., Bosson, J. K., & Thompson, J. K. (2016). Differential impact of upward and downward comparisons on diverse women's disordered eating behaviors and body image. *International Journal of Eating Disorders, 49,* 519–523.

Rangel, C., Dukeshire, S., & MacDonald, L. (2012). Diet and anxiety. An exploration into the Orthorexic Society. *Appetite, 58,* 124–132.

Rasmussen, N. (2012). Weight stigma, addiction, science, and the medication of fatness in mid-twentieth century America. *Sociology of Health & Illness, 34*(6), 880–895. https://doi.org/10.1111/j.1467-9566.2011.01444.x

Ravaldi, C., Vannacci, A., Bolognesi, E., Mancini, S., Faravelli, C., & Ricca, V. (2006). Gender role, eating disorder symptoms, and body image concern in ballet dancers. *Journal of Psychosomatic Research, 61*(4), 529–535. https://doi.org/10.1016/j.jpsychores.2006.04.016

Ricciardelli, L. A., McCabe, M. P., Holt, K. E., & Finemore, J. (2003). A biopcsychomodel. *Applied Developmental Psychology, 24*, 475–495.

Rich, E., Holroyd, R., & Evans, J. (2004). Hungry to be noticed: Young women, anorexia and schooling. In J. Evans, B. Davies, & J. Wright (Eds.), *Body knowledge and control: Studies in the sociology of physical education and health* (pp. 173–190). Routledge.

Rideout, V., & Robb, M. B. (2018). *Social media, social life (2018): Teens reveal their experiences*. Common Sense Media.

Rieger, E., Van Buren, D. J., Bishop, M., Tanofsky-Kraff, M., Welch, R., & Wilfley, D. E. (2010, June). An eating disorder-specific model of interpersonal psychotherapy (IPT-ED): Causal pathways and treatment implications. *Clinical Psychology Review, 30*(4), 400–410. https://doi.org/10.1016/j.cpr.2010.02.001

Riley, S., Frith, H., Wiggins, S., Markula, P., & Burns, M. (2008). Critical Bodies: Discourses of health, gender and consumption. In S. Riley, M. Burns, H. Frith, S. Wiggins, & P. Markula (Eds.), *Critical Bodies: Representations, identities and practices of weight and body management* (pp. 193–203). Palgrave MacMillan.

Robinson, L., Prichard, I., Nikolaidis, A., Drummond, C., Drummond, M., & Tiggemann, M. (2017). Idealised media images: The effect of fitspiration imagery on body satisfaction and exercise behaviour. *Body Image, 22*, 65–71.

Rosenblatt, P. (1999). Ethics of qualitative interviewing in grieving families. In A. Memon & R. Bull (Eds.), *Handbook of the psychology of interviewing* (pp. 197–209). Wiley.

Ross, J. A., & Green, C. (2011). Inside the experience of anorexia nervosa: A narrative thematic analysis. *Counselling and Psychotherapy Research, 11*(2), 112–119.

Russell, G. F. M. (1979). Bulimia nervosa: An ominous variant of anorexia nervosa. *Psychological Medicine, 9*, 429–448. https://doi.org/10.1017/S0033291700031974

Sachdev, P., Mondraty, N., Wen, W., & Gulliford, K. (2008). Brains of anorexia nervosa patients process self-images differently from non-self-images: An fMRI study. *Neuropsychologia, 46*(8), 2161–2168. https://doi.org/10.1016/j.neuropsychologia.2008.02.031

Sadeh-Sharvit, S., Levy-Shiff, R., Ram, A., Gur, E., Zubery, E., Steiner, E., Latzer, Y., & Stein, D. (2016). Mothers with eating disorders: The environmental factors affecting eating-related emotional difficulties in their offspring In *Bio-psycho-social contributions to understanding eating disorders*. Springer International Publishing. https://doi.org/10.1007/978-3-319-32742-6_6

Saguy, A. (2013). *What's wrong with fat*. Oxford University Press.

Saguy, A. C., & Gruys, K. (2010). Morality and health: News media constructions of overweight and eating disorders. *Social Problems, 57*(2), 231–250.

Sahoo, K., Sahoo, B., Choudhury, A. K., Sofi, N. Y., Kumar, R., & Bhadoria, A. S. (2015). Childhood obesity: Causes and consequences. *Journal of Family Medicine and Primary Care, 4*, 187–192. https://doi.org/10.4103/2249-4863.154628

Saldana, J. (2013). *The coding manual for qualitative researchers*. SAGE.

Sarner-Levin, K., Canetti, L., Latzer, Y., Bonne, O., Lerer, B., & Bachar, E. (2018). Anorexia nervosa, selflessness, and gender-role identity: A study of daughters and parents. *Israel Journal of Psychiatry & Related Sciences, 55*, 25–33.

Saukko, P. (2008). 'I feel ridiculous about having had it'—Critical readings of lived and mediated stories on eating disorders. In S. Riley, M. Burns, H. Frith, S. Wiggins, & P. Markula (Eds.), *Critical Bodies*. Palgrave Macmillan. https://doi.org/10.1057/9780230591141_3

Saul, J. S., & Rodgers, R. F. (2018). Adolescent eating disorder risk and the online world. *Child and Adolescent Psychiatric Clinics, 27*(2), 221–228. https://doi.org/10.1016/j.chc.2017.11.011

Sawka, K. J., McCormack, G. R., Nettel-Aguirre, A., & Swanson, K. (2015). Associations between aspects of friendship networks and dietary behavior in youth: Findings from a systematized review. *Eating Behaviors, 18*, 7–15. https://doi.org/10.1016/j.eatbeh.2015.03.002

Schaefer, L. M., & Thompson, J. K. (2018a). The development and validation of the Physical Appearance Comparison Scale–3 (PACS-3). *Psychological Assessment, 30*(10), 1330–1341. https://doi.org/10.1037/pas0000576

Schaefer, L. M., & Thompson, J. K. (2018b). Self-objectification and disordered eating: A meta-analysis. *International Journal of Eating Disorders, 51*(6), 483–502. https://doi.org/10.1002/eat.22854

Schaumberg, K., Zerwas, S., Goodman, E., Yilmaz, Z., Bulik, C. M., & Micali, N. (2019). Anxiety disorder symptoms at age 10 predict eating disorder symptoms and diagnoses in adolescence. *Journal of Child Psychology and Psychiatry, 60*(6), 686–696. https://doi.org/10.1111/jcpp.12984

Schlüter, C., Kraag, G., & Schmidt, J. (2021). Body shaming: An exploratory study on its definition and classification. *International Journal of Bullying Prevention*. https://doi.org/10.1007/s42380-021-00109-3

Schmidt, U. (2003). Aetiology of eating disorders in the 21(st) century: New answers to old questions. *European Child & Adolescent Psychiatry, 12*(Suppl. 1), I30–I37. https://doi.org/10.1007/s00787-003-1105-9

Schmidt, U., & Treasure, J. (2006). Anorexia nervosa: Valued and visible. A cognitive-interpersonal maintenance model and its implications for research and practice. *British Journal of Clinical Psychology, 45*, 1–25.

Segura-Garcia, C., Ramacciotti, C., Rania, M., Aloi, M., Caroleo, M., Bruni, A., Gazzarrini, D., Sinopoli, F., & De Fazio, P. (2015). The prevalence of orthorexia nervosa among eating disorder patients after treatment. *Eating and Weight Disorders, 20*, 161–166. https://doi.org/10.1007/s40519-014-0171-y

Seykes, S. (2017). *Six countries taking steps to tackle super-skinny models*. https://www.euronews.com/2017/09/06/counties-fighting-underweight-modelling

Shafran, R., Fairburn, C. G., Robinson, P., & Lask, B. (2004). Body checking and its avoidance in eating disorders. *International Journal of Eating Disorders, 35*, 93–101.

Sidiropoulos, M. (2007). Anorexia nervosa: The physiological consequences of starvation and the need for primary prevention efforts. *McGill Journal of Medicine MJM: An International Forum for the Advancement of Medical Sciences by Students, 10*(1), 20–25.

Silberstein, L. R., Striegel-Moore, R. H., Timko, C., & Rodin, J. (1988). Behavioral and psychological implications of body dissatisfaction: Do men and women differ? *Sex Roles, 19,* 219–232. https://doi.org/10.1007/BF00290156

Simone, M., Hazzard, V. M., Askew, A. J., Tebbe, E. A., Lipson, S. K., & Pisetsky, E. M. (2022, June). Variability in eating disorder risk and diagnosis in transgender and gender diverse college students. *Annals of Epidemiology, 70,* 53–60. https://doi.org/10.1016/j.annepidem.2022.04.007

Simonich, A. (2007). Perfectionism and eating disorders: Current status and future directions. *Clinical Psychology Review,* 384–405.

Simpson, C. C., & Mazzeo, S. E. (2017). Calorie counting and fitness tracking technology: Associations with eating disorder symptomatology. *Eating Behaviors, 26,* 89–92.

Simpson, J., & Rholes, W. (1994). Stress and secure base relationships in adulthood. In U. K. Bartholomew, & D. Perlman (Eds.), *Attachment processes in adulthood. Advances in personal relationships* (Vol. 5, pp. 181–204). Jessica Kingsley Publishers, Ltd.

Skarderud, F. (2007a). Eating one's words, Part I. "Concretised metaphors" and reflective function in anorexia nervosa – An interview study. *European Eating Disorders Review, 15,* 163–174.

Slišković, A. (2020). Kako istražiti? In A. Slišković & I. Burić (Eds.), *Znanstveno istraživanje u psihologiji: vodič za početnike.* Sveučilište u Zadru.

Smalley, V., Dallos, R., & McKenzie, R. (2017). Young women's experience of anorexia, family dynamics and triangulation. *Contemporary Family Therapy, 39,* 31–42. https://doi.org/10.1007/s10591-016-9398-2

Smink, F. E., van Hoeken, D., & Hoek, H. W. (2012). Epidemiology of eating disorders: Incidence, prevalence and mortality rates. *Current Psychiatry Reports, 14*(4), 406–414.

Smith, L. (1992). Ethical issues in interviewing. *Journal of Advanced Nursing, 17*(1), 98–103.

Smith, A. R., Zuromski, K. L., & Dodd, D. R. (2018, August). Eating disorders and suicidality: What we know, what we don't know, and suggestions for future research. *Current Opinion in Psychology, 22,* 63–67. https://doi.org/10.1016/j.copsyc.2017.08.023

Smolak, L., Levine, M. P., & Schermer, F. (1999). Parental input and weight concern among elementary school children. *International Journal of Eating Disorders, 25,* 263–271.

Smolak, L., & Levine, M. P. (2015). *The Wiley handbook of eating disorders, assessment, prevention, treatment, policy, and future directions.* John Wiley & Sons, Ltd. https://doi.org/10.1002/9781118574089

Smolak, L., & Munstertieger, B. F. (2002). The relationship of gender and voice to depression and eating disorders. *Psychology of Women Quarterly, 26*(3), 234–241. https://doi.org/10.1111/1471-6402.t01-1-00006

Smolak, L., Murnen, S. K., & Ruble, A. E. (2000). Female athletes and eating problems: A meta-analysis. *International Journal of Eating Disorders, 27*(4), 371–380. https://doi.org/10.1002/(sici)1098-108x(200005)27:4<371::aid-eat1>3.0.co;2-y

Smolak, L., & Piran, N. (2012). Gender and the prevention of eating disorders. In G. McVey, M. P. Levine, N. Piran, & H. B. Ferguson (Eds.), *Preventing eating-related and weight-related disorders: Collaborative research, advocacy, and policy change* (pp. 201–224). Wilfred Laurier Press.

Sperling, M. (1978). *Psychosomatic disorders in childhood* (pp. 139–173). Jason Aronson.

Spettigue, W., & Henderson, K. A. (2004). Eating disorders and the role of the media. *The Canadian Child and Adolescent Psychiatry Review* [*La revue canadienne de psychiatrie de l'enfant et de l'adolescent*], *13*(1), 16–19.

Squire, S. (2003). Anorexia and bulimia: Purity and danger. *Australian Feminist Studies, 18*, 17–26.

Stammers, H. R. (2020). The theological language of anorexia: An argument for greater rapprochement between chaplains and physicians. *Feminist Theology, 28*(3), 282–296. https://doi.org/10.1177/0966735020906951

Stanghellini, G., Castellini, G., Brogna, P., Faravelli, C., & Ricca, V. (2012). Identity and eating disorders (IDEA): A questionnaire evaluating identity and embodiment in eating disorder patients. *Psychopathology, 45*(3), 147–158. https://doi.org/10.1159/000330258

Stanghellini, G., Trisolini, F., Castellini, G., Ambrosini, A., Faravelli, C., & Ricca, V. (2015). Is feeling extraneous from one's own body a core vulnerability feature in eating disorders? *Psychopathology, 48*, 18–24. https://doi.org/10.1159/000364882

Staudacher, H. M., & Harer, K. N. (2018). When clean eating goes dirty. *Lancet Gastroenterol Hepatol, 3*, 668. https://doi.org/10.1016/S2468-1253(18)30277-2

Stein, K. F., & Corte, C. (2007). Identity impairment and the eating disorders: Content and organization of the self-concept in women with anorexia nervosa and bulimia nervosa. *European Eating Disorders Review, 15*(1), 58–69. https://doi.org/10.1002/erv.726

Steiner-Adair, C. (1986). The body politic: Normal female adolescent development and the development of eating disorders. *Journal of the American Academy of Psychoanalysis, 14*, 95–114.

Stephens, C. (2019, Kolovoz 7). Why anorexia nervosa can impact your sex drive and what you can do about it. Healthline. https://www.healthline.com/health/eating-disorder-anorexia-sex-drive

Stice, E. (1994). Review of the evidence for a sociocultural model of bulimia nervosa and an exploration of the mechanisms of action. *Clinical Psychology Review, 14*(7), 633–661.

Stice, E. (2001). A prospective test of the dual-pathway model of bulimic pathology: Mediating effects of dieting and negative affect. *Journal of Abnormal Psychology, 110*(1), 124–135. https://doi.org/10.1037//0021-843x.110.1.124

Stice, E., Gau, J. M., Rohde, P., & Shaw, H. (2017). Risk factors that predict future onset of each DSM-5 eating disorder: Predictive specificity in high-risk adolescent females. *Journal of Abnormal Psychology, 126*(1), 38–51. https://doi.org/10.1037/abn0000219

Stice, E., Nemeroff, C., & Shaw, H. E. (1996). Test of the dual pathway model of bulimia nervosa: Evidence for dietary restraint and affect regulation mechanisms. *Journal of Social and Clinical Psychology, 15*, 340–363.

Stice, E., & Presnell, K. (2010). Clinical psychology. In W. S. Agras (Ed.), *The Oxford handbook of eating disorders* (1st ed.). https://doi.org/10.1093/oxfordhb/9780195373622.013.0010

Stice, E., Presnell, K., & Spangler, D. (2002). Risk factors for binge eating onset in adolescent girls: A 2-year prospective investigation. *Health Psychology, 21*(2), 131–138. https://doi.org/10.1037/0278-6133.21.2.131

Stoeber, J., Madigan, D. J., Damian, L. E., Esposito, R. M., & Lombardo, C. (2017). Perfectionism and eating disorder symptoms in female university students: The central role of perfectionistic self-presentation. *Eating and Weight Disorders, 22*(4), 641–648. https://doi.org/10.1007/s40519-016-0297-1

Striegel-Moore, R. H., & Bulik, C. M. (2007). Risk factors for eating disorders. *American Psychologist, 62*(3), 181–198. https://doi.org/10.1037/0003-066X.62.3.181

Striegel-Moore, R. H., Silberstein, L. R., & Rodin, J. (1986). Toward an understanding of risk factors for bulimia. *American Psychologist, 41*, 246–263.

Striegel-Moore, R. H., Silberstein, L. R., & Rodin, J. (1993). The social self in bulimia nervosa: Public self-consciousness, social anxiety, and perceived fraudulence. *Journal of Abnormal Psychology, 102*(2), 297–303. https://doi.org/10.1037/0021-843X.102.2.297

Strober, M. (1986). Anorexia nervosa: History and psychological concept. In K. D. Brownell & J. P. Foret (Eds.), *Handbook of Eating Disorders: Physiology, psychology and treatment of obesity, anorexia and bulimia.* (pp. 231–246). Basic Books.

Strober, M., & Johnson, C. (2012). The need for complex ideas in anorexia nervosa: Why biology, environment, and psyche all matter, why therapists make mistakes, and why clinical benchmarks are needed for managing weight correction. *International Journal of Eating Disorders, 45*(2), 155–178. https://doi.org/10.1002/eat.22005

Sugiati, T. (2019). The influence of body shaming toward FISIP Airlangga University students behaviour pattern. *Indonesian Journal of Social Sciences, 11*(02), 16–24.

Sundgot-Borgen, J., & Torstveit, M. K. (2004). Prevalence of eating disorders in elite athletes is higher than in the general population. *Clinical Journal of Sport Medicine, 14*(1), 25–32. https://doi.org/10.1097/00042752-200401000-00005

Sundgot-Borgen, J., & Torstveit, M. K. (2010). Aspects of disordered eating continuum in elite high-intensity sports. *Scandinavian Journal of Medicine & Science in Sports, 20*, 112–121.

Sutin, A. R., Kerr, J. A., & Terracciano, A. (2017). Temperament and body weight from ages 4 to 15 years. *International Journal of Obesity, 41*(7), 1056–1061. https://doi.org/10.1038/ijo.2017.62

Swartz, L. (1985). Anorexia nervosa as a culture-bound syndrome. *Social Science & Medicine, 20*(7), 725–730. https://doi.org/10.1016/0277-9536(85)90062-0

Tagay, S., Schlottbohm, E., Reyes-Rodriguez, M. L., Repic, N., & Senf, W. (2014). Eating disorders, trauma, PTSD, and psychosocial resources. *Eating Disorders, 22*(1), 33–49. https://doi.org/10.1080/10640266.2014.857517

Tangram wellness blog. (2022) https://tangramwellness.com/blog/tag/eating+disorders

Tasca, G. A., Ritchie, K., Zachariades, F., Proulx, G., Trinneer, A., Balfour, L., Demidenko, N., Hayden, G., Wong, A., & Bissada, H. (2013). Attachment insecurity mediates the relationship between childhood trauma and eating disorder psychopathology in a clinical sample: A structural equation model. *Child Abuse & Neglect, 37*(11), 926–933. https://doi.org/10.1016/j.chiabu.2013.03.004

Thompson, J. K., Heinberg, L. J., Altabe, M., & Tantleff-Dunn, S. (1999). *Exacting beauty: Theory, assessment and treatment of body image disturbance.* American Psychological Association.

Thompson, K. M., & Wonderlich, S. A. (2004). Child sexual abuse and eating disorders. In J. K. Thompson (Ed.), *Handbook of eating disorders and obesity* (pp. 679–694). John Wiley & Sons, Inc.

Thorpe, H., Toffoletti, K., & Bruce, T. (2017). Sportswomen and social media: Bringing third-wave feminism, postfeminism, and neoliberal feminism into conversation. *Journal of Sport & Social Issues.* https://doi.org/10.1177/0193723517730808

Throsby, K. (2012). Obesity surgery and the management of excess: Exploring the body multiple. *Sociology of Health & Illness, 34*(1), 1–15. https://doi.org/10.1111/j.1467-9566.2011.01358.x

Tiggemann, M., & Boundy, M. (2008). Effect of environment and appearance compliment on college women's self-objectification, mood, body shame, and cognitive performance. *Psychology of Women Quarterly, 32*(4), 399–405. https://doi.org/10.1111/j.1471-6402.2008.00453.x

Tiggemann, M., Martins, Y., & Kirkbride, A. (2007). Oh to be lean and muscular: Body image ideals in gay and heterosexual men. *Psychology of Men and Masculinity, 8*(1), 15–24. https://doi.org/10.1037/1524-9220.8.1.15

Tiggemann, M., & Slater, A. (2013). NetGirls: The Internet, Facebook, and body image concern in adolescent girls. *International Journal of Eating Disorders, 46*(6), 630–633. https://doi.org/10.1002/eat.22141

Tiggemann, M., & Williams, E. (2012). The role of self-objectification in disordered eating, depressed mood, and sexual functioning among women: A comprehensive test of objectification theory. *Psychology of Women Quarterly, 36*(1), 66–75. https://doi.org/10.1177/0361684311420250

Toni, G., Berioli, M. G., Cerquiglini, L., Ceccarini, G., GrohmannPrincipi, U. N., & Esposito, S. (2017). Eating disorders and disordered eating symptoms in adolescents with type 1 diabetes. *Nutrients, 9*(8), 906. https://doi.org/10.3390/nu9080906

Toulany, A., Wong, M., Katzman, D. K., Akseer, N., Steinegger, C., Hancock-Howard, R. L., & Coyte, P. C. (2015). Cost analysis of inpatient treatment of anorexia nervosa in adolescents: Hospital and caregiver perspectives. *CMAJ OPEN, 3*(2), E192–E197. https://doi.org/10.9778/cmajo.20140086

Trace, S. E., Baker, J. H., Penas-Lledo, E., & Bulik, C. M. (2013). The genetics of eating disorders. *Annual Review of Clinical Psychology, 9*, 589–620.

Treasure, J., & Cardi, V. (2017). Anorexia nervosa, theory and treatment: Where are we 35 years on from Hilde Bruch's foundation lecture? *European Eating Disorders Review, 25*, 139–147.

Treasure, J., Cardi, V., & Schmidt, U. (2014). Moving to establish the mechanisms underpinning the biopsychiatric models of eating disorders with brain-based translational treatments: From paradigm clash to paradigm complementarity. *Advances in Eating Disorders: Theory, Research and Practice, 2*(2), 171–179. https://doi.org/10.1080/21662630.2013.840085

Treasure, J., Murphy, T., Szmukler, T., Todd, G., Gavan, K., & Joyce, J. (2001). The experience of caregiving for severe mental illness: A comparison between anorexia nervosa and psychosis. *Social Psychiatry and Psychiatric Epidemiology, 36,* 343–347. https://doi.org/10.1007/s001270170039

Tully, L. (2015). Emancipation through emaciation: The pro-ana movement and the creation and control of the feminine subject. *Prescott College.* http://pqdtopen.proquest.com/#viewpdf?dispub=1594379

Tylka, T. L., & Subich, L. M. (1999). Exploring the construct validity of the eating disorder continuum. *Journal of Counseling Psychology, 46*(2), 268–276. https://doi.org/10.1037/0022-0167.46.2.268

van de Wouw, M., Schellekens, H., Dinan, T. G., & Cryan, J. F. (2017). Microbiota-gutbrain axis: Modulator of host metabolism and appetite. *Journal of Nutrition, 147,* 727–745.

van Deth, R., & Vandereycken, W. (1994). Continuity and discontinuity in the history of self-starvation. *European Eating Disorders Review, 2*(1), 47–54. https://doi-org.ezproxy.nsk.hr/10.1002/erv.2400020106

van Eeden, A. E., Hoek, H. W., van Hoeken, D., Deen, M., & Oldehinkel, A. J. (2020). Temperament in preadolescence is associated with weight and eating pathology in young adulthood. *International Journal of Eating Disorders, 53*(5), 736–745. https://doi.org/10.1002/eat.23241

Van Oudenhove, L., McKie, S., Lassman, D., Uddin, B., Paine, P., Coen, S., Gregory, L., Tack, J., & Aziz, Q. (2011). Fatty acid-induced gut-brain signaling attenuates neural and behavioral effects of sad emotion in humans. *Journal of Clinical Investigation, 121*(8), 3094–3099. https://doi.org/10.1172/JCI46380

Van Strien, T., Engels, R. C., Van Leeuwe, J., & Snoek, H. M. (2005). The Stice model of overeating: Tests in clinical and non-clinical samples. *Appetite, 45*(3), 205–213. https://doi.org/10.1016/j.appet.2005.08.004

Vandereycken, W., & Dekerf, A. (2010). Eating-disordered patients' perception of pregnancy in important others and therapists. *Eating and Weight Disorders, 15,* e98.

Vaughan, J. L., King, K. A., & Cottrell, R. R. (2004). Collegiate athletic trainers' confidence in helping female athletes with eating disorders. *Journal of Athletic Training, 39*(1), 71–76.

Vemuri, M., & Steiner, H. (2006). Historical and current conceptualizations of eating disorders: A developmental perspective. In T. Jaffa & B. McDermott (Eds.), *Eating disorders in children and adolescents.* Cambridge University Press.

Veses, A. M., Martínez-Gómez, D., Gómez-Martínez, S., Vicente-Rodriguez, G., Castillo, R., Ortega, F. B., González-Gross, M., Calle, M. E., Veiga, O. L., Marcos, A. & AVENA, AFINOS Study Groups. (2014). AFINOS study groups. physical fitness, overweight and the risk of eating disorders in adolescents. The AVENA and AFINOS studies. *Pediatric Obesity, 9,* 1–9. https://doi.org/10.1111/j.2047-6310.2012.00138.x

Villarejo, C., Fernández-Aranda, F., Jiménez-Murcia, S., Peñas-Lledó, E., Granero, R., Penelo, E., Tinahones, F. J., Sancho, C., Vilarrasa, N., Montserrat-Gil de Bernabé, M., Casanueva, F. F., Fernández-Real, J. M., Frühbeck, G., De la Torre, R., Treasure, J., Botella, C., & Menchón, J. M. (2012). Lifetime obesity in patients with eating disorders: Increasing prevalence, clinical and personality correlates. *European Eating Disorders Review, 20*(3), 250–254. https://doi.org/10.1002/erv.2166

Vollrath, M. E., Tonstad, S., Rothbart, M. K., & Hampson, S. E. (2011). Infant temperament is associated with potentially obesogenic diet at 18 months.

International Journal of Pediatric Obesity, 6(2–2), e408–e414. https://doi.org/ 10.3109/17477166.2010.518240

Volpe, U., Tortorella, A., Manchia, M., Monteleone, A. M., Albert, U., & Monteleone, P. (2016). Eating disorders: What age at onset? *Psychiatry Research*, *238*, 225–227. https://doi.org/10.1016/j.psychres.2016.02.048

de Vries, D. A., Peter, J., de Graaf, H. i, & Nikken, P. (2016). Adolescents' social network site use, peer appearance-related feedback, and body dissatisfaction: Testing a mediation model. *Journal of Youth and Adolescence*, *45*(1), 211–224. https://doi.org/10.1007/s10964-015-0266-4

Wade, T. D., Keski-Rahkonen, A., & Hudson, J. I. (2011). Epidemiology of eating disorders. In T. Ming, M. T. Tsuang, M. Tohen, & B. P. B. PeterJones (Eds.), *Textbook of psychiatric epidemiology*. https://doi.org/10.1002/9780470976739.ch20

Waller, G., Babbs, M., Milligan, R., Meyer, C., Ohanian, V., & Leung, N. (2003). Anger and core beliefs in the eating disorders. *International Journal of Eating Disorders*, *34*(1), 118–124. https://doi.org/10.1002/eat.10163

Ward, A., Ramsay, R., & Treasure, J. (2000). Attachment research in eating disorders. *British Journal of Medical Psychology*, *73*(1), 35–51. https://doi.org/10.1348/ 000711200160282

Ward, A., Ramsay, R., Turnbull, S., Steele, M., Steele, H., & Treasure, J. (2001). Attachment in anorexia nervosa: A transgenerational perspective. *British Journal of Medical Psychology*, *74*, 497–505. https://doi.org/10.1348/000711201161145

Warin, M. (2003). Be-coming clean: The logic of hygiene in anorexia. *A Journal of Social Anthropology and Cultural Studies*, *1*(1), 109–132.

Warin, M. (2010). *Abject relations: Everyday worlds of anorexia New Brunswick*. Rutgers University Press.

Warren, C. S., & Akoury, L. M. (2020). Emphasizing the "cultural" in sociocultural: A systematic review of research on thin-ideal internalization, acculturation, and eating pathology in US ethnic minorities. *Psychology Research and Behavior Management*, *13*, 319–330. https://doi.org/10.2147/PRBM.S204274

Weaver, K., Wuest, J., & Ciliska, D. (2005). Understanding women's journey of recovering from anorexia nervosa. *Qualitative Health Research*, *15*(2), 188–206. https://doi.org/10.1177/1049732304270819

Wechselblatt, T., Gurnick, G., & Simon, R. (2000). Autonomy and relatedness in the development of anorexia nervosa: A clinical case series using grounded theory. *Bulletin of the Menninger Clinic*, *64*, 91–123.

Weltzin, T. E., Weisensel, N., Franczyk, D., Burnett, K., Klitz, C., & Bean, P. (2005). Eating disorders in men: Update. *The Journal of Men's Health & Gender*, *2*, 186–193. https://doi.org/10.1016/j.jmhg.2005.04.008

Wertheim, E. H., Martin, G., Prior, M., & Sanson, A. (2002). Parent influences in the transmission of eating and weight related values and behaviors. *Eating Disorders*, *10*, 321–334.

Whitlock, J. (2010). Self-injurious behavior in adolescents. *PLoS Medicine*, *7*(5), e1000240. https://doi.org/10.1371/journal.pmed.1000240

WHO. (2000). Obesity: Preventing and managing the global epidemic. Report of a WHO consultation. *World Health Organization Technical Report Series*, *894*, i–253.

Wilde, A., & Diekman, A. B. (2005). Cross-cultural similarities and differences in dynamic stereotypes: A comparison between Germany and the United States.

Psychology of Women Quarterly, 29(2), 188–196. https://doi.org/10.1111/j.1471-6402.2005.00181.x

Wildes, J. E., Forbush, K. T., & Markon, K. E. (2013). Characteristics and stability of empirically derived anorexia nervosa subtypes: Towards the identification of homogeneous low-weight eating disorder phenotypes. *Journal of Abnormal Psychology, 122*(4), 1031–1041. https://doi.org/10.1037/a0034676

Williams, S., & Reid, M. (2012). 'It's like there are two people in my head': A phenomenological exploration of anorexia nervosa and its relationship to the self. *Psychology and Health, 27*(7), 798–815. https://doi.org/10.1080/08870446.2011.595488

Williams, R. J., & Ricciardelli, L. A. (2003). Negative perceptions about self-control and identification with gender-role stereotypes related to binge eating, problem drinking, and to comorbidity among adolescent. *Jornal of Adolescent Health, 32*, 66–72.

Wilson, C. P. (1988). The psychoanalytic treatment of anorexia nervosa and bulimia. In B. J. Blinder, B. F. Chaitin, & R. Goldstein (Eds.), *The eating disorders.* Copyright © 1988 PMA Publishing Corp.

Wilson, S. (2020). Fear of self in eating disorders. *Journal of Obsessive Compulsive and Related Disorders, 27*, 100562. https://doi.org/10.1016/j.jocrd.2020.100562

Wilson, C. P., Hogan, C. C., & Mintz, I. L. (1983). *Fear of being fat: The treatment of anorexia nervosa and bulimia* (Vol. 1983, pp. 1–366). Jason Aronson.

Witcomb, G. L., Arcelus, J., & Chen, J. (2013). Can cognitive dissonance methods developed in the West for combatting the 'thin ideal' help slow the rapidly increasing prevalence of eating disorders in non-Western cultures? *Shanghai Archives of Psychiatry, 25*(6), 332–340. https://doi.org/10.3969/j.issn.1002-0829.2013.06.002

Witztum, E., Latzer, Y., & Stein, D. (2008). Anorexia nervosa and bulimia nervosa as idioms of distress: From the historical background to current formulations. *International Journal of Child and Adolescent Health, 4*, 1.

Woitas, M. (2018). "Exercise teaches you the pleasure of discipline" – The female body in Jane Fonda's Aerobics videos. *Historical Social Research, 43*(2), 148–164. https://doi.org/10.12759/hsr.43.2018.2.148-164

Wolf, N. (2002). *The beauty myth: How images of beauty are used against women.* Harper Perennial.

Yap, A. (2016). (Hip) throwing like a girl: Martial arts and norms of feminine body comportment. *The International Journal of Feminist Approaches to Bioethics, 9*(2), 92–114.

Yilmaz, Z., Gottfredson, N. C., Zerwas, S. C., Bulik, C. M., & Micali, N. (2018). Developmental premorbid body mass index trajectories of adolescents with eating disorders in a longitudinal population cohort. *Journal of the American Academy of Child & Adolescent Psychiatry.* https://doi.org/10.1016/j.jaac.2018.11.008

Yilmaz, Z., Hardaway, J. A., & Bulik, C. M. (2015). Genetics and epigenetics of eating disorders. *Advances in Genomics and Genetics, 5*, 131–150.

Yilmaz, Z., Szatkiewicz, J. P., Crowley, J. J., Ancalade, N., Brandys, M. K., van Elburg, A., & Bulik, C. M. (2017). Exploration of large, rare copy number variants associated with psychiatric and neurodevelopmental disorders in individuals with anorexia nervosa. *Psychiatric Genetics, 27*, 152–158.

Young, I. M. (1980). Throwing like a girl: A phenomenology of feminine body comportment motility and spatiality. *Human Studies, 3*(1), 137–156.

Young, S., Rhodes, P., Touyz, S., & Hay, P. (2015). The role of exercise across the lifespan in patients with anorexia nervosa: A narrative inquiry. *Advances in Eating Disorders, 3*(3), 237–250. https://doi.org/10.1080/21662630.2015.1027947

Zachrisson, H. D., & Kulbotten, G. R. (2006). Attachment in anorexia nervosa: An exploration of associations with eating disorder psychopathology and psychiatric symptoms. *Eating and Weight Disorders, 11*(4), 163–170. https://doi.org/10.1007/BF03327567

Zaitsoff, S. L., Geller, J., & Srikameswaran, S. (2002). Silencing the self and suppressed anger: Relationship to eating disorder symptoms in adolescent females. *European Eating Disorders Review, 10*(1), 51–60. https://doi.org/10.1002/erv.418

Ziolko, H. U. (1996). Bulimia: A historical outline. *International Journal of Eating Disorders, 20*, 345–358.

Printed and bound by CPI Group (UK) Ltd, Croydon, CR0 4YY

16/04/2024

14484230-0001